Strategic Planning

Library of Congress Cataloging-in-Publication Data

Simerson, Byron K.
  Strategic planning: a practical guide to strategy formulation and
execution / B. Keith Simerson.
      p. cm.
  Includes bibliographical references and index.
  ISBN 978-0-313-38480-6 (hardcopy: alk. paper)—ISBN 978-0-313-
38481-3 (ebook) 1. Strategic planning. I. Title.
  HD30.28.S4347   2011
  658.4'012—dc22   2010050978

ISBN: 978-0-313-38480-6
EISBN: 978-0-313-38481-3

15   14   13   12   2   3   4   5

This book is also available on the World Wide Web as an eBook.
Visit www.abc-clio.com for details.

Praeger
An Imprint of ABC-CLIO, LLC

ABC-CLIO, LLC
130 Cremona Drive, P.O. Box 1911
Santa Barbara, California 93116-1911

This book is printed on acid-free paper ∞

Manufactured in the United States of America

To Darlie, Jarrett, Brent, and Andrew, thank you for your endless encouragement and support and for the boundless enthusiasm, passion, and zeal you bring to everything you do. To Kristin, our conversations remain exciting and insightful. To Janet, thank you for reviewing the manuscript; your suggestions and recommendations were invaluable.

Contents

Chapter 1

Overview

Strategic planning is extremely important to individuals (regardless of the role they play, their position or title, or their area of responsibility), their teams, and their organizations. This chapter introduces readers to what "planning" typically means and entails, gives examples of how people in different walks of life typically plan, describes how strategic planning differs from but is similar to tactical planning, points out general advantages and challenges of strategic planning, and reveals the implications for strategic planning that served as the impetus for this book.

PLANNING IN OUR DAILY LIVES

Planning is a fundamental part of our lives, whether we are going to commute into town to run errands or make several purchases; travel across town, the state, or the country to visit various historical sites or participate in cultural events; or prepare for and then enter into and navigate through a particular occupation or profession. As used here, planning is a process by which you formulate a particular intent, identify one or more associated goals, and then decide on the actions you will take to realize your intent and achieve your goals.

Planning can be as simple as deciding which purchases you need to make, ensuring that you have adequate funds on hand, determining the stores you frequent that are likely to carry those items as well as the locations of those particular stores, deciding on the most effective and efficient means for traveling from your current address to the stores' location, and taking steps to ensure that your mode of transportation will be available and fully operational at the needed time. Planning in our daily lives can also be somewhat more complex. For example, we might as an individual or as a family develop a plan to help:

- Guide a relatively complex home improvement project by specifying needed equipment and supplies.
- Ensure a safe, enjoyable, and educational vacation by helping us take factors such as weather, scheduled events, motel or hotel vacancy, special offers, and cultural and educational opportunities into consideration.
- Steer our savings and investments so that we can retire in relative comfort.
- Ensure that we receive long-term care as needed and when needed.

Or, we might belong to a local citizens' group or volunteer organization or be a member of a local association or club responsible for creating a plan to help guide:

- Emergency operations should the right conditions, situations, or circumstances emerge.
- The consumption, utilization, and exploitation of local land and resources.
- The local or regional response to a violent and devastating accident involving hazardous materials.

PLANNING: AN IMPORTANT ELEMENT OF ANY ORGANIZATION

With the above points in mind, I—as an adult, husband, parent, and member of my local community—recognize the vital role planning plays in one's personal life. As a consultant with almost two decades of experience working with leaders, executives, managers, supervisors, and individual contributors, and as a member of the faculty of a leading university, I have made observations and had experiences that led me to conclude some time ago that planning is as important to an organization as it is to an individual. Without formal planning, the purpose of the organization might be misunderstood to stakeholders, the intent of the organization might be unclear to employees (at all levels), organizational intelligence and resources might be misapplied, and the sum total of the organization's effort might yield suboptimal results or outcomes or yield optimal results and outcomes that do not directly or indirectly contribute to the organization's purpose for existence.

Several reasons have contributed to planning becoming increasingly important to organizations. Our tumultuous national and global economy has adversely impacted every industry and profession; organizations have downsized and "right-sized" and are now having to do much more work with fewer resources. On a daily basis, executives, managers, supervisors, and individual contributors are being asked to do significantly more; such demands have been magnified by organizational structures such as the matrix, which requires all employees (regardless of their level, area of responsibility, or title) to function in an environment marked by competing priorities and multiple stakeholder groups. Even under the most optimal circumstances, today's organizational realities make it much more essential—perhaps more than at any other point in our history—for the person lower in the organization to quickly make proper and appropriate business decisions. Such complexity showcases the need for clear thinking, clear communication, and a clear directive—all the product of effective planning.

STRATEGIC VERSUS TACTICAL PLANNING

Conversations with numerous executives and students have sensitized me to the importance of understanding the difference between strategic and tactical planning. They have also helped me understand why some people "freeze" because they consider strategic planning something "others" do or because the difference between strategic and tactical planning confuses them. While I will point out other differences later in this section and will describe a practical and easily understandable planning hierarchy in Chapter 2, the primary difference between strategic and tactical planning is that strategic planning typically involves thinking about and making decisions impacting the entire organization and tactical planning typically involves thinking about and making decisions impacting a part of the organization (such as a particular functional group, division, or department). The key point here is that a clear majority of the methodologies, tools, and techniques applied to strategic planning efforts can also be applied to tactical planning efforts. Although some of the questions one must ask might differ according to whether you are developing a strategic or tactical plan, both types of plans require strategic thinking, benefit from the application of certain tools, and are important components of strategic management.

This book is designed to serve as a practical guide to strategy formulation and execution. As such, it provides information useful in and beneficial to conducting strategic or tactical planning, since both involve strategy (defined as the means by which you intend to realize a strategic intent or achieve a strategic goal), formulation (defined as drawing something up carefully and in detail), and execution (defined as the act of successfully carrying out or accomplishing an action).

I focus on strategic rather than tactical planning because strategic planning:

- Requires the broadest perspective. Tactical planning might focus on challenges and opportunities pertaining to a particular function, such as information technology (IT), human resources (HR), or marketing; strategic planning typically involves the analysis and consideration of a broader array of factors, including but not limited to organization-wide business systems, core processes, technology, people capabilities, and culture.
- Takes the longest timeframe into consideration. Tactical planning typically involves goals and actions likely to occur over the course of a year; strategic planning might involve a strategic intent likely to take 10 to 15 years to realize.

- Focuses on the entire (local, regional, national, or global) organization. Tactical planning involves a particular division, department, or unit; each subunit (regardless of what it is called) has a particular focused area of responsibility and as a result might focus on a particular goal, geographic area, business system, core process, technology, people capability, or cultural issue. The impact of strategic planning is much more far-reaching, in that it focuses on all components and elements of the organization.

Planning of any sort involves careful preparation, prudent analysis of information and data, credible decision making, and the utilization of various tools and techniques. The larger and more complex the organization, the more likely the planning endeavor is to be strategic; the more challenging and demanding the business, the more likely the planning effort is to be strategic. Although the concepts, principles, tools, and techniques I introduce throughout this book are appropriate for strategic planning, they will prove equally useful and beneficial to the individual asked to prepare for, conduct, participate in, or review tactical planning.

THE ADVANTAGE OF STRATEGIC PLANNING

Many factors—including those previously listed—showcase the importance of strategic planning to the individual and organization. Strategic planning allows you to take internally and externally focused information into consideration when making a decision, thus maximizing certainty, minimizing risk, and optimizing results and outcomes. While specific benefits are described in greater detail in Chapter 2, strategic planning:

1. In short, provides much-needed focus and direction. As previously stated, uncertainty and ambiguity surround corporate, government, for-profit, and nonprofit positions and areas of responsibility, and employees at all levels are now being asked to perform in an exemplary manner with little managerial or supervisory support or direction. Strategic planning allows the organization to determine what's important and understand what every organizational element—from business systems to human resources—must achieve to contribute to the individual, team, and organizational success. Strategic planning allows the members of the organization to understand what's important and how the role they play and their effort and performance contribute to the organization's short- and long-term success.
2. Allows a new organization to make fundamental decisions about the market in which it will operate; the value it will bring to its clients or customers; the unique knowledge, skills, and abilities its employees must (or do) possess and must (or will) apply to client and customer opportunities and challenges; and how the organization will differentiate itself from its competitors.
3. Allows an existing organization to review its progress to date; recognize, acknowledge, and celebrate noted accomplishments; identify and share lessons

learned and likely best practices; and determine whether its current focus and effort (as well as associated resources) should be directed elsewhere or be emphasized or deemphasized.

4. Gives you an opportunity to take a step back and think strategically about your organization's past, present, and future; existing and emerging issues your organization faces; and external forces and internal factors impacting your organization's ability to succeed now and into the future.

5. Allows you to answer questions relating to your client and customer needs and expectations and your organization's ability to meet or exceed those needs and expectations.

6. Gives you a chance to consider or reconsider your organization's future. For example, it allows you to firm up, confirm, or verify where your organization is heading, what the organization must do to immediately succeed and succeed over time, and how you and your colleagues will (or must prepare to) contribute to your organization's success.

7. Allows you to identify strategies, tactics, tasks, and subtasks that will help your organization attain its strategic intent and achieve its stated objectives. Not only does strategic planning allow you to identify these multilayered, increasingly specific and defined actions, but it also allows you to put these actions into a proper context and organize them in a way that is easily understandable to you and your key stakeholder groups and easily communicated within and throughout your organization.

8. Provides an opportunity for the organization to identify the resources (including budget, people, facilities, equipment, supplies, knowledge, and information) needed to achieve optimal success.

9. Allows you to consider unlikely, unexpected, or unplanned obstacles that may interfere with the organization's performance and decide in advance how you will recognize and subsequently resolve such unexpected occurrences.

10. Provides an excellent forum for the involvement, contribution, and input of a broad cross section of the organization as well as select representatives of the organization's various stakeholder communities.

One of the most, if not the most, important benefits of any strategic planning effort is that it allows your organization to bring its "collective intelligence" together to apply to external forces, internal factors, and the slate of current and emerging challenges and opportunities likely to impede or support the organization's attaining its vision and accomplishing its mission.

THE CHALLENGE OF STRATEGIC PLANNING

The recent downturn in the economy has changed the nature of many roles, positions, and jobs. In the past, many people were responsible for isolated activities

- Regardless of the answer to the previous question, how do you decide who should participate in your company's strategic planning session?
- It seems to me that it would be easier to conduct a strategic planning session if we were a more mature company; what strategic issues should we address since we are a start-up organization?
- It seems to me that it would be easier to conduct a strategic planning session if we were a start-up organization; what strategic issues should we address since we are a more mature organization?

IMPLICATIONS

Planning is a fundamental part of our lives, whether we are going to commute into town, travel across the country, or to prepare for an occupation or profession. If uncertain about the importance of planning to one's welfare, consider the multitude of ways that inadequate planning has disrupted or devastated the lives of people you know. Strategic planning is as important to an organization as it is to an individual. As used here, strategic planning focuses on the entire organization: (1) it is a process by which you formulate a particular intent, identify one or more associated goals, and then decide on the actions you will take to realize your intent and achieve your goals; (2) it also involves careful preparation, prudent analysis of information and data, credible decision making, and the utilization of various tools and techniques.

Strategic planning yields certain advantages that impact individuals, teams, and organizations in a favorable way, and it also has certain inherent challenges that, if not addressed or somehow mitigated, are likely to result in suboptimal results and outcomes. Successful strategy formulation and execution depend, in part, on:

- The organization embracing strategic planning as a useful and beneficial endeavor.
- The organization adopting a strategic planning process likely to capitalize on the advantages typically associated with strategic planning and address, reduce, or mitigate the challenges inherent in strategic planning.
- The individuals responsible for strategic planning putting forth the time and effort to think strategically; consider issues, options, and implications; and come to a credible decision.
- The strategic planning team's willingness to involve others (to help ensure awareness, understanding, buy-in, commitment, and advocacy) and to act in a manner that can be reviewed and evaluated at a later time.
- The strategic planning effort focusing equally on strategy formulation and execution and ensuring that thoughts, discussions, and actions relating to both occur in a planned and purposeful manner.
- Those responsible for strategic planning having access to useful and easily applicable information pertaining to the strategic planning methodology, process, tools, and techniques.

A PRACTICAL GUIDE, IN TERMS OF STRUCTURE

In my conversations with leaders and students about strategic planning and in my own personal reflection from helping facilitate strategic planning sessions, I have found that when it comes to strategic planning, all interested parties have several common desires. Everyone seems to want:

1. The strategic planning endeavor to be worthwhile.
2. The time they and the organization invest in strategic planning to yield optimal results and outcomes.
3. To measure the success of strategic planning in terms of the extent to which the organization's strategic intent is realized and the degree to which its goals are attained.
4. To focus on more than simply the numbers—it is important that how the resulting strategic plan impacts customers, clients, and other stakeholders, as well as organizational members, be taken into account.
5. To do all they can to take full advantage of strategic planning so that the results of the overall strategic planning effort impact organizational systems, processes, technology, people, and culture in a positive way.

The remainder of this book explores concepts, principles, frameworks, models, processes, tools, and techniques that, if applied, (1) will help you and other members of your organization realize the five strategic planning–related desires outlined above; (2) will likely prove useful and beneficial as you help your organization prepare for a strategic planning session, as you participate in a strategic planning session as a facilitator or participant, and/or as you review the results and outcomes of previous strategic planning efforts; and (3) will likely help you form a personal "point of view" pertaining to strategic planning.

While this chapter spotlights why this book was written and how it is designed to be used, Chapter 2 presents additional information on the importance of strategic planning to individuals (regardless of the role they play, their position or title, and their area of responsibility), teams, and organizations. It presents observations, issues, and implications of strategic thinking, strategy formulation, strategic planning, and strategy execution. Topics addressed include:

- Strategic planning versus strategic thinking versus strategic management.
- Strategic planning: what it is and what it is not.
- Benefits of strategic planning and strategic plans.
- Factors to consider when planning.
- Abilities conducive to strategic planning.
- The potentially hazardous outcome of poor planning.

Chapter 2

Background

While the previous chapter provided a brief overview of the purpose and importance of strategic planning, I will now expand on that information by reviewing important factors to consider if you are thinking about embarking on a strategic planning effort and provide information you can use to assess or firm up your current strategic planning activities. Topics covered in this chapter include:

- Strategic planning versus strategic thinking versus strategic management.
- Characteristics of an effective strategic plan.
- Benefits of strategic planning and strategic plans.
- Factors to consider when planning.
- Abilities conducive to strategic planning.
- The potentially hazardous outcome of poor planning.

The following information will prove equally useful to the individual who is developing a strategic plan for the first time; preparing for an upcoming strategic planning session; facilitating or participating in a strategic planning session; or assessing the process, results, or outcomes of a previous strategic planning session. Regardless of the circumstances, having an informed and well-rounded point of view will contribute to and undoubtedly impact your strategic planning endeavor in a positive way. Information in this and the following chapters will give you the information you need to create your personal point of view to apply to current and future strategic planning opportunities.

PLANNING VERSUS THINKING VERSUS MANAGEMENT

My work with executives and graduate students has sensitized me to the need to define and describe the relationship between several terms typically containing the word "strategic." As you begin forming your point of view, consider the differences and similarities between strategic planning, strategic thinking, and strategic management.

Strategic planning is the act (typically occurring during a meeting or session or during a series of meetings or sessions) of creating a strategic plan. The resulting strategic plan provides specific yet comprehensive information on the organization's current situation and circumstances and where the organization hopes to be or what it hopes to become over time. Strategic planning involves preparing for the strategic planning session, analyzing internal and external information, formulating or refining the organization's strategic intent and goals, deciding on a course of action likely to lead to the organization's realizing its strategic intent and achieving its goals and taking other actions during the strategic planning session to increase the likelihood of the resulting plan being successfully executed, and assessing progress and the overall success of execution to determine how to improve the next strategic planning cycle and further position the organization for optimal success.

Strategic planning requires strategic thinking, which involves taking a broad set of facts and information into consideration as you strive to understand the present situation and circumstances, identify future trends and formulate future possibilities, decide on your organization's core values and value proposition, develop or firm up your organization's mission and vision, determine the means you will employ to attain your vision and accomplish your mission, and identify ways to mitigate or address challenges or obstacles likely to impede your progress or sub-optimize your overall success. It involves shifting your viewpoint so that you consider the overall context rather than one particular part, aspect, situation, or circumstance. Strategic thinking requires you to consider a multitude of factors and variables as well as the relationship and interaction between and among those factors and variables. (For example, if you change your human resource capabilities by altering your selection criteria, you may impact your employees' ability to help your organization attain its vision and accomplish its mission.) It involves focusing not only on the present, but also on the past (to identify lessons and best practices to apply now and into the future) and the future (to anticipate changing customer and client needs, changes in technology, and external forces likely to impact the organization's vision, mission, or operational capacity or capability in a positive or negative way).

Strategic planning does not occur in a vacuum; it is one critical element of strategic management. When managing strategically, you (1) typically collaborate with others to make decisions likely to impact the entire organization in the most positive way, consistent with the organization's values and in support of the organization's vision and mission; (2) take a multitude of factors into consideration when assessing the current situation and in determining your organization's strengths, weaknesses, opportunities, and threats; (3) strive to draw valid conclusions and make credible decisions designed to contribute to the organization's short- and long-term success; (4) act personally in a planned and purposeful manner so as to impact the entire organization rather than a particular division, department, or group in a positive way; and (5) give your colleagues and followers the direction and support they need to succeed individually while contributing to the team and organization's success. Strategic management involves constantly asking fundamental questions such as:

- What is our intent or goal?
- How are we doing?
- How might we improve?
- How will we know we have improved?

KEY LEARNING POINT

The answer to "How might we improve?" may require you to choose between two or more follow-up actions. Strategic management involves evaluating such options against predefined criteria. We will review the process for evaluating options and explore potentially useful prioritization tools in Chapter 3.

CHARACTERISTICS OF AN EFFECTIVE STRATEGIC PLAN

You may be trying to decide whether or not strategic planning is needed in your organization (whether it is a business, club, association, or some other organized group) or whether to embark on a strategic planning effort for the first time. When making your decision, think about whether the following information is likely to contribute to your organization's success: a clear description of—

- What the organization will become or where it will be five to 20 years into the future.
- The value (typically in the form of services or products) the organization will provide to customers or clients over a given period, typically 12 months, with the value being consistent with and supportive of what the organization plans to become or where it plans to be in the more distant future.
- Specific goals associated with the value (again, in the form of products and services) that the organization will provide its customers and clients, consistent with and supportive of what the organization plans to become or where it plans to be in the more distant future.

- Specific strategies the organization will employ to achieve its goals.
- The strategies broken down into increasingly more detail and including a timeline, needed resources, and associated tasks and subtasks.
- Steps you are going to take to involve as many individuals as possible in your planning and execution so that a large portion of your colleagues understand, buy into, and commit to contributing to where the organization is headed and what it hopes to become.
- Steps you are going to take to ensure that the strategic planning process and resulting strategic plan do not adversely impact but rather leverage and/or take advantage of the organization's culture.
- How you will monitor deployment, implementation, and execution to ensure that progress is made as expected.
- How you will identify unexpected or unanticipated obstacles, challenges, or barriers and steps you will take to identify and adopt ways of addressing, mitigating, or otherwise addressing the obstacles, challenges, and barriers.
- How you will assess overall progress and success and determine ways to modify the strategic planning process and resulting plan to better position the organization to attain its vision and accomplish its mission.

BENEFITS OF STRATEGIC PLANNING

A strategic plan containing the above information serves as a roadmap to your organization's future. The strategic planning process adds structure to your planning efforts and helps ensure proper analysis, adequate formulation, and successful execution. The strategic planning session (or series of sessions) serves as a forum; it gives you and your colleagues the opportunity to think strategically and to "exercise your strategic management muscle." Strategic planning requires you to consider external and internal factors; evaluate what and where you currently are and where you hope to be or what you hope to become; consider alternate futures, various strategic intents and goals, and different means for attaining the decided-upon intent and achieving the decided-upon goals; recognize resource limitations (including facilities, equipment, supplies, time information, money, and capabilities); recognize uncertainty and therefore formulate contingencies; and prioritize options so that whatever future actions you take are likely to yield the most optimal results and outcomes—those results and outcomes most consistent with and supportive of the organization's mission and vision.

From personal experience, observations, and conversations with executives responsible for and/or involved in strategic planning, I have found that effective strategic planning benefits the organization by ensuring that:

1. Personal biases or blind spots do not overly influence the organization's focus, priorities, or actions.

2. Decisions impacting the organization's success are credible and can be reviewed so that the factors and considerations that went into a particular decision can be determined.

3. Organizational decisions and actions do not occur in a vacuum, but rather within the context of prescribed values, a defined mission, and a clearly articulated (and equally compelling) future.

4. Immediate, short-term actions contribute to the organization's long-term aspirations.

5. All decisions and actions pertaining to the organization's systems, processes, technology, people, and culture contribute to the overall organization's success rather than simply that of a particular functional area, department, or division.

6. Individual learning and increased awareness about everyone's interrelatedness and interdependency occur during and as a result of the strategic planning effort.

7. Decisions pertaining to the organization's value proposition and the services and products offered to clients and customers are not made in a vacuum; rather, they are made with actual stakeholder representative input or stakeholder input obtained through interviews or surveys.

8. During the strategic planning session, participants might advocate for their particular team or subgroup, but when drawing conclusions and making decisions, keep the overall organization's strategic intent and goals in mind.

9. All organizational elements are in alignment: the organization's values and value proposition match customer or client expectations; actions are being taken to take advantage of positive external forces and to address, mitigate, or reduce negative external forces; actions are being taken to leverage positive internal factors and to reduce or address negative internal factors; employees at all levels understand the role they play and what they must do to contribute to the organization's short- and long-term success; and resource capacity and capabilities match requirements associated with where the organization is heading and what the organization hopes to become.

10. A communication plan and, if necessary, a change management plan outlining relevant goals, actions, timelines or critical dates, responsible parties, and assessment criteria are included in the strategic plan or as supplements to it.

FACTORS TO CONSIDER

The above list of benefits can only occur if you proceed forward in a planned and purposeful manner and the strategic planning process you utilize is effective. Information cited above and in the previous chapter emphasizes the importance of strategic planning. Because of its importance, I encourage you to invest the time and energy necessary to ensure that your strategic planning session (or series of sessions) is an effective one. Although the following factors do not represent all the things that might cause your strategic planning process to be ineffective or produce suboptimal results, they are the "critical few" that I encourage you to keep in mind.

Be candid and honest when analyzing information and data about the current state. I frequently work with clients who assume that the current state is what they hoped or previously planned it would be, when in fact external factors have changed and internal factors have not materialized or reached their full potential. As you think about where your organization is heading or what it hopes to become, be creative and stretch yourself, but be sure to start at a proper place. Otherwise, the future you envision may not have any basis in reality; it may not resonate with or may actually seem foreign to your colleagues, clients, customers, and/or stakeholders.

KEY LEARNING POINT

The vision you create during your strategic planning session must be based in and linked to reality. If not, it will not resonate with and may actually seem foreign to your colleagues, customers, and/or stakeholders. Ask this: Is the future we describe a vision, or is it likely to come across to others as a mirage or hallucination?

When you conduct your strategic planning session, have an adequate amount of information and data on hand on which to base assumptions and conclusions. However, do not allow your team to become paralyzed by attempting to identify, gather, analyze, and understand volumes of information and data, or to delay the strategic planning session until all relevant data and information are compiled. An important point to keep in mind is that, because of the nature of information and the way it constantly changes (to reflect ever-changing external forces and internal factors), you and your team will never be able to compile all relevant up-to-the-minute data and information.

As you and your team analyze information and data, be open to team members asking questions and stating divergent views. Such questions and divergent viewpoints allow you to identify challenges or opportunities you might otherwise miss and to find additional, more effective, and more highly creative and innovative ways of attaining your organization's vision and accomplishing its mission. Such involvement on everyone's part also raises their understanding and increases their personal sense of buy-in and commitment.

While conducting your strategic planning session, strive to reach a balance between the "big picture" and isolated events, situations, and circumstances. If your team focuses too heavily on the big picture and pays too little attention to isolated events, situations, and circumstances (for example, the cost of particular supplies or the relationship your organization has with a particular supplier), it might fail to factor a mission-critical trend into your strategic plan. If your team focuses too heavily on isolated events, situations, and circumstances, it might— for example—fail to move beyond one or two problematic areas or issues and miss the opportunity to explore market forces or strengths and weaknesses associated with organization-wide systems, processes, technology, people, and culture.

As you proceed with strategic planning, do not become bogged down on the differences or similarities between strategic planning, long-range planning, tactical planning, and so on. Rather, clarify your need: determine whether you need to plan for your entire organization or plan for a particular subunit (a particular division, department, unit, or functional group) and proceed forward accordingly.

For our purpose, the strategic planning hierarchy has only two levels: the entire organization and its subgroups (division, department, functional area, or group). When developing organization-wide strategic plans, Hrebiniak (a noted professor, author, and researcher) recommends that you strive to answer three basic questions:

1. Are we playing in the right sandbox? Here, one key issue is whether your organization is likely to succeed in the business it's in or should enter a new business. Another issue is whether your organization is offering value likely to resonate with your intended clients and customers or should change its services or products or its client and customer groups. Another issue is whether your organization is offering services and products in the proper locations or should enter new geographic regions.

2. Are we leveraging our capabilities? Here, one key issue is whether you have the facilities, equipment, and supplies you need and whether your employees at all levels have the knowledge, skills, and abilities they need to contribute to the organization's short- and long-term success. Another issue is whether your organization's structure, procedures, processes, or norms are contributing to or interfering with the contributions made by the organization's facilities, equipment, supplies, and people.

3. Are we performing at optimal levels? Here, one key issue is whether you have developed and communicated expectations pertaining to individual, team, and organizational performance and whether technology, systems, and processes are in place to support and reinforce their implementation. Another issue is whether behavioral expectations have been specified in increasing levels of detail so as to increase the likelihood of understanding and implementation: for example, whether your organization has created, communicated, and provided feedback on individual, team, and organizational goals and objectives.

When creating a strategic plan for a subunit (a division, department, functional area, or group) of the organization, Hrebiniak recommends that you strive to understand and:

- Capitalize on industry and market forces. Here, one key issue pertains to whether your services or products are unique and likely to meet or exceed the needs of your clients or customers. A key consideration is whether your customers are able to procure elsewhere the products and services you offer. Another key issue pertains to whether you have consistent and reliable access to all of the inputs (employees, supplies, equipment, etc.) your organization needs to succeed.
- Counter competitor strategies and capabilities. Here, one key issue pertains to whether you are positioned to compete with your competitors and, if so, are likely to win. A key consideration relates to your competitor's ability to take advantage of the positive or counter the negative aspects of your industry and market forces. Another key issue pertains to whether your competitor's strategic thinking, strategic planning, and strategic management give it an advantage over your organization.
- Take advantage of your tangible and intangible assets. Here, one key issue pertains to whether you have and are taking advantage of tangible assets such as your supplier network, the capability and capacity of your employees (at all levels), and facilities, equipment, and supplies. A key consideration relates to whether you have a positive, neutral, or negative reputation and whether you are taking full advantage of a good reputation in the marketplace. Another key issue pertains to whether your employees possess unique knowledge, skills, and abilities and whether your organization is using this intangible asset to its fullest advantage.[1]

Whereas Hrebiniak spotlights factors typically considered when organizations develop organization-wide and subunit (division, department, functional area, or group) strategic plans, Mintzberg (another leading professor, author, and researcher) and his colleagues—in identifying 10 different schools of thought pertaining to strategic planning—in essence showcase the far-reaching consequences of properly designed, effective strategic planning. One might take away from Mintzberg that effective strategic planning should impact your organization in a variety of positive ways, allowing you to:

1. Match your organization's internal strengths to its current and emerging external environment.
2. Explore and develop alternative means for your organization achieving short- and long-term success.
3. Analyze competitive pressures and identify ways of improving your organization's competitive positioning.

4. Create a vision for the future that is compelling and exciting to all stakeholder groups.

5. Analyze current and emerging trends, patterns, tendencies, and movements and identify ways to taking advantage of the positive features and reduce, avoid, or mitigate the negative features.

6. Identify prevailing and prospective best practices and incorporate them into the strategic plan as well as share them with all organizational members so that they duplicate previous successes and do not repeat previous mistakes.

7. Do whatever it takes to address challenges associated with limited resources so that the organization can meet or exceed the needs and expectations of its key stakeholder groups.

8. Take advantage of and further reinforce key cultural norms by, for example, involving individuals from throughout the organization in the strategic planning process or taking steps to ensure that a large portion of organizational members participate, contribute, and/or share input.

9. Monitor and analyze external forces and take steps to take advantage of positive forces and mitigate negative ones.

10. Continuously improve as an organization, such as by transforming from a centralized to a decentralized decision-making structure.[2]

Whereas most strategic planning endeavors focus heavily on identifying ways to "defeat" the competition, Kim and Mauborgne stress the importance of the strategic planning process in allowing you to broaden your perspective to a much more strategic level and asking questions outside the competitor-competition arena. For example, effective strategic planning should allow you to:

- Analyze existing internal factors relating to systems, processes, technology, people, and culture to determine which factors you should eliminate, create, or change.

- Modify and refine your preliminary "to be" strategy based on input you receive from your key stakeholders.

- Analyze the services and products your organization provides to ensure that clients or customers are likely to purchase them because your services and products meet or exceed their needs and expectations.

- Analyze the quality, cost, and availability of the products and services your organization provides to ensure that they meet or exceed your client and customer requirements.

- Analyze all factors impacting your organization's ability to act on its value proposition to ensure, for example, that manufacturing, transportation, and distribution costs and the price of the services and products will allow (1) your clients and customers to purchase them and (2) your organization to realize needed profit margins.[3]

ABILITIES CONDUCIVE TO STRATEGIC PLANNING

Personal observations and experience facilitating strategic planning sessions and conversations with executives responsible for strategic planning have led me to conclude that certain abilities contribute to successful strategic planning. This does not suggest that all of these abilities are required for strategic planning to succeed or that these abilities cannot be further developed over time. However, it is important (1) that a "critical mass" of these abilities be naturally present and contribute to the strategic planning effort, or (2) that methodologies, tools, techniques, and facilitation skills be applied to ensure that proper behaviors surface and contribute to the strategic planning effort.

When it comes to effectively and efficiently developing and subsequently executing a strategic plan, it is beneficial if those who participate in the process are:

- Willing to analyze and act on relatively little information.
- Willing to analyze and act on relatively complex information.
- Willing to make sound decisions.
- Willing to take reasonable risks.
- Willing to ask insightful questions and contribute divergent viewpoints.
- Able to communicate with others and express opinions and ideas in a way that does not upset others.
- Comfortable working with individuals possessing unfamiliar skill sets.
- Comfortable working with individuals of other cultures.
- Comfortable working with individuals from other geographic regions.
- Comfortable working in an environment in which a structured framework is applied.
- Well rounded, in terms of orientation, viewpoint, and perspective.
- Able to manage disagreement and resolve conflict in an efficient and effective manner.

It is unreasonable and quite unrealistic to believe that everyone participating in the strategic planning effort will possess all of the above personal abilities. Reflecting on this information now and sharing it with prospective strategic planning participants in the future will help raise awareness of how your skills and abilities are likely to impact how you contribute to the strategic planning effort. Such insight might prove invaluable; for example, if your organization's strategic planning process requires you to think strategically and you are naturally a tactical thinker, all is not lost. You may simply find the strategic planning process a bit frustrating, and forcing yourself to think strategically may feel a little awkward and perhaps take you a little more time. However, as you "flex your strategic thinking muscle," it will become less challenging, you will begin to feel less awkward, and you will eventually require less effort and time. Recognizing this in advance will allow you to deal with the "down side" in an appropriate way at the appropriate time. In addition, it will compel you to explore various tools and techniques presented throughout this book that are designed to help address personal blind spots and biases and contribute to effective and efficient strategic planning.

THE POTENTIALLY HAZARDOUS OUTCOME OF POOR PLANNING

I mentioned in the previous section that participating in a strategic planning effort might, at times, cause an individual to become frustrated or feel awkward. My experience suggests that a poorly designed strategic planning process will likely yield the following negative results while the planning session is under way:

- Participants feel they are being manipulated and therefore become skeptical of the overall process and question the resulting deliverable.
- Participants withdraw from the strategic planning process and assume no responsibility for or ownership of the deliverables.
- Participants covertly sabotage the strategic planning effort in potentially one of several ways: they withhold suggestions and recommendations; they provide skewed or biased input; they say or do things to slow down or derail the process in other subtle or not-so-subtle ways.
- Participants refuse to actively participate in individual or team activities.
- Participants become frustrated with the other participants and then themselves.

The result of a poorly conducted strategic planning session is a deliverable (i.e., a resulting strategic plan) that:

- Lacks credibility in the eyes of everyone, including those who participated in the strategic planning session.
- Is not likely to be embraced or advocated by anyone, including those who participated in the strategic planning session.
- Lacks credibility and is likely to be rejected by key stakeholders, including the executive or organizational leader who sponsored and who (hopefully) participated in the strategic planning session.
- Does not contribute to the organization's short- or long-term success.
- Or worse, allows the organization to proceed in an inefficient manner or go down an incorrect path.
- May lead key stakeholders to withdraw their support for future strategic planning sessions.
- May lead low- to middle-level employees to exert suboptimal effort when executing associated tasks and subtasks.

• May lead upper- and highest-level employees to subtly or perhaps not so subtly withdraw their support for future strategic planning sessions.

To summarize, in this chapter you have reviewed the purpose and importance of strategic planning and how an effective strategic plan contributes to an organization's short- and long-term success. You have explored how strategic thinking contributes to strategic planning and how strategic planning is a critical element of strategic management. You have reviewed characteristics of an effective strategic plan and how such a plan benefits the individual, team, and organization. You have also explored factors to consider when planning, skills and abilities conducive to strategic planning, and what might happen if your strategic planning effort proves to be suboptimal.

Chapter 3

Planning to Plan

While previous chapters addressed the purpose and importance of strategic planning and factors to consider if you are thinking about embarking on a strategic planning effort or assessing or firming up your current strategic planning activities, this chapter provides comprehensive and detailed information, tools, and techniques you will likely find useful and beneficial if you are developing a strategic plan for the first time or are planning for an upcoming strategic planning session.

Just as you undoubtedly have a toolkit in your house (to use whenever there is a need for certain tools or supplies) or vehicle (to use on those occasions when you might be experiencing unexpected problems when commuting or traveling), the tools and techniques in this and the following chapters should become a part of your strategic planning toolkit to use when unexpected and unplanned challenges surface during your strategic planning preparation, conduct, or follow-up.

SETTING THE STAGE

An effective strategic plan is not created by happenstance; it requires planned and purposeful action resulting from participants (1) following a clearly defined process and (2) contributing their time, energy, thoughts, ideas, suggestions, and recommendations to and throughout the process. A participant's willingness to follow the "prescribed" process and contribute totally and completely does not simply occur; it results from your establishing an atmosphere that supports such actions. As you consider all the factors and issues pertaining to strategic planning and you proceed with your strategic planning endeavor, I encourage you to adopt a personal philosophy centered on the idea that the individuals participating in the strategic planning effort, and those subsequently impacted by the resulting strategic plan, are key to the short- and long-term success of your strategic planning effort and your organization. As you design your strategic planning process and prepare for your strategic planning meeting, aspire to the following principles:

- *Help.* Through the strategic planning process you utilize and the methodologies, tools, and techniques you use, help individuals participating in the strategic planning process and the other members of the organization understand the prevailing situation and circumstances and, based on their understanding, identify, discuss, and agree on how to address the challenges and take advantage of the positives.

- *Help.* Through the vision and mission the participants articulate and the means they identify for realizing the vision and accomplishing the mission, help individuals participating in the strategic planning effort and the other members of your organization succeed. As appropriate, ensure consideration and discussion about how your organization will develop internal capabilities to meet or exceed immediate and future stakeholder needs and expectations. As necessary, ensure development and subsequent implementation of a change management plan. As needed, ensure creation and immediate utilization of a communication plan.

- *Treat.* Through your leadership and/or facilitation style, as well as through the methodologies, tools, and techniques you utilize, treat individuals participating in the strategic planning endeavor and the other members of your organization as adults. Recognize and take advantage of their input, contribution, ideas, suggestions, and recommendations. They may not possess specialty certifications or advanced degrees (although they may), but by being personally involved in and/ or impacted by your organization's systems, technology, processes, people, and culture, they are uniquely positioned to help identify ways to bring the totality of your resources to bear on current and emerging challenges and opportunities and to combine, consolidate, and/or apply them in such a way as to ensure greater short- and long-term individual, team, and organizational success.

- *Use.* Through the process you follow, the methodologies, tools, and techniques you use, and the way you treat individuals participating in the strategic planning process and with everyone throughout the organization as you communicate and share the resulting strategic plan, use the strategic planning effort as an opportunity to introduce and/or further reinforce concepts, principles, and practices relating to strategic thinking, strategy formulation, strategic planning, strategy execution, continuous improvement, decision making, problem solving, disagreement management, conflict resolution, prioritization, teaming, and collaboration.

As you design your strategic planning process and prepare for your strategic planning meeting, strive to introduce and/or reinforce the following key tenets to all members of the organization:

- Strategic thinking and strategic management will be our organization's way of doing business.

- The conclusions we draw and the decisions we make will be based on the analysis of information and data.
- When making important, strategic, mission-critical decisions, we will bring members of our organization together to analyze information, discuss issues, draw conclusions, and make decisions.
- While we as an organization may remain confident and optimistic, we plan and prepare for the unplanned and unexpected by analyzing risks and identifying contingencies.
- As appropriate, we will share our overall strategic planning approach, process, methodologies, tools, and techniques, as well as the logic we apply to our issues and the bases of our conclusions and decisions, with our various stakeholder groups.
- Strategic planning is not complete and cannot be successful until strategies are executed in an effective and efficient manner; we will therefore:
  - Take steps to ensure execution, such as develop concrete goals, identify tasks and subtasks, develop associated metrics (the measure of an organization's activities or performance), and assign responsible parties, critical dates or timeframes, and assessment criteria.
  - As necessary, supplement the strategic plan with a change management plan and, as needed, develop and implement a communication plan.

I introduced the differences, similarities, and relationships between strategic thinking, strategic planning, and strategic management in the last chapter. Strategic thinking is an integral part—and at times the hardest part—of strategic planning. Likewise, subsequent execution of the strategies formulated during the strategic planning process is an integral part—and at times the hardest part—of strategic management. Experience and conversations with countless executives and graduate students reinforce to me that strategic management not only involves deciding on the desired position of an organization in the business environment, but also includes the acquisition of the right capabilities, the allocation of resources, the establishment of performance objectives and the monitoring of metrics, and the constant assessment, feedback, and actions contributing to continuous improvement that make that position a reality. As you proceed with your strategic planning effort, consider the creation of the strategic plan to be the beginning rather than the end of your effort; only through successful execution marked by constant and steady progress, short-term accomplishment of your organization's mission, and the ultimate attainment of your organization's vision will your strategic planning effort be complete and successful. Here, I use the terms "complete" and "successful" with some reservation: your strategic planning effort will never be "complete" in that you will factor the results of your first effort and time period into your next strategic planning cycle, and during the initial effort and time period and throughout subsequent cycles, you will strive to continuously improve your strategic planning process as well as your strategy formulation and execution.

As you prepare to embark on your strategic planning effort or assess your current strategic planning process or the results of previous planning efforts, do so with these key points in mind:

- Develop your strategic planning approach, create your strategic planning meeting agenda, and assemble your strategic planning team with an eye toward eventual execution.

- Act and treat others in a way that reinforces the important role they will play in the strategic planning process and in the subsequent execution.

- Structure and then facilitate the process in a way that encourages participation, involvement, and inclusion.

- Apply tools and techniques that encourage the involvement of many, the sharing of ideas and divergent viewpoints, and the input and contribution of others.

- Take steps to help ensure understanding, buy-in, and commitment; apply tools and techniques to ensure that all voices are heard and all voices are equal. Take steps to ensure that the process you follow is credible and that the steps you take throughout your strategic planning effort yield credible conclusions, valid decisions, and reasonable follow-up actions.

The effort to ensure understanding, buy-in, and commitment begins before you launch your strategic planning effort. Before your strategic planning process has been decided upon or defined, your strategic planning team has been assembled, and the strategic planning meeting agenda has been developed and distributed, you begin setting the stage for effective strategic planning by sharing general information about strategic planning and talking at various forums (such as meetings with superiors, colleagues, direct reports, and key stakeholders). Prior to embarking on your strategic planning effort, it is important that you have created awareness throughout your organization (however small or large it may be) about the importance of strategic planning—stressing that without it, organizations simply cannot gain superiority in the marketplace and that in today's tumultuous economy and competitive environment, organizations must constantly decide:

- Which customers to serve, which products and services to provide, and which resources and capabilities to deploy.

- What they want to achieve in the marketplace, how they will differentiate themselves from current and future competitors in the minds of their customers, and what returns and rewards they wish to attain for their stakeholders.

As you raise awareness about the purpose and importance of strategic planning, consider describing the strategic planning effort as the means by which your organization will articulate what future success entails and the resulting strategic plan as the roadmap your organization will use as it ventures from the present into the future. Emphasize that the strategic planning process will be consistent with and supportive of your organization's culture, will reinforce its underlying values, and will produce a strategic plan that will be concrete enough to provide short- and long-term direction yet flexible enough to accommodate the ever-changing environment in which your organization functions. Also emphasize that the strategic planning process will:

- Establish goals resulting from the analysis of internal strengths and opportunities and external weaknesses and threats.
- Include strategies to help the organization achieve its goals, accomplish its mission, and attain its vision.
- Specify concrete tactics and actions to help ensure that your organization's strategies are successfully deployed.
- Articulate to members of your organization how their decisions and actions will contribute to the tactics and actions outlined in the strategic plan and recognize how the strategic plan will position their organization to succeed, given its internal strengths and weaknesses and the complex and competitive environment within which it operates.

As you begin "spreading the word" about strategic planning through your company, agency, club, association, church, or community organization, it is important that you take advantage of scheduled and unplanned and unexpected opportunities to raise the awareness and interest of others. To take full advantage of these opportunities, keep several key points about strategic planning and about how it will benefit your organization in mind to consistently share with others. To facilitate the sharing of such information, consider creating a 3- by 5-inch billfold or wallet reminder card highlighting seven to 10 key points pertaining to these three questions:

- Why us?
- Why strategic planning?
- Why now?

The size of the reminder card will make it easily transportable and easy to refer to when interacting with your superiors, colleagues, or direct reports. The information you include in your reminder card should relate specifically to your situation and circumstance and emphasize information relevant to your organization. As you create your reminder card, consider including information similar to that outlined in Sample of Application 3.1.

The size, complexity, or nature of your organization may suggest the need for a more direct or formal approach to "spreading the word" to your superiors, colleagues, or direct reports. Rather than finding opportune times to personally

Sample of Application 3.1

BILLFOLD OR WALLET REMINDER CARD

Why Us?

- Although we have been successful, we undoubtedly could be much more successful.
- Strategic planning supports our focus on continuous improvement.
- Strategic planning will help us clarify our thinking, focus our effort and actions, and do all that is needed to ensure short- and long-term future success.

Why Strategic Planning?

- It will allow us to take a multitude of factors into consideration when we decide on our future.
- It will help us make decisions about how our systems, technology, processes, and people will contribute to our future success.
- When it comes to meeting the needs of our clients, strategic planning will help us "do the right things for the right reasons."

Why Now?

- We have historically been challenged—and are being increasingly challenged—when it comes to having adequate money or resources.
- We have previously gone about our business in a rather piecemeal, happenstance way. Strategic planning will provide some much-needed direction as well as the structure we need to be more focused with future decisions and actions.
- Added direction and focus will benefit us, our colleagues, and our clients.

---

share the key points laid out in your reminder card, you might consider developing, sending, and distributing an e-mail or memorandum. This means of sharing information with your key stakeholders is a good one, in that you will be able to provide additional information for them to consider at a time and place that is convenient for them. As with the reminder card, it is essential that the e-mail or memorandum relate specifically to your situation and circumstance and emphasize information relevant to your organization. If you decide to raise awareness and understanding through a memorandum or e-mail, consider including information similar to that outlined in Sample of Application 3.2.

Normally scheduled and conducted forums, along with ad hoc meetings, should provide adequate opportunity for you to raise everyone's awareness of the importance

Sample of Application 3.2

AWARENESS-RAISING E-MAIL OR MEMORANDUM

Date: Today's date

To: Members of our leadership team

From: A. B. Smith

Subject: Results of Research on Strategic Planning

I have completed researching the topic of strategic planning. I have reviewed books written by noted authors and have considered their advice and comments within the context of our organization. Although we feel we have achieved a certain level of success during our three years of existence, we as a leadership team feel confident that we can do better. My research suggests that strategic planning is one tool likely to prove useful as we strive to continuously improve and set the stage for even higher levels of short- and long-term future success!

Advantages of Strategic Planning

A strategic plan, in short, serves as a roadmap to an organization's future. Strategic planning is not new; applications in the public and private sectors have proven time and again that the strategic planning process adds structure to an organization's planning efforts and helps ensure proper analysis, adequate strategy formulation, and successful execution. The strategic planning session (or series of sessions) serves as a forum; it gives members of the organization the opportunity to think strategically and to exercise their "strategic management muscle." Strategic planning requires members of an organization to:

- Consider prevailing and emerging external forces and internal factors.
- Evaluate what they currently do, where they currently are (for example, within the competitive landscape), and where they hope to be or what they hope to become.
- Consider alternate futures, various strategic intents and goals, and different means for realizing the intents and achieving the goals.
- Recognize resource limitations (including facilities, equipment, supplies, time information, money, and capabilities).
- Recognize uncertainty and therefore formulate contingencies.
- Select and prioritize options so that whatever future actions they take are likely to yield results and outcomes consistent with and supportive of the organization's mission and vision.

Advantages to Our Organization

As you know, we have been reflecting on how we function as a leadership team. Within the context of those discussions and based on what I have learned about strategic planning, I sincerely believe that our embarking on a strategic planning effort will benefit our organization in these ways:

- The personal biases of a handful of people will no longer overly influence our organization's focus.
- Decisions impacting the organization's success will become more credible in our eyes and in the eyes of our people.
- The decisions we make in the future will no longer occur in a vacuum, but rather within the context of a clearly defined mission and articulated future.
- We as a leadership team will be more confident that the decisions our executives make pertaining to our systems, processes, technology, and people will contribute to the organization's success rather than the success of a particular division, department, or unit.
- We will stop making decisions about services and products in a vacuum; rather, we will include a stakeholder representative in our process or consider stakeholder input obtained through interviews or surveys.

Next Steps

I encourage you to give some personal thought to this issue and to perhaps explore the topics of strategic thinking, strategic planning, and strategic management. I ask that we devote a portion of our next "Friday Leadership Team Meeting" to the topic of strategic planning, with the objective of deciding whether embarking on a strategic planning effort is likely to benefit our organization, our people, and our clients.

For More Information

Numerous articles, books, and white papers have been written on the topic of strategic planning, and I am confident that a review of the trade journals you typically read will yield quite a few articles on this topic. I found the following three books to be of immense value in my personal learning:

- Hrebiniak, Lawrence G. 2005. *Making Strategy Work.* Upper Saddle River, NJ: Wharton School Publishing.
- Mintzberg, Henry, Joseph Lampel, and Bruce Ahlstrand. 2008. *Strategy Safari: A Guided Tour through the Wilds of Strategic Management.* New York: The Free Press.
- Kim, W. Chan, and Renee Mauborgne. 2005. *Blue Ocean Strategy.* Boston: Harvard Business School Press.

of strategic planning. Your objective is to build enough interest, excitement, and enthusiasm to offset the concern that employees (at all levels) might have with the uncertainty and ambiguity that accompany any first-time effort, activity, or offering and to counter their desire to continue doing what they have previously done and further uphold and maintain the status quo.

Conversations with key stakeholders and meetings with members of your various stakeholder groups will allow you to build interest, excitement, and enthusiasm for moving forward with strategic planning. Unfortunately, interest, excitement, and enthusiasm alone are not enough. While setting the stage for strategic planning, it is important to ensure that your organization is prepared to move forward in these three critical ways:

- As has been stressed throughout the previous section of this chapter, it is important that members of your organization have the "heart" to proceed forward; that is, they must have the desire to, for example, set time aside from the already busy day to analyze your organization's current state; to consider, discuss, and make decisions about your organization's future; and to formulate the means of progressing from the present to the future. Because your strategic planning process will involve their ongoing input and contribution, it important that the members of your organization buy into the process and personally commit to helping make the strategic planning effort a success.
- It is important that members of your organization have the "mind" to proceed forward; that is, they must possess the knowledge to help create, deploy, and/or implement the organization's strategic plan.
- Although having the desire and requisite knowledge is extremely important, my experience working with organizations has shown that it is equally important that members of your organization have the "hands" to proceed forward in developing and implementing your organization's strategic plan. That is, they must have the skills, abilities, tools, and techniques to analyze the current state; to consider, discuss, and make decisions about your organization's future; and to formulate the means of progressing from the present to the future.

While meeting with key stakeholders and members of your various stakeholder groups, determine whether the organization is prepared to move forward with strategic planning. Listen closely to what individuals ask and say; their words will give you insight as to whether:

- Senior leadership considers strategic planning to be an important cornerstone of your organization's future and therefore is willing to encourage everyone to contribute to the strategic planning effort.
- Executives and managers consider strategic planning to be an important part of strategic management and therefore an endeavor to which they will commit personal and team member time and energy.

- Supervisors consider strategic planning to contribute to organizational performance and continuous improvement and so encourage their team members to assist and support the strategic planning effort.
- All members of your organization recognize the importance of strategic planning to the organization's—and thus to their personal—success and therefore an endeavor that they will personally assist and support.
- Members of your organization understand what strategy formulation entails, in terms of concepts and principles that typically contribute to successful strategy formulation and execution.
- Members of your organization possess tools and techniques likely to prove useful in formulating strategy, preparing the organization for execution, and implementing and deploying the resulting strategic plan.

The extent to which your senior leaders, executives, managers, supervisors, and individual contributors possess the requisite knowledge, skills, and abilities (as well as the associated tools and techniques) will impact the actions you must take to further set the stage for strategic planning to successfully occur within your organization. Table 3.1 lists actions you might take if your organization is not ready to proceed with strategic planning.

Given the advantages of strategic planning and how it benefits organizations in such a positive manner, you will be able to move forward once you have invested the time and energy required (1) to raise the awareness and understanding of your superiors, colleagues, direct reports, and key stakeholders and (2) to ensure that all parties involved in helping develop and execute strategy possess the needed knowledge, skills, and abilities. Once you make the decision to proceed with strategic planning, you must immediately start planning to plan.

PREPARING THE FRAMEWORK

You have invested time and effort to raise awareness and understanding of the importance of strategic planning, how it typically benefits organizations in general, and how it will likely benefit your organization in particular. You feel you have garnered the interest, excitement, and enthusiasm of others. You have

---

KEY LEARNING POINT

If the questions being asked and the comments being made suggest that you lack adequate support, do not move forward. Circle back and take additional steps to raise awareness and understanding and to garner the needed support. Move forward once you feel you have garnered the interest, excitement, and enthusiasm of others.

Table 3.1   Likely Challenges and Potential Solutions

If you discover that . . .	Consider . . .
Senior leadership does not consider strategic planning to be important to your organization's future.	• Arrange for your leader and/or leadership team to meet with or speak to strategic planning thought leaders (researchers, authors, and icons of your particular industry or profession). • Send key members of your leadership team to strategic planning workshops or sessions sponsored by respected institutes, colleges, universities, think tanks, or consultancies. • Share additional information with the leader and/or leadership team during private meetings. • Brief the leader and/or leadership team during normally scheduled business meetings. • Seek out information about the experience that board members have pertaining to strategic planning and share the information with the leader and/or leadership team. • Share articles on strategic planning from professional journals to which the leader and/or leadership team subscribe. • Share white papers on strategic planning from professional associations to which the leader and/or leadership team belong.
Executives and managers do not understand strategic management or do not consider strategic planning to be an important part of strategic management.	• Arrange for key executives or managers to speak with a strategic planning thought leader in a respected college or university. • Arrange for key executives or managers to speak with their counterparts in similar (but noncompeting) organizations that recently tackled strategic planning. • Share additional information with executives and managers who are held in exceptionally high regard by their fellow executives and managers. • Share additional information with executives and managers during normally scheduled executive and management team meetings.

(Continued)

Table 3.1 (Continued)

	• Find out from your organization's training department (if it has one) if it has any materials or courses on strategic planning; if so, share the materials or information with the executives and managers or ask the training department to offer a special briefing or to offer the briefing during a normally scheduled executive or management team meeting. • Share articles on strategic planning from professional journals, emphasizing to the executives and managers that the articles are from professional journals to which the leader and/or leadership team subscribe. • Share white papers on strategic planning from professional associations, emphasizing to the executives and managers that the papers are from professional associations to which the leader and/or leadership team belong. • If your organization's leaders and/or leadership team recognize the importance of strategic planning and agree to advocate strategy formulation and execution, ask the leader or select members of the leadership team to meet with the executives or managers to emphasize to them the importance of strategic planning to the organization and why it is important that executives and managers commit personal and team member time and energy to the strategic planning endeavor.
Supervisors do not consider strategic planning to contribute to organizational performance or continuous improvement.	• Arrange for key supervisors (i.e., in a core area of the organization, from one of the larger stakeholder groups, or a supervisor who is held in exceptionally high regard by superiors, colleagues, and direct reports) to speak with a strategic planning thought leader in a respected college or university. • Arrange for key supervisors to speak with their counterparts in similar (but noncompeting) organizations that recently tackled strategic planning. • Using a variety of means and forums, share additional information with those supervisors held in exceptionally high regard by their fellow supervisors and through direct reports. • Share additional information with all supervisors during normally scheduled meetings. • Find out from your organization's training department (if it has one) if it has any materials or courses on strategic planning; if so, share the materials or information with supervisors or ask the training department to offer a special workshop.

	• Share articles on strategic planning from professional journals, emphasizing to the supervisors that the articles are from professional journals to which the leadership, executive, or management team subscribe.
• Share white papers on strategic planning from professional associations, emphasizing to the supervisors that the papers are from professional associations to which the leadership, executive, or management team belong.
• If your organization's leadership team recognizes the importance of strategic planning and agrees to advocate strategy formulation and execution, ask a select member of the leadership team, accompanied by one or more executives or managers, to meet with the supervisors to emphasize to them the importance of strategic planning to the organization and why it is important that they commit personal and team member time and energy to the strategic planning endeavor.
Members of your organization do not recognize the importance of strategic planning to the organization's—and thus to their personal—success.	• Conduct informational meetings or sessions throughout the organization.
• If your organization has a cafeteria or formal break areas, set up information desks when a large portion of the organization is likely to see and most likely to approach individuals staffing the desks.
• Share additional information with key members (i.e., the informal leaders) of your organization who are held in exceptionally high regard by their superiors, colleagues, associates, and/or direct reports.
• Share additional information with members of your organization during normally scheduled "all-hands" meetings.
• Find out from your organization's training department (if it has one) if it has any materials or courses on strategic planning; if so, include materials or information in normally scheduled or "special circumstance" newsletters.
• Find out from your organization's training department if it has any materials or courses on strategic planning; if so, ask it to offer special or additional sessions and/or showcase the information and materials during normally scheduled business programs or business meetings.
• Share articles on strategic planning from professional journals to which a large segment of your organization subscribe.

(Continued)

37

Table 3.1 (Continued)

	• Share white papers on strategic planning from professional associations to which a large segment of your organization belong. • If your organization's leaders and/or leadership team recognize the importance of strategic planning and agree to advocate strategy formulation and execution, ask the leader or members of the leadership team, accompanied by select executives, managers, and supervisors, to conduct special meetings (perhaps an all-hands meeting or a series of department or division meetings) to emphasize to everyone the importance of strategic planning to the organization and why it is important for everyone to personally commit to supporting and assisting with the strategic planning endeavor.
Members of your organization do not possess tools and techniques likely to prove useful in formulating strategy, preparing the organization for execution, and implementing and deploying the resulting strategic plan.	• Add books on strategic planning models, frameworks, approaches, principles, tools, and techniques to your organization's library. Add professional journals containing articles on strategic planning models, frameworks, approaches, principles, tools, and techniques to your organization's library. If your organization does not have a library, purchase a bookcase and place it (and the relevant reading material) in an area that many of your leaders, executives, managers, supervisors, and individual contributors are likely to visit. • Distribute a reading list of materials on and about strategic planning models, frameworks, approaches, principles, tools, and techniques throughout your organization and make it easy for everyone to borrow books or journals containing information on strategic planning. • Send representatives to public courses or workshops on strategic planning models, frameworks, approaches, principles, tools, and techniques. • Conduct informational meetings or sessions on strategic planning models, frameworks, approaches, principles, tools, and techniques throughout the organization. • If your organization has a cafeteria or formal break areas, set up information desks (showcasing sample strategic planning models, frameworks, approaches, principles, tools, and techniques) when a large portion of the organization is likely to see and most likely to approach individuals staffing the desks.

also assessed the organization to ensure that everyone involved in helping develop and execute strategy possesses the needed knowledge, skills, and abilities. Where the organization lacked the necessary readiness, you took steps to enhance capabilities and otherwise to ensure that needed planning tools and techniques will be available when needed.

You can now proceed with strategic planning in a structured and purposeful way. You must solidify your thinking about the elements your strategic planning framework will contain and the components your strategic plan will include. It is important that you consider these issues (1) within the context of your organization's culture and (2) in light of the factors your organization will likely consider to be of paramount importance when ultimately deciding whether the process you follow is credible and the resulting strategic plan is worthwhile.

The Strategic Planning Framework

Professional services firms offer strategic planning services to clients in all conceivable industries and professions. Many of these firms' strategic planning methodologies can be accessed on their Web sites. Doing so, along with reviewing books and articles on the subject, quickly reveals an interesting observation: approaches to strategic planning are very similar, and the steps strategic planning processes typically follow are also similar. This observation should not be surprising because (1) strategic planning has a particular purpose regardless of where or by whom it is applied; (2) accomplishing the purpose of strategic planning in a credible manner requires one to explore certain fundamental issues and answer certain core questions; and (3) the exploration of such issues and the pursuit of the answers to such questions naturally follow a certain path and involve the use of similar methodologies, tools, and techniques.

The strategic planning framework I introduce below is therefore likely to prove useful and beneficial to you. You will undoubtedly need to modify the process to meet your particular needs or to match the cultural norms or the thinking and decision-making style of your organization. Prior to adopting this or any strategic planning approach, I encourage you to review it carefully and modify it to ensure that it will address your specific needs and meet your organization's requirements and expectations.

Regardless of the specific strategic planning framework, model, or process you ultimately use, it is likely to prove credible if the steps it contains allow you and your colleagues to analyze information and also consider and discuss issues relating to, and subsequently decide on and/or specify:

- The value (in the form of services or products) your organization will provide to customers or clients over a short-term period, typically 12 to 18 months.
- What your organization will become or where it will be five to 20 years into the future.

- Specific goals associated with the value (again, in the form of products and services) your organization will provide its customers and clients over the short term, consistent with and supportive of what your organization plans to become or where it plans to be in the more distant future.

- Specific strategies your organization will employ to achieve its goals.

- The strategies broken down into increasingly more detail and including a timeline, needed resources, and associated tasks and subtasks.

- Steps you will take to involve as many individuals as possible in your planning and execution so that a large portion of your colleagues understand, buy into, and commit to contributing to where the organization is headed and what it hopes to become.

- Steps you will take to ensure that the strategic planning process and resulting strategic plan do not adversely impact but rather leverage and/or take advantage of the organization's culture.

- How you will monitor deployment, implementation, and execution to ensure that progress is made as expected.

- How you will identify unexpected or unanticipated obstacles, challenges, or barriers, and steps you will take to identify and adopt ways of addressing, mitigating, or otherwise addressing the obstacles, challenges, and barriers.

- How you will assess overall progress and success and determine ways to modify the strategic planning process and resulting plan to better position the organization to accomplish its mission and attain its vision.

KEY LEARNING POINT

Do not exhaust your time, effort, and energy searching for the one ideal or perfect generic framework, model, or process to apply to your strategic planning endeavor. Create a new approach or adopt or modify an existing one to answer these important questions within the context of your organization, industry, and environment. You will then have the strategic planning framework, model, or process you need and will be able to move forward in a confident manner.

A strategic planning framework containing the following nine elements will help you perform the above tasks and thus help your organization realize the associated benefits:

1. *Gather, analyze, and summarize information.* Identify the kind of internal and external information and data your planning team needs to consider as it determines your organization's internal strengths and weaknesses and identifies

current and emerging threats and opportunities that exist in the environment within which your organization functions. Identify sources of the needed data and information; collect, analyze, and summarize the data and information.

2. *Analyze information relating to the organization's value proposition and the internal factors and external forces likely to impact its short- and long-term success.* Analyze the above data and information to determine the extent to which your organization is delivering on its value proposition and to identify your internal strengths (S) and weaknesses (W) and the current and emerging opportunities (O) and threats (T) presented by the external environment within which your organization functions.

3. *Create (or verify) your organization's mission, vision, and sweet spot.* Your mission statement indicates what the organization will strive to accomplish over the short term, whereas the vision statement indicates what the organization will strive to become or where it hopes to be in the future. Your organization's "sweet spot" is where its passion, abilities, and purpose or reason for existence intersect.

4. *Create strategic goal statements.* Based on your analysis of—and in support of—the organization's mission and vision statements, create goal statements describing (and adding clarity and specificity to) your mission and vision statements.

5. *Identify and prioritize the means by which you will achieve the strategic goals.* With your mission and vision statements in mind, determine the various means by which you will achieve your strategic goals.

6. *Identify tactics, assign roles and responsibilities, establish timelines, and define metrics.* For each strategy, identify the tactics necessary to accomplish that strategy along with associated roles, responsibilities, and timelines. For each strategy, define the metrics necessary to determine if you are making anticipated progress and are on track for achieving your strategic goals.

7. *Plan for the unexpected and unanticipated.* Describe how your organization will monitor deployment and implementation so that unexpected or unanticipated impediments can be identified and addressed. Taking the strategic goals and related tactics into consideration, identify challenges likely to impede implementation and identify countermeasures for each of these obstacles.

8. *Take steps to ensure constant and consistent execution throughout the entire organization.* Realizing the importance of individual involvement and contribution, describe how your organization will help ensure that everyone has the needed levels of awareness, understanding, buy-in, commitment, and advocacy.

9. *Take steps to continuously improve.* Describe what your organization will do to continuously improve its strategic planning process and how it will attempt to improve the way it deploys and implements the resulting strategies to help ensure increasingly more effective and efficient execution.

Table 3.2   The Focus and Elements of Strategic Planning

Focus	Associated Elements
Analysis	1. Gather, analyze, and summarize information. 2. Analyze information relating to the organization's value proposition and internal factors and external forces likely to impact its short- and long-term success.
Formulation	3. Create (or verify) your organization's mission, vision, and sweet spot. 4. Create strategic goal statements. 5. Identify and prioritize the means by which you will achieve the strategic goals.
Action Planning	6. Identify tactics, assign roles and responsibilities, establish timelines, and define metrics 7. Plan for the unexpected and unanticipated.
Execution	8. Take steps to ensure constant and consistent execution throughout the entire organization.
Continuous Improvement	9. Take steps to continuously improve.

Table 3.2 shows the focus and elements of strategic planning.

A strategic planning framework containing the above nine elements will allow your organization to consider factors, analyze and address issues, and answer questions relating to its short- and long-term success. As previously mentioned, I encourage you to modify the framework you use to match your situation and circumstance, to emphasize those factors, issues, and/or questions your leadership team and key stakeholders consider to be of the utmost importance, or to deemphasize those factors, issues, and/or questions your key stakeholders and leadership team consider to be of less importance at this particular point in time. Table 3.3 illustrates elements of the strategic planning framework your organization might emphasize to address certain prevailing questions or challenges.

Conceptually, the recommended strategic planning framework will allow you to gather, analyze, and summarize information and data on which to make valid and credible decisions. The framework then allows you to use that information and data in determining whether a multitude of forces and factors are contributing to or impeding your organization's ability to deliver on its value proposition. Once that determination is made, the framework allows you to create or verify your organization's mission, vision, and "sweet spot" (where your organization's passion, abilities, and purpose or reason for existence intersect) and to identify ways to take advantage of the positive factors and forces and mitigate, reduce, avoid, or otherwise address the negative ones. The framework provides the structure that organizations typically need to ensure that subsequent action takes place in a timely and efficient manner and in a way that will likely yield optimal results

Table 3.3   Issues and Strategic Planning Elements to Emphasize

If . . .	Focus on . . .
	Analysis
• The leaders and managers of your organization base their business decisions on personal opinions. • Leaders, managers, or supervisors base their decisions on anecdotal information. • Decisions made are based on isolated incidents, situations, or circumstances. • Your organization focuses too heavily on internal matters and too little on its competitors or customers.	• Replace personal opinions and anecdotal information with concrete data and information. • Analyze information relating to your value proposition. • Identify external forces and internal factors likely to impact your organization's short- and long-term success. • Conduct a SWOT analysis (strengths, weaknesses, opportunities, and threats).
	Formulation
• Your organization inconsistently stresses the importance of cost or quality to suppliers, employees, and distributors. • From your customer's viewpoint, you and your colleagues do not possess the knowledge, skills, or abilities to succeed. • Your leadership or management team switches from product to product or emphasizes a particular service one week and a different service the next. • Your organization seems to have the right "big" idea but does not know how to move the idea forward.	• Create (or verify) your organization's mission and vision and its "sweet spot." • Create strategic goal statements. • Identify and prioritize the means by which you will achieve the strategic goals.
	Action Planning
• Individuals do not understand how they personally will contribute to your organization's success. • Things needing to get done go unattended and no one in the organization understands why. • Individuals in your organization do not know who is supposed to do what. • Individuals in your organization do not know when certain products are to be delivered. • Individuals do not know if they, their team, or the organization as a whole has succeeded. • Individuals, teams, or the entire organization seems to be caught off guard when something unexpected happens.	• Identify tactics, assign roles and responsibilities, establish timelines, and define metrics. • Plan for the unexpected and unplanned.

(Continued)

Table 3.3   (Continued)

	Execution
• Silos of passion and commitment exist in various parts of, but not throughout, the organization. • Silos of indifference and mediocre performance exist in various parts of, but not throughout, the organization. • Certain individuals or teams contribute heavily to the organization's success, while other individuals and teams do not. • Certain individuals or teams contribute marginally to the organization's success, while other individuals and teams do not. • The awareness, understanding, buy-in, and commitment of individuals (at all levels) are inconsistent. • The participation, contribution, and input of individuals (at all levels) are inconsistent.	• Take steps to ensure constant and consistent execution throughout the entire organization.
	Continuous Improvement
• The organization—in terms of innovation, effectiveness, or efficiency—appears to have hit a plateau and cannot seem to get beyond it. • The organization's strategic planning framework has set the stage for moderate—but not stellar—success. • Strategies and tactics are executed, but the execution is not flawless and as a result disappoints customers or clients.	• Take steps to continuously improve.

and outcomes. Recognizing that optimal performance in the real world typically involves learning, identifying, and applying lessons learned and best practices, the framework recognizes the importance of and sets the stage for planned and purposeful continuous improvement. Figure 3.1 illustrates the recommended strategic planning framework.

Any strategic planning endeavor involving the recommended framework will require the involvement, contribution, and input of many people. This naturally leads one to wonder about the amount of time that various functions, departments, or members of the organization may be asked to devote to the strategic planning process. Table 3.4 describes the amount of time that key departments, functions, and members of your organization will likely need to devote to your strategic planning effort. This description and estimate are based on my observations

Figure 3.1   The Strategic Planning Framework

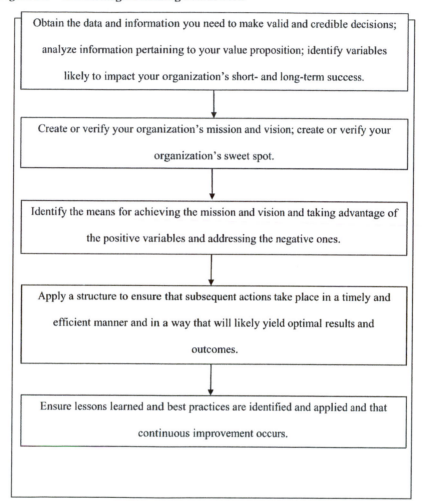

Obtain the data and information you need to make valid and credible decisions; analyze information pertaining to your value proposition; identify variables likely to impact your organization's short- and long-term success.

Create or verify your organization's mission and vision; create or verify your organization's sweet spot.

Identify the means for achieving the mission and vision and taking advantage of the positive variables and addressing the negative ones.

Apply a structure to ensure that subsequent actions take place in a timely and efficient manner and in a way that will likely yield optimal results and outcomes.

Ensure lessons learned and best practices are identified and applied and that continuous improvement occurs.

and experience. The magnitude of involvement and the actual investment of time that your strategic planning effort requires will depend on a number of factors, including the size and complexity of your company, club, association, church, or community organization; the current level of awareness and understanding about strategic planning that your leaders, executives, and managers currently possess; the amount of emphasis (and thus, time) you will give to each of the strategic planning elements; the availability of information and data sources; the complexity of the issues you have before you; the extent to which your organization typically involves its employees (at all levels) in such activities

Table 3.4 An Estimate of Time Required for Strategic Planning

This activity . . .	May require . . .
Brief leadership, executive, and/or management team on the advantages and importance of strategic planning.	A one- to two-hour meeting or conference call involving the organization's leaders, executives, and/or managers. You may need to supplement this briefing with a series of 30- to 45-minute meetings with key stakeholders to answer questions they may have and to provide additional information relating specifically to them or their area of responsibility.
Leaders, executives, and/or managers learn more about the benefits of, and your organization's approach to, strategic planning.	Leaders, executives, and/or managers devote eight to 12 hours reading select articles, book chapters, and/or white papers.
Decide on the type of information and data to gather for the strategic planning effort.	A two-hour meeting or conference call to determine information needs and requirements involving data sources and individuals responsible for your organization's databases.
Gather, consolidate, and summarize data and information prior to the strategic planning session.	Your data sources and individuals responsible for your organization's databases will probably devote three to five days gathering, consolidating, and summarizing information and data.
Conduct the strategic planning session.	This will depend on the size and complexity of your organization and the extent to which you strive to involve key stakeholder groups in the strategic planning effort. A session using the recommended strategic planning framework typically requires three full days. However, you can extend and expand the session two or more additional days, bring key stakeholder groups into the session to help you review and refine the strategies, and add specificity to the tactics and actions. The length of the strategic planning session will also depend on the emphasis you wish to place on various issues or topics; for example, if your organization faces a turbulent and/or mission- or vision-threatening environment, you might wish to devote one or more days exclusively to contingency planning.

Table 3.4   (Continued)

Execution	While the strategic planning session may be a discreet activity, the results of strategic planning are important elements of strategic management. As suggested in previous chapters, I encourage leaders and executives to consider strategy execution to be part of what they and their organization do on a daily basis. Strategy execution therefore occurs throughout the normal workday and encompasses the multitude of decisions that are made and actions that occur.
Continuous Improvement	Optimal performance typically involves lifelong learning and the identification and application of lessons learned and best practices. I consider continuous improvement an important element of organization performance and therefore encourage employees at all levels to seek out and take advantage of opportunities for continuous improvement.

(thus, impacting their capabilities, self-confidence, and self-motivation); and the extent to which your organization adds specificity to the resulting strategies, tactics, and actions.

The Strategic Plan

The strategic plan that is created using the recommended framework will serve as a guide for future decisions and actions and will prove useful in several ways. It will summarize the process followed and decisions made during the strategic planning session; provide the guidance the organization will need as it moves forward; provide an accurate record, should a key stakeholder wish to "audit" the organization's strategic planning endeavor; and give those not involved in the strategic planning session insight on how certain conclusions were drawn and how certain decisions were made.

To optimize usefulness and benefit, I recommend that your strategic plan (at a minimum) contain these eight elements:

1. Analysis of the current state, relating to your organization's—
   a. Value proposition.
   b. Internal strengths (S) and weaknesses (W).
   c. External opportunities (O) and threats (T).

2. Development, verification, or refinement of your organization's purpose, as defined by your organization's—

    a. Mission: what your organization will strive to accomplish over the short term.

    b. Vision: what your organization will strive to become or where it hopes to be in the future.

    c. Sweet spot: where your organization's passion, abilities, and purpose or reason for existence intersect.

3. Development, verification, or refinement of your organization's strategic goals, to add clarity and specificity to what your organization will strive to accomplish in terms of—

    a. Customer service.

    b. Product development.

    c. Growth.

    d. Quality.

    e. Innovation.

    f. Human resource capabilities.

4. Identification and prioritization of the means (i.e., the strategies) by which your organization will achieve its strategic goals.

5. An action plan built around the strategies, consisting of the—

    a. Identification of tactics.

    b. Assignment of responsibilities.

    c. Establishment of timelines.

    d. Delineated metrics.

6. A contingency plan, consisting of the identification of—

    a. Challenges likely to impede implementation.

    b. Viable countermeasures for each of the obstacles.

7. Execution considerations, consisting of a description of—

    a. What your organization will do to ensure constant and consistent execution throughout the entire organization.

    b. How your organization will help ensure that everyone has the needed levels of awareness, understanding, buy-in, commitment, and advocacy.

8. Continuous improvement considerations that describe—

    a. What your organization will do throughout execution to improve the way it deploys and implements its strategies to help ensure increasingly more effective and efficient execution.

    b. Steps your organization will take to improve its next strategic planning endeavor.

In summary, you have now raised awareness and understanding of the importance of strategic planning and garnered the interest, excitement, and enthusiasm of others. You have also taken steps to ensure that all individuals helping formulate strategy possess the needed knowledge, skills, and abilities and have adopted, created, or refined your strategic planning framework, model, or process so that it is likely to prove useful and beneficial and produce the expected results and outcomes.

Chapter 4

Preparing to Plan

You can now begin preparing for strategic planning, realizing that the steps you take will help ensure that your organization's strategic focus, analysis, conclusions, and decisions are valid, credible, and worthwhile. In preparing for your strategic planning endeavor, it is important that you answer these important questions:

- When and where should we conduct our strategic planning session?
- Who should we ask to participate in the process?
- How should we invite individuals to participate in the strategic planning session?
- What should individuals do to prepare to participate in the strategic planning session?
- How should we structure the agenda?
- In terms of preparation, what activities likely to "set the stage" for optimal success might we include in the agenda?
- What else might we do during preparation to "set the stage" for optimal success?
- What should we tell those who will not be participating in the session but who will be asked to help execute the resulting strategies?
- How should the room in which the strategic planning session is held be set up, and what equipment and supplies will we need?

WHEN AND WHERE TO CONDUCT THE STRATEGIC PLANNING SESSION

Approach your strategic planning session as you would any other important business meeting. In deciding when to conduct the session, I recommend that you attempt to select a date that causes minimum disruption and inconvenience. Keep in mind that individuals (and their teams) have only a certain amount of time and energy to devote to business activities and meetings; if your organization faces an especially hectic or busy time, consider postponing your strategic planning session until things settle down or become more stable. With this underlying principle in mind, if you are a relatively small organization and your strategic planning session will involve a relatively small number of people, try to select a date that works for everyone. If that proves difficult or impossible, identify the dates that work best for your senior-level people and attempt to make those dates work for everyone else. While setting the stage for your strategic planning endeavor, you may brief your leadership or executive team and/or supplement that briefing with personal, one-on-one meetings with key stakeholders. If you plan to meet with senior-level teams or individuals in such a manner, consider using this forum to discuss or set the date for your strategic planning session. Keep in mind that because your meeting will involve more than one person, you may find it impossible to accommodate everyone's schedule; simply do the best you can and then move on from there.

I recommend that you set the meeting start and finish times as you do other important business meetings. Since your strategic planning session will in all likelihood involve senior-level members of your organization, will disrupt their (and the other participants') workday, and may involve travel and travel expenses, most organizations try to schedule as much into the strategic planning workday as possible, within the context of the organization's culture (some organizations prefer not to go beyond the 8:00 A.M. to 5:00 P.M. workday, whereas other organizations do not hesitate to do so) and the participants' desire or stamina (some organizations will gladly extend the strategic planning session beyond the typical 5:00 P.M. workday, whereas other organizations feel that doing so will yield diminishing returns because of lack of interest or diminished energy). I also recommend that you consider your organization's work style when setting the start and finish times. I have worked with teams that preferred to start the morning session early so they could finish the afternoon session at the normal "close of business" hour, whereas other teams were not concerned with the start and finish times as long as participants were given a 90-minute lunch hour so that e-mails could be picked up and calls could be answered. As you consider the start and finish times, keep in mind that there are tradeoffs: early morning starts or late evening finishes may allow you to shorten the session by four hours or a full day; however, they may also result in the need for extra overnight accommodations.

Your organization's strategic planning session will require everyone's attention, focus, input, and contribution. To ensure optimal success, you must take steps to limit the likelihood of distractions and disruptions. This single factor will most likely help you decide whether to conduct the strategic planning session on site or at a nearby (or distant) conference center, resort, or hotel. Although off-site settings are typically more expensive and require more time to arrange (due, in part, to your not having control of the facilities, space, or support staff), they do, by virtue of distance, reduce the likelihood of participants being distracted by daily business. Such distance also reduces the likelihood of someone walking by—or a support staff member walking into—the meeting room and overhearing sensitive information or an intense exchange. Here, the concern is not that sensitive information is overheard or an intense exchange is observed; rather, it is that the individual might hear the information or see the exchange "out of context" and as a result inadvertently draw the wrong inferences or conclusions. For these reasons, I typically recommend that organizations conduct their strategic planning sessions off site.

KEY LEARNING POINT

Your organization's strategic planning session will require everyone's attention, focus, input, and contribution. To ensure optimal success, you must take steps to limit the likelihood of distractions and disruptions. This is the single most important factor in deciding whether to conduct the strategic planning session on site or at a nearby (or distant) conference center, resort, or hotel.

WHO SHOULD PARTICIPATE IN THE STRATEGIC PLANNING SESSION?

As previously suggested, I encourage organizations to allow as many stakeholders as possible to participate in the strategic planning session. Such an inclusive approach to strategic planning:

- Enhances involvement, resulting in greater awareness, understanding, buy-in, and commitment.
- Ensures that creative and innovative ideas will surface for translating conceptual plans into concrete action.
- Mirrors the democratic ideal of inclusivity.
- Ensures that the linkage between strategy, tactics, and tasks is not lost during execution.
- Ensures that executives, managers, and first-line supervisors take steps to help strategies cascade all the way down and throughout the entire organization.
- Increases the likelihood that people already struggling with numerous and frequently competing responsibilities embrace change brought about by the strategic planning process.

The individuals asked to participate in your strategic planning session should be asked to do so for a reason. Table 4.1 summarizes reasons why organizations typically ask individuals to participate in their strategic planning session.

Table 4.1   Reasons for Asking Individuals to Participate in Strategic Planning

To help the strategic planning team . . .	By . . .
Analyze existing data and information.	• Sharing financial, quality, and production data. • Providing access to databases and reports. • Providing access to white papers, journal articles, and industry reports. • Providing insight or information pertaining to current and emerging external forces and internal factors impacting the organization's short- and long-term success.
Articulate (or verify) the organization's purpose.	• Identifying customer needs and expectations. • Providing insight into the history of the organization, its mission, or its vision. • Providing anecdotal information reflecting the organization's sweet spot.
Identify forces and factors contributing to or impeding the organization's ability to succeed.	• Sharing "intel" about competitors and/or market forces. • Sharing knowledge of pending regulatory requirements. • Sharing expert knowledge of technological, business process, systems, culture, or human resources capacity or capabilities.
Ensure that strategies and tactics take place in a timely and efficient manner and in a way that will likely yield optimal results and outcomes.	• Identifying or committing needed resources (people, facilities, equipment, supplies, and/or budgets). • Providing insight into likely challenges (needing to be addressed) or opportunities (needing to be leveraged or capitalized upon). • Providing insight into biases or blind spots likely to impact the organization's ability to execute strategies and tactics. • Providing insight into potential impediments and associated countermeasures.
Ensure that continuous improvement occurs.	• Identifying current or likely pockets of exemplary behavior and where lessons learned and best practices are likely to materialize. • Contributing suggestions and recommendations for improving the organization's strategic planning framework, methodologies, tools, and techniques.

Figure 4.1   Strategic Planning Session Participant Matrix

Name	Will Provide Access to Intel or Specialty Knowledge	Will Help Identify Forces and Factors Impacting Our Ability to Succeed	Will Help Set the Stage for Effective and Efficient Execution	Will Help Identify Impediments and Associated Countermeasures	Will Help Us Continuously Improve
Vans	▪		▪		▪
Scott		▪	▪	▪	
Sims	▪	▪	▪	▪	▪

As you consider likely participants for your strategic planning session, you might find a matrix similar to the one presented in Figure 4.1 useful and beneficial. This particular matrix was developed by a federal government agency that was selecting individuals to participate in its first strategic planning session (the names of the participants have been changed to protect the organization's identity). A review of the matrix reveals that individuals being asked to participate in the strategic planning session provided value in three or more ways.

HOW PARTICIPANTS SHOULD BE INVITED

Individuals participating in your strategic planning session should know why they were selected to participate. Such knowledge sets the expectation for personal input and contribution and helps participants prepare for the session, attend the session knowing that they will have something of value to give, and depart from the session knowing how they helped the strategic planning team. I therefore recommend that you send a notification e-mail or message to those selected to participate (see Sample of Application 4.1).

Sample of Application 4.1

PARTICIPANT NOTIFICATION E-MAIL OR MEMORANDUM

Date: Today's date

To: Dale Litaker

From: A. B. Smith

Subject: Invitation to Participate in Strategic Planning

This correspondence follows up the briefing I gave to the executive team last month and the face-to-face meeting you and I had last week. As you know, we are about to embark on a strategic planning endeavor that will initially involve a five-day meeting being conducted October 15–19 at the Ridgeway Conference Center. The accompanying agenda provides detailed information on the focus of the week, issues the planning team will address, topics of discussion, and decisions we plan to make throughout the meeting. As you and I concluded last week, although this meeting and subsequent actions will require an investment of time and effort on everyone's part, strategic planning is a natural continuation of all we have previously done to achieve our current level of success and will undoubtedly prove useful as we strive to continuously improve and set the stage for even higher levels of short- and long-term future success.

You are being asked to participate in the upcoming strategic planning session; we believe your input will be invaluable and that you will prove especially useful in helping the planning team:

- Understand the people, process, and technological capabilities that will allow us to accelerate our process of designing and building a strategic plan.
- Analyze and interpret information and data pertaining to our internal strengths and weaknesses and external threats and opportunities.
- Recognize and address factors impacting our ability to deliver quality products and services to our customers in a timely and cost-effective manner.

Meeting Specifications

Dates: October 15–19

Place: Ridgeway Conference Center, Pine Tree Meeting Room

Breakfast: 6:30 A.M., continental breakfast will be set up in the meeting room

Meeting Start Time: 7:00 A.M.

Lunch: 12:00 P.M. to 1:30 P.M. (to allow you to check e-mails and voice mails)

Finish Time: 7:00 P.M.

Needed Equipment and Supplies: Bring your laptop; all other materials will be provided

To Prepare

We encourage you to give some personal thought to strategic planning as it relates to our organization and to strategic thinking, strategic planning, and strategic management in general. Between now and the strategic planning session, we ask that you:

- Review the strategic planning handouts I distributed during last month's executive briefing.

- Review the "Strategic Imperative" memorandum Dave Conlin sent last week.
- Review last December's "Year-in Review" document.
- Review the quarterly report from the last 12 months.
- Consider and come prepared to discuss the following:
  - Factors relating to systems, processes, technology, people, and culture our organization should eliminate, create, or change.
  - Feedback, information, and any other type of input you have received from your key stakeholders.
  - Information or data you have pertaining to whether our clients or customers are likely to purchase our services and products because our services and products meet or exceed their needs and expectations.
  - Information or data you have pertaining to the quality, cost, and availability of our products and services and whether our products and services meet or exceed our client or customer requirements on these three important fronts.
  - Factors impacting our organization's ability to act on its value proposition to ensure, for example, that manufacturing, transportation, and distribution costs and the price of our services and products will allow (1) our clients and customers to purchase them and (2) our organization to realize needed profit.

For More Information

For general information on strategic planning, we recommend that you review the trade journals you typically read to find articles on this topic. I found the following three books to be of immense value in my personal learning:

- Hrebiniak, Lawrence G. 2005. *Making Strategy Work*. Upper Saddle River, NJ: Wharton School Publishing.
- Mintzberg, Henry, Joseph Lampel, and Bruce Ahlstrand. 2008. *Strategy Safari: A Guided Tour through the Wilds of Strategic Management*. New York: The Free Press.
- Kim, W. Chan, and Renee Mauborgne. 2005. *Blue Ocean Strategy*. Boston: Harvard Business School Press.

Contact me at IC123-4 if you would like to meet to discuss anything relating to this memo or to your participating in our upcoming strategic planning session.

We look forward to seeing you at 7:30 A.M. on October 15!

HOW PARTICIPANTS SHOULD PREPARE FOR THE PLANNING SESSION

When notifying individuals that they will participate in the strategic planning session, you should immediately set the stage for a successful session by sensitizing them to the reason for their being selected or invited to participate in the meeting. This allows participants to give some thought to how they should properly prepare for the session and what they might do during the session to meet or exceed the previously established expectation. For example, the Participant Notification E-mail or Memorandum (Sample of Application 4.1) sensitizes participants to the expectation that their input will prove invaluable and that they will undoubtedly help the planning team:

- Understand the people, process, and technological capabilities that would allow their organization to accelerate its process of designing and building the strategic plan.
- Analyze and interpret information and data pertaining to the organization's internal strengths and weaknesses and external threats and opportunities.
- Recognize and address factors impacting the organization's ability to deliver quality products and services to its customers in a timely and cost-effective manner.

When notifying participants, I recommend that you provide information on how they might prepare for strategic planning in general and for your upcoming strategic planning session in particular. For example, the Participant Notification (Sample of Application 4.1) recommends that participants give personal thought to strategic thinking, strategic planning, and strategic management in general. For general information on strategic planning, participants are encouraged to review trade journals they typically read to find articles on this topic, and, if interested, are directed to three books considered to be of potential use and benefit:

- Hrebiniak, Lawrence G. 2005. *Making Strategy Work*. Upper Saddle River, NJ: Wharton School Publishing.
- Mintzberg, Henry, Joseph Lampel, and Bruce Ahlstrand. 2008. *Strategy Safari: A Guided Tour through the Wilds of Strategic Management*. New York: The Free Press.
- Kim, W. Chan, and Renee Mauborgne. 2005. *Blue Ocean Strategy*. Boston: Harvard Business School Press.

I also recommend that you share information for the participants to review prior to the strategic planning session or direct them to the types of information to review or issues to consider. Here, we keep in mind the issues and considerations raised or implied by Hrebiniak, Mintzberg, Kim, and Mauborgne (and reported in Chapter 2).

If your upcoming strategic planning session focuses on organization-wide strategies, suggest that the participants consider and come to the session prepared to discuss these topics:

- Whether your organization is likely to succeed in the business it's in or whether it should consider entering a new business. Other issues to consider are whether your organization is offering—
  o Value likely to resonate with your intended clients and customers or should change its services or products or client or customer groups.
  o Services and products in the proper locations or should enter new geographic regions.
- Whether your organization has the facilities, equipment, and supplies you need and whether your employees at all levels have the knowledge, skills, and abilities they need to contribute to the organization's short- and long-term success.
- Whether your organization's structure, procedures, processes, or norms are contributing to or interfering with the effort made by facilities, equipment, supplies, and people to help the organization succeed.
- Whether your organization has developed and communicated expectations pertaining to individual, team, and organizational performance and whether technology, systems, and processes are in place to support and reinforce their implementation.
- Whether your organization has specified or defined behavioral expectations in increasing levels of detail so as to increase the likelihood of understanding and implementation.
- Whether your organization has created, communicated, and provided timely feedback on individual, team, and organizational goals and objectives.

If your upcoming strategic planning session focuses on formulating strategies for a key subunit (a division, department, functional area, or group) of the organization, suggest that the participants consider and come to the session prepared to discuss these topics:

- Whether the services or products the organization provides are unique and likely to meet or exceed the needs of your clients or customers. Key issues to explore are whether—
  o Your customers are able to procure products and services elsewhere that are similar to the products and services you offer.
  o You have consistent and reliable access to all of the inputs (employees, supplies, equipment, etc.) your organization needs to succeed.

- Whether your organization is positioned to compete with its competitors and, if so, whether it is likely to win. In this connection, you should consider:
  - Your competitor's ability to take advantage of the positive or counter the negative aspects of your industry and market forces.
  - Whether your competitor's strategic thinking, strategic planning, and strategic management give it an advantage over your organization.
- Whether your organization has and is taking advantage of tangible assets such as a supplier network, the capability and capacity of your employees (at all levels), and facilities, equipment, and supplies. Key considerations include whether your—
  - Organization has a positive, neutral, or negative reputation and you are taking full advantage of it in the marketplace.
  - Employees possess unique knowledge, skills, and abilities and your organization is using this intangible asset to its fullest advantage.

Regardless of the focus of your upcoming strategic planning session, I recommend that you encourage the participants to reflect on the past and present, give thought to the future, and come to the session prepared to:

- Explore how your organization might match its internal strengths to its current and emerging external environment.
- Explore and develop alternative means for your organization to achieve short- and long-term success.
- Analyze competitive pressures and identify ways of improving your organization's competitive positioning.
- Create a vision for the future that is compelling and exciting to all stakeholder groups.
- Analyze current and emerging trends, patterns, tendencies, and movements and identify ways to take advantage of the positive features and reduce, avoid, or mitigate the negative features.
- Identify prevailing and prospective best practices and incorporate them into the strategic plan, as well as share them with all organizational members so that they duplicate previous successes and do not repeat previous mistakes.
- Identify actions the organization might take to address challenges associated with limited resources so that it can meet or exceed the needs and expectations of its key stakeholder groups.
- Take advantage of and further reinforce key cultural norms by, for example, identifying and recommending ways—
  - To further involve individuals from throughout the organization in the strategic planning session.
  - To ensure that a large number of organizational members participate, contribute, and share input throughout the strategic planning endeavor.

- Explore and recommend ways the organization might—
  - Monitor and analyze external forces and work to take advantage of positive forces and mitigate negative ones.
  - Continuously improve as an entity, for example, by considering whether transforming from a centralized to a decentralized decision-making structure might further contribute to the organization's short- and long-term success.

Throughout the process of enhancing understanding, garnering interest, and building enthusiasm for strategic planning, I recommend that you take steps to make it easy for your key stakeholders to join and then accompany you on your journey. This effort does not end when you are preparing for your strategic planning session. Maintain close contact with all key stakeholders and even closer contact with individuals selected or asked to participate in the strategic planning session. Orchestrate opportunities to meet or speak with them, to ensure they recognize the important role they will be playing in your organization's strategic planning endeavor, and to reinforce the value they are expected to bring to the strategic planning session. To help support their preparation for the planning session, be sure to encourage them to contact you should they have any questions or concerns. The Participant Notification (Sample of Application 4.1) reinforces this message by encouraging participants to contact the strategic planning coordinator if they would like to discuss anything relating to the notification or to participating in the organization's upcoming strategic planning session.

THE AGENDA FOR THE STRATEGIC PLANNING SESSION

As with any important business meeting, I recommend that you develop an agenda to help provide structure to your organization's strategic planning session. Creating the agenda allows you to further consider:

- The objectives for the strategic planning session.
- Questions, topics, or issues to be addressed during the planning session.
- The individual who will be facilitating or leading the discussion pertaining to each question, topic, or issue.
- The amount of time each question, topic, or issue will require.

The agenda will prove useful in letting participants know how to prepare for the session and what to expect at the beginning of the session, in serving as a roadmap during the session, and in functioning as a checklist at various points to ensure that progress is being made, session goals are being achieved, and questions, topics, or issues are being addressed.

I recommend that you create an agenda containing three sections: meeting objectives, premeeting work, and the daily agenda. The daily agenda should include at least four sections: time, topic, process/action/tool, and result. The *time* section helps ensure that you allocate an adequate amount of time for the key questions to be answered, the topics to be covered, and the issues to be addressed. During the session, the time section allows the leader, facilitator, and/or participants to monitor progress and to ensure that adequate time remains for the consideration and resolution of topics, issues, and questions yet to be addressed. The *topic* section helps focus everyone's attention and the planning team's conversation; without adequate focus, discussion may center on recent issues or occurrences rather than on the topics, issues, and/or questions that need to be considered and addressed. During the session, the topic section allows the leader, facilitator, and/or participants to monitor their focus and discussion to ensure they are helping the planning team achieve the session goals. The *process/action/tool* section helps ensure that the process the planning team follows, the actions it takes, and the tools it uses help it answer the relevant questions or address the relevant issues in an effective and efficient manner. During the session, the process/action/tool section allows the leader, facilitator, and/or participants to apply the proper tool at the correct time, contributing to a credible process and valid decisions. Finally, the *result* section helps ensure that the planning team's effort yields a useful and beneficial product. In total, the results—the conclusions that are reached, the decisions that are made, and the deliverables that are created—represent the purpose for which the strategic planning session was held and the value the planning session was expected to produce.

While creating the agenda, you will need to identify the individual or individuals who will facilitate or lead the discussion pertaining to each question, topic, or issue. If you plan to use a variety of individuals throughout the strategic planning session, consider adding a fifth section—a leader/facilitator section—to your daily agenda; if one person will be leading or facilitating most or all of the strategic planning session, the fifth section is not required. This leader/facilitator section would allow you to alert individuals to their facilitation and/or leadership responsibilities and sensitize them to when they should be ready and prepared to help the group consider a particular issue, cover a certain topic, or answer a particular question. If this section is included in the daily agenda, to avoid confusion on everyone's part (and to avoid concerns being raised if the strategic planning session is "audited" at some point in the future), the leader/facilitator guiding the strategic planning session should match the name of the person listed in the daily agenda.

Once the agenda is set, I recommend that you distribute it to all participants prior to the session, being sure to give the participants enough time to prepare for the strategic planning session. I am providing three samples of strategic planning session agendas for you to review and consider. Figure 4.2 illustrates an agenda prepared for a newly formed subunit of a well-established global organization. The division's newly formed leadership team, meeting for the first time, needed to (1) firm up its team through team-building activities and (2) discuss topics, address issues, and answer questions to set the stage for the organization's short- and long-term success.

Figure 4.2   Sample Agenda: Strategic Planning Session for a Newly Formed Subunit

Strategic Planning Session

Date of Session

Location of Session

Meeting Objectives

- Gain a better understanding of factors contributing to, and "blind spots" associated with, the leadership team's ability to communicate, make decisions, manage change, and manage conflict.
- Gain a better understanding of the leadership team's underlying assumptions, expectations, guiding principles, and values.
- Develop a purpose statement for our division that dovetails off of the corporate mission statement by drawing on various perspectives and capitalizing on differing viewpoints.
- Develop strategies for our division that are consistent with, and supportive of, the 11 strategies currently in place for the corporation.
- Issue a management and planning pocket guide to each leadership team member and give them an opportunity to apply several management and planning tools in a safe, nonthreatening environment.

Meeting Pre-work

- Within the context of our corporate mission statement, think about the key features of a mission statement for our division and come prepared to discuss them.
- Review the 11 strategies currently in place for the corporation and come fully prepared to factor them into our conversations.

Daily Agenda

Time	Topic	Process/Action/Tool	Result
Day 1			
8:00–8:15	• Meeting overview	• Share meeting objectives • Establish meeting ground rules	• Purpose of meeting is understood • Boundaries within which the meeting will proceed are clarified
8:15–9:15	• Team warm-up activities	• Leadership team tackles the "matrix" • Leadership team reviews information pertaining to high-performing teams • Leadership team creates its "rules of engagement"	• Leadership team members recognize the strengths of the group and mitigate the group's "blind spots" • Leadership team members adopt rules of engagement, in part to address or mitigate blind spots and capitalize on strengths

(Continued)

Figure 4.2   (Continued)

Time			

9:15–1:00 (includes break)	• Personality: a key factor
	• Complete individual and team worksheets
		• Introduce personality and how it contributes to individual and team success
		• Review personality report
		• Review and process:
		  ○ Team dynamics process
		  ○ Team individual worksheet
		  ○ Team dynamics worksheet
		  ○ Team demographics sheet
		  ○ Team scale
			• Increased awareness of how one's personality impacts one's thinking and behavior
			• Increased awareness of how one's personality impacts other individuals and the team
			• Increased awareness of personal strengths and blind spots
			• Increased awareness of team strengths and blind spots
			• A plan for capitalizing on the strengths and minimizing the blind spots

Day 2			
8:00–8:15	• Review results of Day 1	• Conduct a "gallery walk" of flip charts • Participants comment on key insights	• Recognition of learnings, for incorporation in the Day 2 proceedings
8:15–12:00	• Leadership team develops its purpose statement	• Review information pertaining to purpose statements • Review the corporate mission statement • Leadership team members discuss their purpose • Following a structured process, leadership team members work together to develop a purpose statement	• A purpose statement that (1) describes the division's purpose, (2) is consistent with what corporate is asking the division to do, and (3) will resonate with key stakeholders, as well as the expanded management team
12:00–1:00	Lunch		
1:00–5:00 (includes break)	• The leadership team develops its strategies	• Review the 11 strategies currently in place for the corporation • Review information shared when leadership	• Strategies are identified that (1) describe at a high level how the division will achieve its purpose, (2) are consistent with and

Figure 4.2   (Continued)

		team members discussed their purpose	supportive of the corporate strategies,
		• Review the purpose statement developed earlier in the day; discuss implications	and (3) are feasible and doable
		• Following a structured process, team members work together to develop division strategies	
Day 3			
8:00–8:15	• Review results of Day 2	• Conduct a "gallery walk" of flip charts • Participants comment on key insights	• Recognition of learnings, for incorporation in the Day 3 proceedings
8:15–10:30	• Identify information needing to be shared about the strategic planning session and deliverables	• Participants develop a communications matrix • Participants conduct a stakeholder analysis and, if needed, an influence plan	• A completed communications matrix • A completed stakeholder analysis • If needed, a completed influence plan
10:30–12:30 (includes break)	• Identify potential obstacles and develop feasible countermeasures	• Using a contingency matrix, participants identify obstacles and develop countermeasures	• A completed contingency matrix
12:30–1:00	• Action items and next steps	• Identify actions needing to be taken to support the team's effort (responsible parties, critical dates, and success measures) • Agree on immediate next steps	• Action items are agreed upon • Next steps are identified and agreed upon

Figure 4.3 illustrates an agenda prepared for a well-established global organization. I provide this sample because it illustrates a strategic planning session driven primarily by strategic questions rather than a series of issues or topics. Many of the questions considered during this particular strategic planning session were

Figure 4.3   Sample Agenda: Question-Centered Corporate Planning Session

Strategic Planning Session

Date of Session

Location of Session

Meeting Objectives

- Keeping the corporate mission and values in mind, further develop key areas of our vision for 2020.
- Define strategic issues coming from the results of a visioning exercise and a SWOT (strengths, weaknesses, opportunities, and threats) analysis.
- Define shared services as it relates to our corporation, the implications of a shared services strategy, and the direction to be given to the businesses.
- Discuss the merits of our growth strategies (acquisition and organic) and requirements for further segment strategy development.
- Define the people issues that are involved with the attainment of our strategies.
- Continue to enhance our effectiveness as the enterprise leadership team.

Meeting Pre-work

- Identify three companies or industries adjacent to our current businesses that we should acquire or move into within the next three years. Be prepared to discuss the rationale for your selection.
- Think through the visioning exercise material and come prepared to discuss your ideas with the group.
- Review conclusions from last year's strategic planning session.
- Review your assessment and goals from the leadership team analysis.

Daily Agenda

Time	Topic	Process/Action/Tool	Result
Day 1			

1:00–5:00	• A casual conversation about our corporation	• This conversation is intended to stimulate thinking and interaction
		• There is no set time limit; discuss until you or these questions are exhausted
		• Questions for discussion:
		  ○ What factors (such as corporate competencies) have contributed to our previous success?
		  ○ What could we have previously done better?
		  ○ What is/has been holding us back?
			• Stimulated thinking
			• Heightened interaction
			• Considerations for upcoming exercises and activities

Day 2			
8:00–8:30	• Kick-off	• Share opening remarks • Share meeting objectives • Review team dynamics and establish ground rules	• Purpose of meeting understood • Clarity gained regarding boundaries within which the meeting will proceed

8:30–10:30	• What are our:
	  ○ Strengths?
	  ○ Weaknesses?
	  ○ Opportunities?
	  ○ Threats?
		• Conduct a SWOT analysis for the corporation (high level), not the segments
		• Use prior SWOT analyses as a memory jogger but create new analyses
		• Highlight patterns of agreement and disagreement
			• Shared understanding of the "pushes" impacting the organization
			• Strengths and weaknesses unique to our corporation are identified

10:30–10:45	Break		

(Continued)

Figure 4.3 (Continued)

10:45–12:15	• What is our corporate vision for 2020?	• A vision for the organization • Shared understanding of the "pulls" impacting the organization

	• Conduct a future scenario
	• Participants focus on the corporation, not the individual businesses
	• Describe the corporation in 2020 in these key areas (pre-meeting work assigned):
	  ○ Operations
	  ○ Information systems
	  ○ People
	  ○ Processes
	  ○ Culture	

12:15–1:00	Lunch	
1:00–2:00	• Taking the results of the visioning exercise and SWOT analysis into consideration, what key "pushes" and "pulls" are impacting the organization?	• Shared understanding of the key "pushes" and "pulls" impacting the organization
	• Use weighted voting to identify key items • Highlight patterns of agreement and disagreement • Link SWOT results/items to the various facets of the vision • Identify points unique to our corporation from a competitive standpoint: weaknesses to address and strengths to exploit	

2:00–5:15 (includes break)	• What key strategic issues relate to the 2020 vision?
	• What key strategic issues relate to our:
	  ○ Strengths?
	  ○ Weaknesses?
	  ○ Opportunities
	  ○ Threats?
		• Shared understanding of how we plan to attain the vision, capitalize on the opportunities and strengths, and address the weaknesses and threats
		• Shared understanding of the advantages and

	• Discuss how to attain the 2020 vision, how to capitalize on the opportunities and strengths, and how to address weaknesses and threats
	• Discuss the impact on:
	  ○ Shared services
	  ○ Research
	  ○ Competencies needed	

Time	Topic	Activity	Outcomes
			disadvantages of the various approaches • Shared understanding of how the various approaches will impact shared services, R&D, and competencies needed
5:15–5:30	Conclude Day 2	• Summarize results of the day • Closing remarks	• Everyone is set for Day 3
Day 3			
8:00–8:15	Review Day 2 results and Day 3 agenda	• Conduct a gallery walk to review flip charts • Review agenda	• Purpose of the day is understood • Insights from Day 2 are applied to the Day 3 topics
8:15–10:00	How should shared services relate to our corporation?	• Define shared services for our corporation • Discuss which functions should fall under the shared services umbrella and where it should be located (internal or outsourced strategy) • Identify weaknesses associated with shared services; identify actions to address barriers and obstacles • Discuss what will be expected from the segments with regard to their strategies and actions and adherence to a corporate shared services strategy	• Shared definition of shared services for our corporation in the context of the 2020 vision • Shared services linked to the results of the SWOT analysis • Corporate direction to the segments regarding expectations for shared services going forward as they implement separate ERP systems

(Continued)

69

Figure 4.3 (Continued)

Time		

10:15–12:15 (includes break)	• What are the merits of growth through acquisition, new markets, new products, and new technology?	• Discuss:
		  ○ Organic growth versus growth through acquisition
		  ○ How to define innovation for our corporation
		  ○ New channels
		• Discuss each individual's ideas regarding acquisition targets in adjacent markets
		• Define what corporate will expect from the segments during their strategic planning process regarding growth:
		  ○ Use of benchmarks
		  ○ Milestones
		  ○ Metrics
			• Identify deliverables from the segment strategic plans regarding how the company will grow through acquisition, new markets, new products, and new technology

12:15–1:00	Lunch		

1:00–2:00	• Continue discussing the merits of growth through acquisition, new markets, new products, and new technology	• Discuss:
		  ○ Organic growth versus growth through acquisition
		  ○ How to define innovation for our corporation
		  ○ New channels
		• Discuss each individual's ideas regarding acquisition targets in adjacent markets
		• Define what corporate will expect from the segments during their strategic planning process regarding growth:
		  ○ Use of benchmarks
		  ○ Milestones
		  ○ Metrics
			• Identify deliverables from the segment strategic plans regarding how the company will grow through acquisition, new markets, new products, and new technology

Time	Agenda	Expected Outcome

1:00–4:30 (includes break)	• What people issues are inherent in the 2020 vision?
	
	• Discuss strategic people issues such as:
	  ○ The capabilities we will need to execute the agreed-upon corporate strategies
	  ○ "People" barriers to optimally achieving agreed-upon corporate strategies
	  ○ Capabilities that should be groomed from within versus recruited from outside
	  ○ Actions needing to be taken to align people with the corporate priorities
	  ○ In terms of people, what it takes to be successful in emerging markets
		• Definition of people issues and next steps for corporate functions or segments to further develop these actions

4:45–5:30	• Conclude meeting • Review results of the meeting and draw conclusions • Decide on next steps • Share closing comments • Overflow from other topics if necessary	• Next steps are understood by everyone

raised by the company's board of directors. As with the organization showcased in the previous sample agenda, this organization considers the strategic planning session an opportunity to further develop the leadership team.

Figure 4.4 illustrates an agenda prepared for a small team of entrepreneurs gathering to decide on the merits of working together to form a new company. This sample illustrates the nature and scope of topics that need to be explored, issues that need to be addressed, and questions that need to be answered to ensure the initial short-term and subsequent long-term success of such an endeavor.

The above three agendas serve as good examples of how you might structure the agenda you prepare for your strategic planning session and the topics you might include in the session if you are launching a subunit, needing to answer specific strategic questions or address specific strategic issues, or starting up an organization. Although these agendas serve as good examples, they do not reflect all that you might include in your agenda to ensure a successful strategic planning session.

DESIGNING SUCCESS INTO THE AGENDA

While preparing for your strategic planning session, I recommend that you assess the capabilities, self-confidence, and self-motivation of the individual participants as well as the dynamics of the team you are bringing together to formulate your organization's strategy. You might conclude that the individual participants have certain common blind spots (for example, regarding decision making or conflict resolution) and therefore allocate time for a special briefing at the beginning of the session. You might conclude that the team dynamic may be suboptimal because the participants do not know one another and therefore that you should allocate time for ice-breaker exercises at the beginning of the session.

My experiences and observations suggest that certain actions and activities increase the likelihood of the session being optimally successful; I therefore recommend that, at a minimum, you allocate time in your agenda for the establishment of ground rules at the beginning of the session and that you allocate time for check points (points at which progress is checked) at the beginning and end of each day.

The establishment of ground rules helps set an expectation about how participants individually and as a team will behave throughout the strategic planning session. Ground rules typically include such behavioral expectations as:

- Challenge the idea rather than the person.
- Treat each other with mutual respect.
- We agree to disagree.

Figure 4.4 Sample Agenda: Strategic Planning Session for a Start-up

Strategic Planning Session

Date of Session

Location of Session

Meeting Objectives

- Conduct an environmental scan of existing and emerging opportunities and threats to verify that general conditions are conducive to establishing the new organization.
- Review our existing strengths and weaknesses to ensure that there is "critical mass" for moving forward.
- Analyze the market and competitive forces to verify that those forces are conducive to establishing the new organization.
- Given the existing environmental conditions, our interests, passion, and capabilities, develop a mission and vision for the new organization.
- Identify the corporate values that will help ensure our short- and long-term success.
- Given the existing environmental conditions, our mission, vision, and values, and the results of the market and competitive analysis, articulate the value proposition for the new organization.
- Identify the means by which the new organization will accomplish its mission and attain its vision.
- Within the context of the defined strategies, identify critical success factors relating to the organization's structure, business model, operational plan, and financial strategy.
- Create an action plan for moving forward.

Meeting Pre-work

- Conduct the research you have been assigned, summarize the results, and come prepared to share your findings with the rest of the group.
- Reflect on our previous discussions, give some additional thought about what you envision for our organization's future, and come prepared to discuss your ideas with the group.
- Given our previous conversations, give additional thought to the role you would like to play in this endeavor and come prepared to discuss your ideas—and the rationale behind them—with the group.

(Continued)

Figure 4.4 (Continued)

Daily Agenda

Time	Topic	Process/Action/Tool	Result
Day 1			
7:00–7:30	• Kick-off	• Review meeting objectives	• Purpose of meeting understood
7:30–12:00	• What are our: ○ Strengths? ○ Weaknesses? ○ Opportunities? ○ Threats?	• Conduct a SWOT analysis (strengths, weaknesses, opportunities, and threats)	• Shared understanding of existing and emerging opportunities and threats to verify that general conditions are conducive to moving forward • Shared understanding of existing strengths and weaknesses to ensure that there is a "critical mass" for moving forward
12:00–1:30	Lunch		
1:30–6:30	• Analyze the market and competitive forces to verify that those forces are conducive to establishing the new organization	• Each participant presents the results of the research he or she was asked to conduct prior to the session • Participants review information and data pertaining to, but not limited to, the following: ○ Target market size and growth rate ○ The industry cost structure ○ Existing and/or viable distribution channels ○ Existing and/or viable suppliers	Shared understanding that the market and competitive forces are conducive to establishing the new organization

74

	○ Plus/Delta market analysis, competitor analysis, supplier analysis, and distribution channel analysis ○ Companies competing in a related market or offering related products ○ Companies using related technologies ○ Competitors or organizations with the capability and capacity to compete	
Day 2		
7:00–7:30	• Review the results of Day 1	• Common understanding of factors to consider throughout Day 2
7:30–10:00	• Conduct a gallery walk	• A mission statement for the organization
	• Consider and discuss the results of Day 1	
	• Consider what we are passionate about, our capabilities, our ideals	
	• Our mission will guide our short-term: ○ Intent ○ Focus ○ Decisions ○ Actions	
	• Our mission will impact—and will be impacted by—these key areas: ○ Strategies ○ Systems ○ People ○ Processes ○ Culture	

(*Continued*)

Figure 4.4 (Continued)

Time	Topic	Activities	Outcomes

10:00–12:30	• What is our vision for 2020?	• Conduct a future scenario
		• Describe the organization in 2020, taking these key areas into consideration:
		  ◦ Strategies
		  ◦ Systems
		  ◦ People
		  ◦ Processes
		  ◦ Culture
			• A vision for the organization
			• Shared understanding of the "pulls" impacting the organization

12:30–1:30	Lunch		
1:30–3:00	• Identify corporate values that will help ensure our success	• Consider our mission and vision; each participant identifies and shares "draft" values with the group • Highlight patterns of agreement and disagreement • Identify points unique to our organization from a competitive standpoint: potential strengths to exploit • Select our "core" corporate values	• Shared understanding of the "core" corporate values for the organization

3:00–6:15 (includes break)	• Articulate the organization's value proposition	• Taking all factors into consideration, determine whether we will strive to:
		  ◦ Provide cutting-edge innovative products
		  ◦ Be a cost leader
		  ◦ Be the absolute best at meeting or exceeding the needs and expectations of our customers
			• Shared understanding of the organization's value proposition

76

○ Serve a particular target market in an exceptional manner

○ Offer a product or service that is clearly unique, as compared to the products and services offered by others

Day 3

Time	Activity		Outcome
7:00–7:30	• Review the results of Day 2	• Conduct a gallery walk	• Common understanding of factors to consider throughout Day 3
7:30–12:30 (includes break)	• Identify the means (i.e., the strategies) by which the organization will accomplish its mission, attain its vision, and deliver on its value proposition	• Discuss how to accomplish the mission, attain the 2020 vision, and deliver on our value proposition; how to capitalize on the opportunities and strengths; and how to address weaknesses and threats	• Shared understanding of how we plan to accomplish the mission, attain the vision, deliver on our value proposition, capitalize on the opportunities and strengths, and address the weaknesses and threats
12:30–1:30	Lunch		
1:30–6:45	• Identify critical success factors for our short- and long-term success	• Discuss and identify critical success factors relating to the: ○ Organizational structure ○ Business model ○ Operational plan ○ Financial strategy	• Critical success factors are recognized and will be factored into future decisions and actions

(Continued)

77

Figure 4.4 (Continued)

Day 4

Time	Activity	Outcome
7:00–7:15	• Review Day 3 results and Day 4 agenda	• Conduct a gallery walk to review flip charts • Review agenda	• Purpose of the day is understood • Insights from Day 3 are applied to the Day 4 topics

7:15–12:00	• Create an action plan for moving forward	• Given the results of the previous three days of work, create an action plan for moving forward, including:
		  ○ Actions needing to occur
		  ○ Individual(s) responsible for each action
		  ○ Critical or due dates for each action
		  ○ Criteria for assessing the success of each action
		• Identify obstacles or impediments that are likely to impact our effort as well as viable countermeasures for each
			• Understanding of our action plan
			• Contingencies identified for likely impediments

12:00–1:30	Lunch, reflections on the strategic planning session, final questions, and closing comments		

- Although I may disagree during the discussion, I will ultimately support decisions we make during the strategic planning session.
- Although I may not agree with every point, I will discuss and negotiate it until I am willing to "live with" the final decision.
- Differentiate opinion from fact.
- Do not let a side conversation distract or disrupt others, and if it is about an important point, share the conversation with others.
- Silence cell phones so they do not distract or disrupt others.
- Do not use laptop computers during the strategic planning session unless their use directly relates to an agenda item or item under discussion or consideration.
- Watch the words we use; for example, saying "I will argue that point" in some cases will lead to an argument.

To enhance the influence the ground rules have on the strategic planning session, state in the agenda that the ground rules will be posted in the meeting room, will be reviewed at the beginning of each day, and will be referred to as necessary during the session.

Check points at the beginning and end of each day will require 10 to 15 minutes of the planning team's time. Although this activity may seem unnecessary, it allows the strategic planning team to:

- Review the strategic planning session objectives being addressed during the day.
- Review the agenda and understand the issues being addressed, the questions being answered, or the topics being covered during the day.
- Reflect on and gain insights from the previous day's actions and activities.
- Evaluate the strategic planning framework being used, the process being followed, and the tools being applied, and identify opportunities for improvement.
- Evaluate individual and team behavior against the pre-established ground rules, and identify opportunities for improvement.
- If another day is scheduled, prepare, organize, and/or set up for the next day.
- On the last day of the session, solidify understanding and agreement of next steps.

I also recommend that the individual facilitating the strategic planning session conduct process check points throughout the session. These check points are typically ad hoc in nature and therefore are not noted in the agenda.

SETTING THE STAGE FOR OPTIMAL SUCCESS

My experience working with organizations that have varying levels of experience in strategic planning suggests that it is important for you to solicit information, suggestions, and recommendations from individuals who:

• Have participated in previous strategic planning efforts.
• Will be participating in the upcoming strategic planning effort.
• Will be impacted by the strategic planning effort.

Such input will alert you to needs and expectations relating to strategic planning and may reveal issues that, if properly addressed, will (1) contribute to a more effective strategic planning session and (2) generate the buy-in and commitment needed to drive subsequent execution.

If your organization has not previously been involved in a strategic planning effort, consider soliciting information from individuals in the organization who have been or are currently involved in strategy formulation and execution elsewhere. If your organization has previously formulated and executed strategies, it is important that you learn from the past and identify and incorporate lessons learned and best practices into your upcoming strategic planning effort. Consider interviewing individuals who participated in previous strategic planning sessions to solicit their feedback, suggestions, and recommendations on themes to be considered, topics to be discussed, issues to be addressed, and questions to be answered during the session. I recommend that you create a short list of questions prior to interviewing these individuals and that you follow the list when meeting with them; doing so will help ensure efficient use of everyone's time and will help you allocate enough time for each question. Prior to developing the agenda for a four-day strategic planning session, one organization asked the planning team members who had participated in their previous session the five questions included in Sample of Application 4.2.

The agenda you create for your strategic planning session will prove beneficial because it will help the leader, facilitator, and/or participants focus throughout the session. While serving as a useful tool, it cannot be fully detailed because it needs to (1) be relatively brief and (2) provide information of interest and use to the greatest number of people. Although the agenda helps ensure focus and provides guidance, my experience and observations suggest that the individual leading and/or facilitating the strategic planning session requires additional direction, which might come in the form of a strategic planning session leader's guide (for an example, see Sample of Application 4.3). While similar to an agenda, the leader's guide provides detailed notes that the leader or facilitator uses throughout the session to ensure that the process flows smoothly and participants effectively and efficiently answer the questions under consideration, address the issues under review, and cover the intended topics.

Sample of Application 4.2

PLANNING TEAM INTERVIEW QUESTIONS

1. As we strive to build on the success of last year's strategic planning effort, what would you like to see changed or included in this year's strategic planning session?

2. Factors such as board of director expectations, recent critical events, the needs and expectations of your business groups, and corporate-wide initiatives carrying over into next year create the context for this year's strategic planning session. From your viewpoint, what other factors are helping "set the stage" for this year's session?

3. This year's strategic planning session involves planning team members gathering and presenting information that will allow you to analyze areas such as internal strengths and weaknesses, external opportunities and threats, your leveraging capabilities, your focus on quality and customers, current trends relating to your market growth, your exit strategies, and challenges associated with globalization. What other factors or areas do you think should be included in your analysis? Presenters: How much time will it take you to share this information during the strategic planning session?

4. We plan to structure the strategic planning session so that you can discuss issues and information pertaining to human resources, information technology, finance, and the global supply chain. What other factors or issues do you think should be included in this discussion?

5. The strategic planning session gives the planning team the opportunity to enjoy time together and to "decompress" with some social or recreational activity. From your viewpoint, what is the optimal amount of time (for example, a half-day, a full day) in a four-day session that should be spent on such activities?

Sample of Application 4.3

STRATEGIC PLANNING SESSION LEADER'S GUIDE

Day 1

Preparation

- Check with conference center to see if anyone has called to cancel
- Check voice mails and e-mails to see if anyone has called to cancel
- Arrive at meeting room at 5:30
- Verify that primary conference room is set up as planned

- Verify that breakout rooms are available and set up as planned
- Verify that equipment and supplies are available in the primary conference room
- Verify that equipment and supplies are available in each breakout room
- Check to make sure that equipment works properly
- Check to make sure that handout materials and participant notebooks are available and organized
- Welcome participants as they arrive; answer questions and address concerns

Kick-off Session

- Thirty-minute session
- Chairman and CEO shares a few comments (15 minutes)
- Describe overall intent of session
- Describe role of facilitator
- Walk through the agenda, highlighting topical areas, questions being answered, issues being addressed
- Point out the session objectives that are being addressed today
- Develop ground rules; capture on flip chart and post in room

Identification of Strengths, Weaknesses, Opportunities, and Threats (SWOT Analysis)

- Monitor emotions closely and respond appropriately and decisively
- Four-hour session
- Participants remain in one large group
- Describe purpose of session and provide definitions
- List headings on flip chart; work through SWOTs in a structured manner
- Capture input on flip charts; number pages; post in room

Further Development of the Corporate Vision for 2020

- Warning! Two-hour session
- Describe purpose of the visioning exercise and talk about "pulls"
- Break group out into two teams
- Hand out visioning exercise guide
- Facilitator monitors status and progress of both teams
- As slides are shown, the facilitator captures key points on flip charts
- Consolidate the results of the visioning exercise and SWOT; identify key pushes and pulls

- Monitor emotions closely and respond appropriately and decisively
- Warning! Ninety-minute session
- Facilitator leads 30- to 45-minute consolidation or synthesis of vision
- Facilitator sets up multi-voting exercise (refer to resource material)
- Participants vote; votes are tabulated; key pushes and pulls are noted on a separate flip chart sheet
  - Prepare work surface for vote tabulation
  - Highlight patterns of agreement and disagreement
  - Link SWOT results and items to the various facets of the vision
  - Identify points unique to the corporation from a competitive standpoint

Definition of Key Strategic Issues Relating to the 2020 Vision and SWOT

- Monitor emotions closely and respond appropriately and decisively
- Three-hour session
- Refer to and review pre-read materials
  - Discuss the pros and cons of various strategic options (one-half to one hour); capture results on flip charts
  - Review the pros and cons of each strategy in relation to our vision and our SWOT. How does our SWOT or vision impact the direction we go? (15 minutes)
  - Discuss how each strategy fits in with our 2020 strategic imperatives. Does one strategy or the other lend itself better to those imperatives? (30 minutes)
  - Even if we reach consensus (or if we don't), is there a need to have an external party provide us with pros and cons of strategies and/or recommendations from a shareholder value point of view? (15 minutes)
  - Discuss next steps or action plans to take away from this meeting (15 minutes)
- Monitor emotions closely and respond appropriately and decisively

Conclude Day 1

- Insights from today's session
- Framework being used, process being followed, and tools being applied: are there opportunities for improvement?
- Individual and team behavior against the preestablished ground rules: are there opportunities for improvement?
- Review the focus of day; describe how to prepare, organize, and/or set up for Day 2

ALERTING THE REMAINDER OF THE ORGANIZATION

You have now taken steps to involve as many individuals as possible in the strategic planning session, and the Participant Matrix (see Figure 4.1) verifies that the right stakeholders will be involved in the session. Unless your organization is the exception to the rule, some individuals will not be participating in the session but will be asked to help execute the resulting strategies. It is critical that you share information with this group prior to the strategic planning session so that they:

- Do not misinterpret the purpose of the strategic planning session.
- When given the chance, will willingly contribute to the strategic planning effort.
- When asked to do so, will enthusiastically help execute the resulting strategies.

KEY LEARNING POINT

Today's turbulent business environment magnifies the importance of sharing information about your strategic planning effort (and your other efforts, for that matter) with the entire organization. Otherwise, do not be surprised to hear later that the rumor back at the office is that your team is off site deciding who will stay and who will survive an upcoming reduction in workforce.

Although you have shared general information with the entire organization when generating interest in the strategic planning endeavor, I recommend that you work with a member of your organization's leadership team to send a Strategic Planning Launch Notification e-mail or message to all members of your organization seven to 10 days before the strategic planning session begins (see Sample of Application 4.4).

ROOM SETUP AND NEEDED EQUIPMENT AND SUPPLIES

Once the agenda has been set, the strategic planning session topics, issues, and questions have been formulated, and the tools and techniques to help facilitate analysis, discussion, and decision making have been selected, you are ready to decide on the room setup and the equipment and supplies to have available throughout the session. If you are conducting your strategic planning session within your facility, I encourage you to work closely with your facilities organization to ensure that the room is set up and that equipment and supplies are made available to allow the planning session to flow smoothly and as anticipated. If you will be conducting your strategic planning session elsewhere, it is of paramount importance that you work closely with hotel, conference center, or meeting facility

Sample of Application 4.4

STRATEGIC PLANNING LAUNCH NOTIFICATION
E-MAIL OR MEMORANDUM

Date: Today's date

To: All organizational members

From: A member of the leadership team

Subject: Launch of Our Strategic Planning Endeavor

This correspondence supplements the information we have previously shared with you regarding our embarking on a strategic planning endeavor. An important milestone for us will be the initial five-day strategic planning session being held on October 15–19 at the Ridgeway Conference Center.
  The session will allow our strategic planning team to:

- Review the strengths, weaknesses, opportunities, and threats impacting our ability to provide our services and products to our customers.

- Analyze the market and competitive forces to understand how they are impacting our ability to provide services and products to our customers.

- Develop mission and vision statements for our organization, to help us focus on what's important when making decisions and taking action.

- Identify corporate values that will help ensure our short- and long-term success, to be factored into our performance management system.

- Given the existing environmental conditions; our mission, vision, and values; and the results of the market and competitive analysis, to further refine our value proposition.

- Identify the means (i.e., the strategies) by which we will accomplish our short-term mission and attain our long-term vision.

- Create an action plan for moving forward that identifies related actions, responsible parties, and critical dates for each strategy.

We have taken steps to involve as many members of our organization as possible in this meeting. Although you may not be participating in this meeting as a member of the strategic planning team, you will be asked to review and comment on the results of the meeting; your input and contribution are vital to our effort, and we look forward to involving you in this endeavor in the coming weeks and months. In addition to involving individuals from throughout our organization, we have solicited information from our customers to be used during the session. This information will help ensure that our analysis is not overly internally focused and that resulting decisions and actions are in our customer's—and thus, our own—best interest.

We are very excited about our strategic planning effort in general and the upcoming strategic planning session in particular; although this meeting and subsequent actions will require an investment of time and effort on everyone's part, strategic planning is a natural continuation of all we have previously done to achieve our current level of success and will undoubtedly prove useful as we strive to continuously improve and set the stage for even higher levels of short- and long-term future success.

For More Information

For general information on strategic planning, we recommend that you drop by the corporate library and review the articles we have collected on this topic. If you are interested in learning more, consider checking out one of the following books we currently have available in the library:

- Hrebiniak, Lawrence G. 2005. *Making Strategy Work.* Upper Saddle River, NJ: Wharton School Publishing.
- Mintzberg, Henry, Joseph Lampel, and Bruce Ahlstrand. 2008. *Strategy Safari: A Guided Tour through the Wilds of Strategic Management.* New York: The Free Press.
- Kim, W. Chan, and Renee Mauborgne. 2005. *Blue Ocean Strategy.* Boston: Harvard Business School Press.

If you have questions about the upcoming strategic planning session or how you might contribute and share input, contact me at IC123-4 and I will gladly share additional information with you or let you know how you might be able to assist in this important effort.

representatives to help ensure that the proper facility is reserved for the proper number of days and is properly set up, with equipment and supplies available to allow the strategic planning session to flow smoothly and as anticipated.

Whether conducting the session in your facility or elsewhere, reserve the meeting space well in advance, work closely with your colleagues or facility representatives to set up and equip the meeting room, check on the meeting room the day before the strategic planning session, and arrive at the site early on the day of the session to make sure that all preparations are complete and according to plan.

FROM PREPARATION TO STRATEGIC PLANNING

As the date of your organization's strategic planning session approaches, it is important that you:

- Identify the kind of internal and external information and data your planning team will need to consider as it determines your organization's internal strengths and weaknesses and identifies the current and emerging threats and opportunities that exist in the environment within which your organization functions.

- Identify sources of the needed data and information.
- Collect, organize, summarize, and "package" the data and information the strategic planning team will consider throughout the strategic planning session.

Once the needed data and information are available and the date of your strategic planning session arrives, your strategic planning team will be set to work together to:

- Analyze information relating to the organization's value proposition and the internal factors and external forces likely to impact its short- and long-term success.
- Create (or verify) your organization's mission, vision, and sweet spot.
- Create strategic goal statements.
- Identify and prioritize the means by which you will achieve the strategic goals.
- Identify tactics, assign roles and responsibilities, establish timelines, and define metrics.
- Plan for the unexpected and unanticipated.
- Take steps to ensure successful execution.
- Take steps to continuously improve.

Chapter 5

Gathering and Analyzing Data and Information

One underlying principle of credible and trustworthy strategic planning is that decisions are not based on opinion or hearsay but rather on data and solid information. In getting things in order for your upcoming strategic planning session, you must give careful thought to:

- The nature and scope of the information and data your strategic planning session requires.
- How you will obtain that information and data.
- How you will make the information and data available to the strategic planning team so it is easily understood and used.
- How the planning team will prepare by analyzing the relevant data and information.

THE NATURE AND SCOPE OF STRATEGIC PLANNING DATA AND INFORMATION

The nature and scope of the information and data your strategic planning session requires will depend on your industry, your profession, or the area in which your organization specializes. When preparing to conduct your strategic planning session, you will need to collect data on a variety of factors likely to impact your organization's short- and long-term success. Internal factors impacting your organization's success include but are not limited to:

- The financial strength of your organization.
- The extent to which your organization has access to capital.

- The knowledge, skills, and abilities of employees (at all levels).
- The leadership, managerial, and supervisory skills within your organization.
- Your organization's capacity to develop and ship products and/or provide services.
- Union issues and the relationship your management team has with union leadership.
- Issues pertaining to—
  - Safety.
  - Legality.
  - Warranty.
  - Quality.
- Information technology, specifically—
  - The availability and capability of technology.
  - Knowledge management and knowledge sharing.
  - Internet usage (e.g., when managing excess or deficient capacity).
- Your organization's research and development efforts.
- Geographic location(s).
- The relationship your organization has with its suppliers.
- Distribution channels your organization has capitalized upon.
- The relationship your organization has with its distributors.
- Supplier relationships.
- Your organization's pricing strategy.

Porter[1] and David[2] identify a multitude of external forces impacting your organization's short- and long-term success, including but not limited to:

- Your competitors—
  - The size of each competitor, in comparison to your organization.
  - Your competitor's capabilities and capacity.
  - The reputation your competitor has within the marketplace.
  - The manner in which your competitor is likely to "counter" your current and emerging strategies.
- Market conditions—
  - Market segment growth potential and rate.
  - Threat of new competitors entering the target market.
  - Current and emerging price pressures being exerted on the industry or profession.

- Labor market demographics.
- Government—
  - Regulations.
  - Rules.
  - Incentives.
  - Controls.
- Technology trends potentially influencing (1) your ability to produce products or deliver services and (2) the needs and expectations of your customers and clients.
- Lifestyle trends potentially influencing (1) the availability and commitment of employees and (2) the needs and expectations of your customers and clients.
- The impact of the economy on the buying patterns of your customers and clients.
- Your suppliers' power (e.g., to withhold the material you need or raise the price of your supplies).
- Buyers' power (e.g., to purchase duplicate products or services elsewhere at a comparable or more favorable cost).

While the above factors impact an organization's short- and long-term success, the nature and scope of the information and data your strategic planning session requires will depend on your particular industry, profession, or area in which your organization specializes. For example, when preparing to facilitate a regional strategic planning session for a particular branch of the U.S. military, we collected information and data relating specifically to that particular branch, its particular mission, and the specific challenges and opportunities it had before it (see Figure 5.1).

Figure 5.1   Information and Data Used in Regional Strategic Planning

Internal Factors	External Factors
Business processes	Fishing industry trends
Systems	Foreign fishing vessels
Technology	Freight transport
Culture	Government and political trends
People	Migrant interdictions
	Natural disasters
	Offshore oil and gas trends
	Passenger transport industry
	Ports and waterways
	Recreational boating
	Tank, chemical, and gas vessels
	Towing industry

Table 5.1   Likely Sources of Internal Information and Data

Functional Area	Information and Data
Human resources	People, culture
Operations, manufacturing, or research and development	Business processes
Operations, manufacturing, research and development, or information technology	Systems, technology

OBTAINING THE NEEDED INFORMATION AND DATA

Your organization's various functional groups in all likelihood collect and retain certain information and data that the strategic planning team will need to consider during the planning session. I therefore recommend that you meet with representatives from each of the functional areas to discuss the information and data the strategic planning team will require and determine the nature and scope of the information and data readily available. Although data sources may vary, Table 5.1 lists likely sources of internal information and data.

Internal information and data you collect may include, but not be limited to, the following:

- Management issues: whether your management team—
  - Solicits and accepts the advice of others (e.g., accountants, attorneys, economists, etc.).
  - Is willing and able to make decisions in a timely manner.
  - Has the means of attaining, analyzing, and basing decisions on valid and credible data and information.
  - Makes management decisions and actions that are consistent with previous decisions and actions.
  - Has created and reinforces the appropriate balance between—
    - Responsibility and authority.
    - Autonomy and teamwork.
    - Controls and incentives.
  - Has empowered employees (at all levels) to make prudent decisions and take needed action.
- Financial issues: whether your organization—
  - Has access to needed capital.
  - Properly and appropriately spends money.
  - Has enough money to—
    - Install, maintain, and/or update its systems, processes, and technology.

- Support the research, development, manufacturing, and sales to meet or exceed revenue and profit margin requirements.
  - Manages cash flow in an effective and efficient manner.
  - Is generating enough revenue to repay its loans.
- Operations issues: whether your organization's—
  - Inputs (in terms of raw materials, supplies, equipment, and people) meet or exceed manufacturing and/or sales requirements.
  - Systems, processes, and technology are producing products and/or services in an efficient and effective manner.
  - Products and services match or exceed customer or client requirements.
- Human resources issues: whether your employees (at all levels)—
  - Possess the needed knowledge, skills, and abilities.
  - Possess and exhibit the needed levels of self-confidence and self-motivation.
  - Are sufficient in number to support needed growth and expansion.
  - Understand your organization's mission and vision.
  - Strive to behave in a manner that is consistent with and supportive of your organization's core values.
  - Are properly and appropriately—
    - Selected.
    - Assimilated into the organization.
    - Managed and supervised.
    - Evaluated.
    - Disciplined (as and when needed).
    - Compensated.
    - Recognized and rewarded.
    - Promoted.
  - Remain with the organization, so they do not resign to join competitors or become competitors.

Your organization's functional groups in all likelihood also collect and retain certain externally focused information and data that the strategic planning team will need to consider during the planning session. Externally focused information and data you collect may include, but not be limited to, the following:

- Market issues: whether marketplace—
  - Size is increasing, decreasing, or remaining static.
  - Demand is increasing, decreasing, or remaining static.

- o Demand is matching, exceeding, or lagging behind the quantity of product you can produce or the service you can provide.
- o Product or service needs and/or expectations are changing or remaining static.
- o Purchase decisions are based on cost, innovation, or customer service considerations and whether those considerations are changing or remaining static.
- o Price requirements are changing or remaining static.
- • Competitive issues, pertaining to—
- o Current and prospective competitors.
- o Each competitor's—
  - ▪ Business model and strategies.
  - ▪ Supply chain and distribution network.
  - ▪ Market share.
  - ▪ Customer base.
  - ▪ Market growth rate.
- o How each competitor—
  - ▪ Seeks to enter the market or increase its market share.
  - ▪ Differentiates its products and services.
  - ▪ Has previously countered your organization's strategies or how it might counter your future strategies.
- o The capacity and capabilities of each competitor.

Data and information relating to market and competitive issues will help you analyze external factors impacting your current business, product portfolio, and/or service offerings and increase the likelihood of your defeating your competitors. However, building on what we learned from Kim and Mauborgne in Chapter 2, it is important that you broaden your perspective to a much more strategic level, step outside the competitor-competition arena, and collect data that will allow your strategic planning team to:

- • Study current and emerging trends and patterns to identify customer and client needs and expectations yet to be investigated, understood, or addressed.
- • Analyze advances in systems, processes, and technology to identify opportunities to eliminate, create, or change the way you currently conduct business, provide services, and develop, sell, and distribute products.
- • Analyze the services and products that organizations, industries, or professions similar to yours offer to explore implications for your organization's purpose, mission and vision, and the value your organization brings to its various stakeholder groups.

- Explore the unknown, unrealized, and/or unrecognized needs and expectations of your clients or customers to determine what else your organization might do to meet or exceed those particular needs and expectations.

- Analyze all external factors impacting your organization's ability to act on its value proposition to ensure, for example, that manufacturing, transportation, and distribution costs and the price of the services and products will allow (1) your clients and customers to purchase them and (2) your organization to realize needed profit margins.

KEY LEARNING POINT

The type and amount of information and data to collect for your strategic planning session depend on the information your team needs to draw conclusions and to make decisions that your various stakeholder groups will consider valid and credible. Collecting more information and data than that is inefficient and unnecessary; collecting less is inadequate and jeopardizes optimal success.

While you will probably collect most of the information and data you need from your various functional groups, you may (1) discover that you need to augment existing information and data or (2) decide to further engage your employees (at all levels) in the strategic planning endeavor by conducting an employee opinion survey. Such a survey will produce information likely to prove useful to the strategic planning team and will provide invaluable insight into the perceptions of employees (at all levels) on a variety of topics as well as the extent to which they buy into and commit to your organization's strategic imperatives and initiatives. More specifically, an employee opinion survey will allow you to explore perceptions and attitudes in areas such as:

- Mission, vision, and values.
- Management capabilities, imperatives, and initiatives.
- Commitment, self-confidence, and self-motivation.
- Operations and performance.
- Organizational capabilities and capacity.
- Interpersonal and organizational communication.
- Quality assurance and improvement.

A properly structured and administered survey will—while maintaining the level of anonymity required to ensure completion and submission—help you identify areas, levels, or positions that are helping drive or enable the organization's imperatives and initiatives and those areas needing additional information, guidance, and/or support. If you decide to use an employee opinion survey to obtain information, I encourage you to ask individuals within your organization who have testing and measurement expertise to help you design and conduct the survey or arrange for an outside consultant or vendor to assist you in this matter. Whether using an internal or external resource, your employee survey will in all likelihood include these steps:

- Define the overall purpose of the survey—the overarching topic, issue, or question to be explored.
- Identify the target audience for the survey—who will be asked to complete and submit the survey or be asked to participate in an interview.
- Determine how the survey will be administered—the survey can be conducted using a paper or electronic questionnaire or using face-to-face (one-on-one or group) interviews.
- Decide on questions to be asked—questions to be included in the interview guide or questionnaire.
- Create a draft survey and test it using a sample audience; to the extent needed, modify the survey—to ensure the survey is clear and concise, that recipients or interviewees are likely to participate fully, and that the results are likely to prove useful and beneficial.
- Prepare the audience for the survey—including needed information about the purpose of the survey, the nature and scope of the information it will solicit, the amount of time it will take, and how the results will be used.
- Administer the survey, and analyze and summarize the results—summarize the results in a format that is likely to prove useful and beneficial to the strategic planning team.

You may also need to conduct research outside your organization to collect additional information and data on external trends impacting your organization's short- and long-term success. One essential but frequently overlooked data source is your organization's end-users, that is, current customers, clients, or individuals who benefit from the products your organization produces or the services your organization provides. Consider conducting an end-user survey if you need to supplement or augment the information your organization currently has on its customers or clients. This survey will allow you to further develop or strengthen the relationship you have with your end-users and provide information likely to prove useful to the strategic planning team. For example, an end-user survey will allow you to find out:

- Why customers or clients buy your products; for example, is it because—
  ○ Your products are innovative?

- ○ Your products meet or exceed the end-user's specifications or requirements?
- ○ Your products are of good quality?
- ○ Your products are the least expensive to buy or use, operate, deploy, or implement?
- ○ Your products are simply not available elsewhere?
- ○ The end-user receives a high level of service while shopping, buying, or following up on a purchase?
- • Why customers or clients procure your services; for example, is it because—
  - ○ Your organization or employees have a good reputation?
  - ○ Your employees possess good knowledge, skills, and abilities?
  - ○ Your employees exhibit high self-confidence or self-motivation?
  - ○ The services your organization provides are of good quality?
  - ○ The services you provide are the least expensive?
  - ○ Your services are simply not available elsewhere?
  - ○ The end-user receives a high level of service throughout the engagement process?
- • The opinion your customers or clients have of your products or services versus the opinion they have of your competitors' products or services.
- • Other products your customers or clients are likely to purchase or other services they are likely to procure.
- • Other products your customers or clients would like you to produce or other services they would like you to offer.

As with an internally focused survey, a properly structured and administered end-user survey will help you identify the capabilities, imperatives, and initiatives that are helping drive or enable the organization's short- and long-term success and those factors that need to be emphasized, modified, or deemphasized. If you decide to use an end-user survey to obtain information, as with the internally focused survey, I encourage you to seek the assistance of individuals within your organization who have testing and measurement expertise or arrange for an outside consultant or vendor to assist you in this matter. Whether using an internal or external resource, your end-user survey will in all likelihood include these steps:

- • Define the overall purpose of the survey—the overarching topic, issue, or question to be explored.
- • Identify the target audience for the survey—who will be asked to complete and submit the survey or be asked to participate in an interview.
- • Determine how the survey will be administered—whether conducted using a paper or electronic questionnaire or using face-to-face (one-on-one or group)

interviews, note that meeting with customers or clients at their home or place of business may provide additional insight regarding current and emerging needs and expectations.

- Decide on questions to be asked—questions to be included in the interview guide or questionnaire.
- Create a draft survey and test it using a sample audience; as needed, modify the survey—to ensure the survey is clear and concise, that recipients or interviewees are likely to participate fully, and that the results are likely to prove useful and beneficial.
- Properly introduce the survey and set the stage for an adequate and proper response—including information about the purpose of the survey, the nature and scope of the information it solicits, the amount of time it will take, and how the results will be used.
- Administer the survey, analyze it, and then summarize the results in a format that is likely to prove useful and beneficial to the strategic planning team.

There are countless other sources of external data and information; access the ones most likely to provide the information and data you need and that your stakeholders are likely to consider credible. A visit to your local college, university, or federal depository public library will reveal dozens of databases containing information likely to prove useful and beneficial to your strategic planning effort, including Bloomberg,[3] ORBIS,[4] Gartner,[5] and Hoover's.[6]

In conducting your research, I encourage you to rely on two other important sources of information: the Internet and individuals you know and/or with whom you work. The Internet might be an efficient and effective way to collect information and data on your competitors. Enter any competitor's Web site and you will likely find the following data and information readily, legally, and ethically available to the public:

- Analyst reports.
- Financial statements and Securities and Exchange Commission (SEC) filings.
- Annual shareholder reports.
- Press releases.

Input from individuals you know and with whom you work in the following areas will provide additional insight as to each competitor's intent, capability, and capacity:

- The personalities, biases, and blind spots of the competitor's leaders and executives.
- The competitor's—
  - Organizational structure, leadership, and governance.
  - Growth strategy (e.g., organic or through mergers and acquisitions).

- Marketing and sales strategies.
- Supplier and distributor networks.

- The emphasis the competitor places on cost, innovation, and customer satisfaction.
- The breadth and depth of the competitor's products and/or services.
- The effectiveness and efficiency of the competitor's systems, processes, and technology.
- The level of competency, self-confidence, and self-motivation the competitor's employees (at all levels) possess and exhibit.
- Research and development efforts and new products or services the competitor is currently developing.
- Quality assurance and/or improvement systems or processes the competitor has in place.

Although the above externally focused information will serve as a foundation for your strategic planning team's analysis, you in all likelihood will need to supplement it with additional environmental trend data and information. For example, while we were preparing for the military's regional strategic planning session, meetings with key stakeholders revealed their need to focus on a slate of external trends impacting the military's short- and long-term success. To help guide our external research focus and effort, we developed the trend data and information matrix illustrated in Figure 5.2. Please note that the list presented in Figure 5.2 is condensed and does not contain sensitive or confidential information.

The external sources of information and data your strategic planning team requires will largely depend on your industry, your profession, or the area in which your organization specializes. For example, we collected information and data from more than three dozen external sources when preparing to facilitate the military's regional strategic planning session. A condensed list of data sources is presented in Figure 5.3; please note that it does not contain sensitive or confidential information.

When identifying external sources of information and data, I encourage you to strive to collect information from and/or about leading performers in your industry or profession or in an industry or profession similar to yours. Information and data from such "best-in-class" organizations can provide insight into how your strategies, systems, processes, people, and culture compare to the best-in-class organization's strategies, systems, processes, people, and culture. The results of this comparison may reveal:

- Biases that your organization's leadership or planning team members have that cause them to place too much emphasis on developing, maintaining, and/or improving certain aspects, elements, or components of your organization's strategies, systems, processes, people, and culture.

Figure 5.2   Trend Data and Information for Regional Strategic Planning

Research Area	Associated Trend Data and Information
Fishing	• Weather trends • Number of fishing vessels
Freight vessels	• TEUs (20-foot-equivalent units) entering port • Size of vessels
Government	• Impact of current legislation • Possibility of new legislation
Natural disasters	• Nature and scope of interventions, based on previous incidents • Future predictions based on the magnitude, frequency, and duration of previous natural disasters
Passenger ships	• Number of cruises and ferries • Physical size of vessels
Ports and waterways	• Port development plans • Channel development plans
Recreational boating	• Number of people participating • Number of boats and watercraft

- Blind spots that your organization's leadership or planning team members have that cause them to neglect to develop, maintain, and/or improve certain aspects, elements, or components of your organization's strategies, systems, processes, people, and culture.
- Strengths pertaining to your organization's strategies, systems, processes, people, and culture that should be leveraged or capitalized upon.
- Weaknesses or limitations pertaining to your organization's strategies, systems, processes, people, and culture that should be reduced, mitigated, or somehow addressed.

Synthesizing, Consolidating, and Summarizing Information and Data

Experience and observations reinforce the edict that people can only absorb and apply a certain amount of information and data. It is therefore important that you synthesize, consolidate, and summarize the results of your data-gathering activities. Doing less may result in your strategic planning team getting bogged down in too many details and potentially "freezing" rather than basing their conclusions and

Figure 5.3   External Sources of Information for a Strategic Planning Session

Agencies and Departments
• Scientific Committee on Oceanic Research (SCOR)
• National Oceanic and Atmospheric Administration (NOAA)

Societies and Associations
• Society of Naval Architects and Marine Engineers (SNAME)
• Navy League of the United States

Colleges and Universities
• U.S. Merchant Marine Academy
• U.S. Naval Academy

Institutes
• International Risk Management Institute (IRMI)
• Office of Research Services, National Institutes of Health

Periodicals
• *American Shipbuilder*
• *Journal of Ship Production*

Reports
• "Shipbuilding and Repair Industry Report"
• "Double Hull Tanker Legislation"

Individuals
• Director of Research and Scholarship, U.S. Naval Academy Research Center
• Deputy Director of Research and Scholarship, U.S. Naval Academy Research Center

decisions on valid and credible information and data. In deciding what information and data to emphasize or showcase and how much information and data to share with the strategic planning team, I recommend that you take five factors into consideration:

1. How information and data are generally shared within your organization.
2. The amount of information members of your organization typically require when drawing conclusions or making decisions.
3. The kind of information members of your organization typically require when drawing conclusions or making decisions.
4. The kind of information and data the members of your organization might likely consider to be valid and credible.
5. The kind and amount of information and data that you feel a nonbiased third party might expect a strategic planning team to use when drawing such conclusions and making such decisions.

Consider synthesizing, combining, and summarizing some of the results of your data-gathering activities and sharing them with several strategic planning team members. Ask the team members to compare the abridged materials with the complete information and data and to provide feedback regarding the adequacy of the materials as well as suggestions and recommendations for improvement. Be sure to retain the source materials as you merge, blend, combine, and otherwise abridge the data and information. Have at least one copy of the source materials at the strategic planning session so you can refer to or cite baseline information or data if called upon to do so or if doing so will add clarity or credibility to the process.

PACKAGING AND PRESENTING THE INFORMATION AND DATA

As the previous section suggests, it is important that you properly package and present information and data to the planning team to ensure optimal under-standing, interpretation, and utilization. This effort typically involves organizing, sequencing, or arranging the information and data so that strategic planning team members can easily access and refer to it throughout the session. If the information and data are voluminous and/or complex, supplement text and numbers with charts and graphs to emphasize key data, trends, and patterns and to help team members compare changes and relationships.[7]

If your strategic planning team members are likely to expect a formal report rather than or in addition to spreadsheets, raw data, charts, and/or graphs, I recommend that you create one following the protocol and/or style generally used in your organization. Absent such a prevailing practice, consider creating a document containing these elements:

- Cover page, including subject and date.
- Table of contents.
- Executive summary, if the length or complexity of the document suggests the need for one.
- Clearly defined sections, including—
  - Background or introduction, providing an overview and explaining the nature and scope of the information and data presented in the document.
  - Findings, providing detailed information and data on the factors or forces being reported on.
  - Conclusions, providing a summary of the main findings or emphasizing or showcasing key points.
  - References, providing information that will allow further exploration or analysis.
  - Appendices, providing data and information in the form of tables, graphs, charts, figures, spreadsheets, and so on.

MOVING FORWARD WITH INITIAL ANALYSES AND DECISIONS

You are now ready for the strategic planning team to come together to move forward with the strategic planning agenda (which may or may not be similar to the ones presented earlier in this chapter). Using the data and information you have collected and organized, your strategic planning team will initially focus on the organization's value proposition as well as internal factors and external forces likely to impact its short- and long-term success.

Deciding on a Decision-Making Process

Prior to beginning its review, analysis, and examination of the package(s) of information and data, I recommend that your strategic planning team decide on the decision-making process it will follow throughout the strategic planning process. A quick assessment of previous meetings may reveal the various ways your team arrives at a decision; for example, it might:

- Make a decision by—through mutual agreement or action—failing to make a decision.
- Let the individual in charge of the session or the highest-ranking leader in attendance make the decision.
- Defer to the loudest voice or to the individual willing to advocate a particular position or point for the longest period of time.
- Let the opinion or desire of the majority influence the decision through voting.
- Make the decision by allowing the team members to come to consensus.

It is important that your strategic planning team consider the advantages and disadvantages of each approach and decide which approach is most appropriate, given the purpose of the strategic planning session, the challenge the strategic planning team has before it, and the culture of the organization. With those factors in mind, I encourage you to strongly consider using consensus as your decision-making process. Given the goals (and the underlying importance) of your strategic planning session, it will be important for the planning team to make valid and credible decisions and for participants and key stakeholders to buy into and otherwise support the resulting strategies, tactics, and actions. These desired outcomes spotlight the need for adequate and proper analysis, discussion, negotiation, and consideration and for all planning team members to consent to "live with" a decision even though they may not be in 100 percent agreement with every aspect of the decision. Although voting may be more efficient, consensus allows the strategic planning team to have the necessary dialogue and debate, draw needed conclusions, make needed decisions, and move forward with the needed level of buy-in and commitment.

> **KEY LEARNING POINT**
>
> Your organization's success hinges on the decisions your team makes throughout the strategic planning session. It is important that your strategic planning team select and apply the most appropriate decision-making technique, given the purpose of the strategic planning session, the challenge the planning team has before it, and the culture of the organization.

The Organization's Purpose and Value Proposition

You may wonder why the strategic planning team should begin its analysis by reviewing the organization's purpose and value proposition. Understanding, verifying, or confirming the organization's purpose and value proposition is important because it sets the context within which the planning team's analysis and examination occur. For example, information and data pertaining to your customers or competitors cannot be interpreted properly and/or is relatively meaningless unless members of the strategic planning team understand and agree on:

- The purpose of the organization: what the organization is attempting to do.
- How the organization is attempting to benefit or bring value to the customer or client.
- How the organization is attempting to differentiate itself from its competitors.

Organizations are not formed simply out of happenstance, nor do they function haphazardly. Rather, they consist of individuals working together in a planned and purposeful way to ensure that the organization's predetermined purpose is accomplished. The purpose of your organization may be stated in a previously created mission or vision statement. If such statements do not exist, the strategic planning committee should consider reviewing information shared with stakeholders (such as board members, investors, and prospective employees), regulatory filings, organizational charters, or partnership agreements. While such documents describe an organization's official purpose and what it is formally attempting to do, an analysis of which expenditures are approved and how monies are allocated in quarterly or annual financial reports—especially when money is scarce and programs, imperatives, and initiatives must be prioritized—will reveal an organization's true purpose and what it is actually doing (versus what it is hoping, intending, or attempting to do).

Organizations have limitations pertaining to finances, time, and resources. They therefore cannot be all things to all people; they must decide how best to differentiate themselves from their competition and provide the services and/or products most likely to prove useful and beneficial to their target client or customer. Your organization's purpose, along with the manner in which it differentiates itself from its competition and attempts to provide services and/or products to its target clients and customers, will establish the overall context within which your strategic planning team will assess the current state, envision the desired future state, and identify and assess the means for accomplishing the current state (its mission) and realizing the future (its vision).

Treacy and Wiersema created a framework that your strategic planning committee might find useful in reviewing how your organization differentiates itself from its competition and attempts to provide services and/or products to its clients and customers. Their value disciplines model[8] suggests that customers and clients typically obtain products or services from an organization that emphasizes:

- Operational excellence. These organizations strive to conduct efficient operations and provide services and products at a relatively low price. If your organization emphasizes operational excellence, the strategic planning committee will focus on external forces and internal factors impacting your organization's ability to—
  - Manage the quantity and quality (while controlling the cost) of the raw materials entering the organization.
  - Maximize the productivity of your organization's employees (at all levels).
  - Increase the speed of production while minimizing waste and the need for rework.
- Product leadership. These organizations emphasize the design, development, and marketing of innovative products and services. If your organization emphasizes product leadership, your strategic planning team will focus on external forces and internal factors impacting your organization's ability to—
  - Research and develop products and services your target clients and customers are likely to consider "cutting edge."
  - Manufacture products your target clients and customers are likely to consider "cutting edge."
  - Provide services your target clients and customers are likely to consider "cutting edge."
- Customer intimacy. These organizations emphasize excellent customer service throughout the sales process and strive to provide products and services likely to meet or exceed the client or customer's requirements or expectations. If your organization emphasizes customer intimacy, your strategic planning team will focus on external forces and internal factors impacting your organization's ability to—
  - Understand and respond to the customer or client's needs and expectations before, during, and after the sale.
  - Develop, maintain, and further develop the relationship it has with its target clients or customers.

- o Create products and services likely to meet or exceed customer or client expectations, requirements, or specifications.
- o Deliver products and services in a way that exceeds the client or customer's needs and expectations.

Once the strategic planning team members agree on your organization's purpose and the manner in which it differentiates itself from its competition and attempts to provide services and/or products to its target clients and customers, they can begin to analyze data and information collected prior to the strategic planning session.

Analyzing Research Data and Information

The strategic planning team should obtain and analyze data and information it believes will allow it to understand, discuss, draw conclusions from, and make decisions about the issues, topics, and questions your organization considers to be of utmost importance. The strategic planning team members will have to answer the questions of "what" data and information are right and "how much" data and information are enough. To help the strategic team members answer these two important questions, I encourage you to keep the following two points in mind:

1. The strategic planning team's conclusions and decisions must be valid and credible. Planning team members must believe that the information and data they consider are sufficient to support the conclusions they draw and the decisions they make. To help ensure the availability and application of sufficient information and data, prior to proceeding forward from each decision point, the planning team should verify that all team members are in general agreement that the decision made is a valid and credible one and that the decision was based on a sufficient amount of information and data.

2. The strategic planning team members must properly interpret the data and information. This data and information must be shared with the team in a manner that team members are likely to understand. To help ensure proper interpretation, planning team members should periodically "test" their individual interpretations.

Data and information considered during a strategic planning session relate to the topics being considered, the issues being addressed, and the questions needing to be answered. For example, a group of investors recently explored whether external conditions and internal factors were favorable for the establishment of a new residential real estate management and sales organization. Given the tumultuous business environment and prevailing industry pressures, it was essential that the investment group take broad-based and multifaceted information and data into consideration. Figure 5.4 presents some of the key information and data the

Figure 5.4   Investment Group Information and Data Considerations

Background

The trend leading up to the 2008 subprime mortgage-driven housing crisis was as staggering as the housing crisis itself: housing prices had risen on average about 45 percent from 2000 to 2007. By contrast, the median income for working-age households (homes headed by someone under 65) plummeted 4 percent over that same period.

Market Analysis

This market analysis takes these factors into consideration:

- Market size.
- Market growth rate.
- Market profitability.
- Industry cost structure.
- Distribution channels.
- Market trends.

Market Size

Data reveal that 51.4 percent of the target market population is of the age considered likely to rent, lease, or purchase a residential property and that the median age in the target market is 35, in the age range likely to rent, lease, or purchase a residential property. Home ownership rates in the region in which the target market is located further verify the above data.

An analysis of the following geographically focused data also verifies the following:

- Percentage of residents living in same house in 1995 and 2000: 37.4.
- Number of housing units as of 2008: 1,065,197.

Target market data suggest a continued upward trend, with 2009 data revealing:

- Total housing units: 228,139.
- Occupied housing units: 204,688, or 89.7 percent.
- Median family income: $57,471.
- Per capita income: $24,887.

Our business model would be designed to provide the most value to prospective home owners residing in the target market who still have the dream of one day owning a home. Data sources suggest these statistics for our target market:

- 17.3 percent of ARMs resetting within the next 12 months.
- House vacancies stand at 6.7 percent.

Market Growth Rate

Our target market is one of the fastest-growing areas in the United States. Over a 10-year period, the population increased 86.3 percent, while the U.S. population increased 13.3 percent. We predict a continued upward trend, with more than 2,000 people moving into our target market each month.

(Continued)

Figure 5.4   (Continued)

Current trends are likely to continue unless significant changes occur in the housing market or with the employment rate in our target market.

Although a potential decline in growth due to price pressure caused by competition may eventually occur, the following entry barriers will likely delay or prohibit its occurrence:

- Strategic network of professionals to implement the needed infrastructure and business methodology.
- The implementation of the systems and policies to drive needed behaviors and performance.

Market Profitability

These factors help ensure optimal market profitability:

- A price point likely to match what customers can afford.
- Services that meet or exceed customer expectations.

Industry Cost Structure

Over the past 12 months, 97 percent of the homes rented in our target market fell in the $2,300/month or less monthly rental range, while 68 percent of the homes sold in the market fell in the $125,000–$175,000 price range. The largest single cohort (39 percent) of home buyers in the market purchased homes in the $150,000–$200,000 band, which we presume supports a $2,300 or so monthly rental fee.

Research reveals that the following property management fee is to be expected within the target market: an initial fee that equals 75 percent of the first month's payment and then a monthly fee that equals 18 percent of the monthly payment.

Distribution Channels

Existing Distribution Channels

- 250 local real estate companies.
- Three local real estate investment trust (REIT) companies.

Trends and Emerging Channels

The housing industry is experiencing a crisis of historic proportions. This crisis, coupled with high unemployment rates, reduces the attractiveness (from our competitor's point of view) of the target market. Those external forces, along with our unique value proposition and business model, give us a distinct competitive advantage.

Channel Power Structure

We have established a strategic alliance and through the enhancement of these trusting relationships have captured "most preferred" billing rates and fee structures.

Market Trends

Our target market is one of the fastest growing in the United States. However, with the current financial crisis and downward pressure on the housing market, our target

Figure 5.4   (Continued)

market now maintains a housing vacancy rate of 23 percent for rentals and 9 percent for homes.

Current and Future Competitive Threats

- Companies competing in a related product or market:
  - 250 local real estate companies.
  - 44 local property managers.
- Companies using related technologies: 31 regional REIT companies.
- Companies targeting our market segment with related services: 32 institutional investors.

Barriers to Entry

- The strategic network of professionals to create and implement the needed infrastructure and business methodology.
- The reinforcement of business practices to drive needed results and outcomes.

Competitor Analysis

Taking our most likely competitor into consideration, the following analysis demonstrates that the business we establish will be uniquely suited and positioned to enter and control this industry or market. To determine the likelihood of entry into our industry or target market, we:

- Defined the nature and scope of the industry.
- Determined the critical success factors for our industry.
- Identified our most likely competitors.
- Evaluated our organization and our most likely competitor against the critical success factors to determine the relative strength of each organization.
- Used the results to determine the overall likelihood of competitor entry and to identify the forces and factors that must be leveraged and/or reduced, mitigated, or avoided.

This analysis reveals that the organization we create will be rated higher than our leading competitor on the price point, product, and performance requirements, as well as on our strategic alliances, infrastructure, value proposition, and investment sources. Overall, our organization will be rated much higher than our leading competitor (80 versus 65.5 raw score and 10.0 versus 8.1285 weighted score).

Competitive Risks

- Service features.
- Warranty and lease agreements.

Given the nature and scope of the industry and target market and the nature and scope of the risks, we will identify countermeasures to nullify the risks and reduce the likelihood of entry by our competitors.

investment group considered in deciding whether to establish the new real estate firm; please note that information and data were omitted and modified to protect sensitive and/or confidential material.

Analyzing Employee Opinion Survey Information

Your strategic planning team may find it useful and beneficial to supplement research results with information obtained through an employee opinion survey. The individual, team, or vendor administering the survey will in all likelihood summarize the results and showcase key employee perceptions as well as the extent to which they buy into and commit to your organization's strategic imperatives and initiatives.

Experience and observations suggest that your strategic planning team will find such information invaluable in helping it explore perceptions and attitudes in the areas of:

- Mission, vision, and values.
- Management capabilities, imperatives, and initiatives.
- Commitment, self-confidence, and self-motivation.
- Operations and performance issues.
- Organizational capabilities and capacity.
- Interpersonal and organizational communication.
- Quality assurance and improvement.

A leading medical center, when preparing to review and refine its strategic plan, recognized the importance of engaging employees and obtaining their perceptions of previous strategic management decisions and their suggestions for future organizational imperatives and initiatives. More specifically, the medical center's executive team decided to conduct an employee opinion survey to:

- Obtain feedback on the medical center's organization, management, operation, quality of patient care, and work environment.
- Ask questions about the level of buy-in, ownership, and commitment for key strategic management imperatives and initiatives existing throughout the medical center.
- Ask questions about external forces and internal factors likely to impede the medical center's short- and long-term success.
- Gather information on ways the medical center might leverage or otherwise take advantage of its strengths and how it might mitigate, reduce, or otherwise address its weaknesses and limitations.
- Obtain suggestions and recommendations to apply toward the medical center's continuous quality improvement efforts.

- Obtain baseline information against which the effectiveness of future strategic decisions and actions might be assessed.

All members of the medical center—from the individuals working in the boiler room to individuals sitting in the boardroom—were asked to complete the employee opinion survey. The team administering the survey analyzed and summarized the results and shared participation statistics and survey results with the strategic planning team.

The medical center survey administrators tracked response rates so that (1) gaps in levels of understanding, buy-in, and commitment could be identified and addressed and (2) potential best practices could be identified, leveraged, and capitalized upon. For this employee opinion survey, respondents were asked to provide information pertaining to a number of demographic variables, including:

- Gender.
- Ethnic group status.
- Position held within the organization.
- Length of service with the medical center.
- Shift typically worked at the medical center.
- Division or department in which the respondent works.

Although the demographic information was designed to reveal gaps in levels of understanding, buy-in, and commitment and/or a possible lack of thought leaders and potential best practices, employees across all demographic categories for the most part had consistent views of the organization; there were very few differences in employee opinions across genders, ethnic groups, service lengths, shifts worked, and divisions or departments. The strategic planning team felt that this information reflected positively on the medical center's communication policies and practices. The lack of thought leaders and the absence of potential best practices were also considered to be important data points, which the strategic planning team committed to exploring further.

Given the important role that human resources plays in health care, it was essential that the planning team take employee opinion survey results into consideration. Figure 5.5 presents some of the key survey findings the planning team considered as it reviewed and refined the medical center's strategic plan. Please note that some information was omitted from Figure 5.5 and that some of the information presented was modified to protect sensitive and/or confidential material.

Analyzing End-User Survey Information

Your strategic planning team may also find it useful and beneficial to supplement research results with information obtained through an end-user survey.

Figure 5.5   Results of Medical Center Employee Opinion Survey

Key Findings

1. A clear majority of employees at all levels feel that the medical center provides high-quality services to its patients and the patients' families.
2. A clear majority of employees at all levels feel that the medical center is a leader in the national health care profession.
3. Most employees feel that the medical center has a positive reputation and that patients recommend the medical center to their family and friends.
4. A clear majority of employees at all levels commit to personally contributing to the medical center's mission and vision.
5. Most employees understand the role they play in helping the medical center achieve short- and long-term success.
6. A clear majority of employees feel that their colleagues understand, buy into, and commit to personally supporting the medical center's mission and vision.
7. Some employees feel that the medical center's current communications policies and practices interfere with or otherwise impede the flow of communication.
8. Some employees feel that the current performance management and employee evaluation system is inconsistent with and does not support the medical center's strategies.
9. Some employees feel that current technology and information systems are inadequate.
10. A majority of employees believe that management is trying to improve the current quality of the technology and information systems.

The individual, team, or vendor administering the survey will in all likelihood summarize the results and showcase end-user perceptions as well as the extent to which they buy into and otherwise support your organization's value proposition.

Experience and observations suggest that your strategic planning team will find such information invaluable in helping it explore:

- Why customers or clients buy your products.
- Why customers or clients procure your services.
- The opinion your customers or clients have of your products or services versus the opinion they have of your competitors' products or services.
- Other products your customers or clients are likely to purchase or other services they are likely to procure.
- Other products your customers or clients would like you to produce or other services they would like you to offer.

Most leading professional services firms recognize the importance of establishing, maintaining, and enhancing relationships with their clients. As part of the relationship management process, many firms invest a great deal of time and effort in obtaining data and information about their clients' needs and expectations and the extent to which they address those needs and meet or exceed those expectations. Firms typically conduct end-user surveys to obtain concrete feedback from clients on their ability to:

1. Provide services and products that address the clients' needs and meet or exceed the clients' expectations.
2. Provide services and products the clients consider to be worth the fees the firm charges.
3. Recognize and help the clients respond to emerging challenges, impediments, and obstacles within the clients' industry and/or market.
4. Recognize and help the clients respond to emerging challenges, impediments, and obstacles within the clients' organization.
5. Inform the clients of current or emerging issues, challenges, opportunities, and/or threats that must be considered and acted upon.
6. Manage turnover within the client engagement team to ensure continuity of knowledge and service.
7. Offer creative and innovative solutions.
8. Deliver technical expertise that matches program requirements.
9. Work effectively and efficiently with the clients.
10. Provide suggestions and recommendations that prove to be useful and beneficial.

All of a firm's clients—regardless of the amount of revenue they bring to the firm—are typically asked to complete an end-user survey at various times throughout the year; although this may be rather time consuming, professional services firm management teams recognize the importance of the resulting data and information. Taking the time to solicit and analyze such information from small clients may not seem to be cost-effective, but firm management teams typically adhere to the adage that "a majority of the giants in industry were once small" and therefore consider this to be a wise investment. A team (frequently consisting of internal specialists and an external vendor) administering the end-user survey typically analyzes and summarizes the results and then shares the results with the firm's strategic management team.

Strategic management teams for professional services firms typically meet monthly or quarterly to discuss end-user survey results and factor that information into operational decisions; firm leadership also typically considers end-user results during quarterly or annual strategy review sessions. While management team members typically focus on high-level findings and associated implications, they also periodically review responses to specific questions to obtain the detailed information they need to formulate strategy, tactics, or countermeasures. Figure 5.6 presents questions that professional services firms typically include in their end-user surveys.

Figure 5.6   Survey Questions for Professional Services Firm End-Users

On providing services and products that address the client's needs and meet or exceed the client's expectations:

- In general, do we understand your needs and expectations?
- What services and products do we offer that you find to be exceptionally useful and beneficial?
- What specific needs or expectations do you have that we have not addressed?
- What would we need to do to exceed your expectations?

On providing services and products the client considers to be worth the fees the firm charges:

- In general, do you feel that the services and products we provide match the fees we charge?
- What would it take for you to feel that the services and products we provide are worth the fees we charge?
- When it comes to providing services and products that match the fees we charge—
  - What should we start doing?
  - What should we stop doing?
  - What should we continue doing?

On recognizing and helping the client respond to emerging challenges, impediments, and obstacles within the client's industry and/or market:

- In general, have we helped you recognize and respond to external challenges, impediments, and obstacles?
- What external challenges, impediments, or obstacles—
  - Did we fail to help you recognize?
  - Should we have provided additional support or assistance for?
- What other steps should we take to help you identify and respond to external challenges, impediments, or obstacles?

On recognizing and helping the client respond to emerging challenges, impediments, and obstacles within the client's organization:

- In general, have we helped you recognize and respond to internal challenges, impediments, and obstacles?
- What internal challenges, impediments, or obstacles—
  - Did we fail to help you recognize?
  - Should we have provided additional support or assistance for?
- What other steps should we take to help you identify and respond to internal challenges, impediments, or obstacles?

On offering creative and innovative solutions:

- In general, have we helped you address challenges and opportunities in a creative or innovative way?
- What challenges or opportunities—
  - Could we have helped you address in a more creative or innovative way?
  - Do you typically encounter that are conducive to a creative or innovative solution?

Analysis of end-user survey results and revenue generation, write-offs, and discounts can be quite revealing. For example, such an analysis might show that:

• Client dissatisfaction in certain areas increases the likelihood of write-offs or discounts.

• Satisfaction in a few "key" areas increases the likelihood of invoices being paid "in full and on time."

• Client satisfaction in certain areas increases the likelihood of retaining the client over time and/or being able to extend the current contract or engagement.

• Improving client satisfaction in a few "key" areas will influence the client's overall satisfaction with the services and products you provide.

Using a SWOT Analysis to Showcase Key Data and Information

Your strategic planning team has reviewed and discussed information and data coming from a variety of data sources (an environmental scan, employee opinion survey, and end-user survey, to name just a few). Your team must now synthesize and consolidate this information and data and put it in a (more) useful form. Your planning team may find a SWOT (strengths, weaknesses, opportunities, and threats) analysis to be a useful way to summarize and display the key data and information it will consider throughout the remainder of the strategic planning session.

The SWOT analysis is both a technique and a tool: as a technique, it will help your strategic planning team explore and identify forces and factors most likely to impact your organization's short- and long-term success; as a tool, it will help your strategic planning team record the results of its review and analysis. The SWOT analysis will help ensure that your strategic planning team takes multifaceted variables into consideration; more specifically, it will help your team identify and record key:

• Internal strengths: any existing or potential internal resource or capability that if properly capitalized upon may provide an advantage to the organization.

• Internal weaknesses: any existing or potential internal force that if not properly addressed may inhibit the organization's success.

• External opportunities: any existing or emerging force in the external environment that if properly exploited may provide an advantage to the organization.

• External threats: any existing or emerging force in the external environment that if not properly addressed may inhibit the organization's success.

The SWOT analysis will help your strategic planning team summarize, note, and then subsequently consider a multitude of "key" external forces and internal factors impacting your organization's short- and long-term success. These forces and factors typically include, but are not limited to, those listed in Figure 5.7.

Taking all information and data previously reviewed and discussed into consideration, your strategic planning team will list key strengths, weaknesses, opportunities, and threats (SWOTs). It is important that the SWOT analysis be framed as the team's attempt to identify key forces and factors it must consider throughout the remainder of the strategic planning session. Although there is in all likelihood a multitude of variables impacting your organization's short- and long-term success, it is important that your strategic planning team members:

1. Review and discuss the information and data they have before them.
2. Identify and agree on the variables most likely to have the most impact or influence on your organization's short- and long-term success.
3. Create a list of strengths, weaknesses, opportunities, and threats that is both manageable and likely to prove useful throughout the remainder of the strategic planning session.

Data and information your strategic planning team notes and subsequently displays in its SWOT analysis should include external forces and internal factors most likely to have the most impact or influence on your organization's short- and

Figure 5.7   Internal Factors and External Forces

Internal Factors	External Forces
• Financial strength	• Competition:
• Access to capital	○ Comparative size
• Skills of employees	○ Strength
• Managerial or leadership skills	○ Capacity
• Facility capacity	○ Reputation
• Union issues	○ Likelihood of retaliation
• Safety	• Market conditions:
• Legal issues	○ Growth potential
• Warranty and quality	○ Growth rate
• Customer satisfaction	○ Threat of new entrants
• Information technology	○ Price pressures
• Internet usage	• Labor market demographics
• Research and development	• Government regulations, rules, and controls
• Geographic location	• Technology trends
• Distribution channels	• Lifestyle trends
• Supplier relationships	• Impact of economy on buying patterns
• Pricing	• Supplier's power
	• Buyer's power

long-term success. Your strategic planning team will refer to the SWOT analysis and will take the data and information it contains into consideration as it covers topics, addresses issues, and answers questions throughout the remainder of the strategic planning session.

Each strategic planning team's SWOT analysis will contain variables relating specifically to (1) its organization, industry, market, and/or area of specialization and (2) strategic topics being considered, strategic issues being addressed, and strategic questions being answered throughout the strategic planning endeavor. For example, the leadership team of a heavy machinery manufacturing company recently explored external conditions and internal factors likely to impact their organization's short- and long-term success. The team had several volumes of information and data to review and discuss throughout its strategic planning session. To help manage the information and data and to make it more accessible, useful, and applicable, the team synthesized and consolidated the information into a SWOT analysis. While recognizing the large number of variables impacting and influencing the organization's success, the leadership team identified and agreed on the key variables displayed in Figure 5.8. Please note that some information

Figure 5.8   Corporate SWOT Analysis

Strengths
- Passion for our business
- Genuine corporate values
- Long-term relationship with our customers
- Tendency to take action
- Disciplined growth

Weaknesses
- Weak coordination of product life-cycle management
- Reluctance to pursue joint ventures
- Poor product quality and process efficiency through the design-build cycle
- Poor portfolio mix
- Inadequate bench talent

Opportunities
- The downturn or down cycle
- Strong emerging markets for our products
- Expansion of nuclear power
- Low-cost engineering
- Currency shifts

Threats
- Disruptive technologies developed by our competitors
- Global recession
- Increased cost of commodities
- Increased regulatory requirements in certain markets
- Changing demographics

Figure 5.9   Leadership Team's Five Most Important SWOT Variables

Ranking	Area of Focus	S, W, O, or T
1	Forecasting	W
2	Brand, No. 1 position, market leader	O
3	Emerging competition	T
4	Corporate culture and focus	S
5	Taking full advantage of emerging markets	O

and data were omitted from Figure 5.8 and that some data and information were modified to protect sensitive and/or confidential material.

The leadership team realized that it had identified a relatively large number of external forces and internal factors. Concerned with not being able to focus on such a large number of variables throughout the strategic planning session, the team reviewed the results of the SWOT analysis and identified the five variables most likely to impact the organization's short- and long-term success (listed in Figure 5.9).

Chapter 6

Strategizing Your Organization's Future

Your strategic planning team can now verify or create your organization's mission and vision statements, verify or clarify your organization's sweet spot, establish goal statements, and identify and prioritize the means by which your organization will achieve short- and long-term success. As your planning team moves forward, it is important that it do so with the results of all previous reviews, analyses, and discussions in mind. I encourage strategic planning teams to note key findings, conclusions, and decisions on flip chart pads and post them on walls so they are clearly visible to planning team members. I then recommend that team members review the charts at the beginning and ending of each day, periodically throughout the strategic planning session, and whenever questions relating to previous findings, conclusions, or decisions surface during the session.

YOUR ORGANIZATION'S MISSION STATEMENT

If your organization has a mission statement, your strategic planning team should verify its existence, review it, and discuss how it will influence strategy formulation and execution. If your organization does not have a mission statement, your planning team should create one, keeping the following information in mind.

Your organization was not formed simply out of happenstance, nor does it operate haphazardly. Rather, it consists of you and your colleagues working together in a planned and purposeful way to ensure the accomplishment of your organization's purpose. Each formal organization (whether a club, a corporation, a government agency, an institution of higher learning, or any other group of individuals coming together in a planned and purposeful way to accomplish a particular purpose) has a particular function, endeavor, aim, or reason for existence.

KEY LEARNING POINT

Your organization was not formed simply out of happenstance, nor does it operate haphazardly. Rather, it consists of employees (at all levels) working together in a planned and purposeful way to help your organization accomplish its mission.

Mission statements describe the overarching intent of an organization. It is important that your strategic planning team take this intent into consideration when establishing strategic goals for your organization and the means by which it will accomplish its goals. Your planning team should therefore review your organization's mission prior to proceeding forward and take it (and all that it implies) into consideration as it formulates and subsequently executes your organization's strategies. If your organization does not currently have a mission statement, the strategic planning team should create one. A properly formulated and worded mission statement is important to an organization; it:

• Defines the nature, focus, and intent of the organization.
• Provides boundaries within which the organization will operate, potentially including—
    ○ Opportunities or threats the organization will address.
    ○ Needs or expectations the organization will fulfill.
    ○ Services and/or products the organization will provide.
    ○ The market or geographic area the organization will target.
    ○ The impression the organization hopes to make on its clients, customers, and community.
• Sets expectations on how all members of the organization should behave and perform and inspires them to do the right thing for the right reasons when making decisions and conducting business (whatever that business might be).
• Helps employees (at all levels) understand—
    ○ Why they are being asked to do what they do on a daily basis.
    ○ How what they do on a daily basis helps the organization achieve its mission.
• Helps customers and clients know what to expect from the organization, in terms of—
    ○ How they are to be treated when speaking to or meeting with members of the organization.
    ○ The services and products they are likely to receive from the organization or what needs or requirements the organization is likely to fulfill.

- Sends a clear and concise message about the organization's intention to various stakeholders (such as board members, investors, and prospective employees).
- Helps establish mutual understanding of an organization's function and intention in regulatory filings, organizational charters, and/or partnership agreements.
- Helps guide decision making and actions (relating to, for example, how monies are allocated—especially when money is scarce and programs, imperatives, and initiatives must be prioritized).

Creating Your Organization's Mission Statement

A standard, single, best, or most effective way to create a mission statement does not exist. My experience and observations suggest that your strategic planning team members should work together to create your organization's mission statement and that the team should use an iterative process. A process your strategic planning team might find useful involves:

- Dividing the team into two or three subgroups.
- Each subgroup creating a draft mission statement, taking these questions into consideration—
  - What are the underlying nature, focus, and intent of our organization?
  - What opportunities or threats does our organization strive to address?
  - What needs or expectations does our organization strive to fulfill?
  - What services does our organization provide and/or what products does our organization produce?
  - What market and/or geographic area does our organization target?
  - What impression do we hope our organization makes on our clients, customers, and community?
  - How do we expect the members of our organization to behave when speaking to or meeting with our clients and customers?
  - How do we expect the members of our organization to behave when speaking to or working with their colleagues and associates?
  - In terms of how we allocate our time, effort, and money, what are we actually attempting to accomplish on a daily basis?
  - What should our customers and clients expect when speaking to or meeting with members of the organization?
  - What services and products are our customers and clients likely to receive from our organization?
  - What customer and client needs or requirements is our organization likely to fulfill?

- o What message about our organization's intention do we want to emphasize to our various stakeholders (board members, investors, and prospective employees)?
- o What values do we want employees (at all levels) to emphasize when making decisions and taking action (for example, when allocating monies when money is scarce and programs, imperatives, and initiatives must be prioritized)?
- The subgroups reforming into a single strategic planning team and presenting their draft mission statements to the entire team.
- Each subgroup receiving input from and answering questions raised by the entire team.
- Each subgroup reforming to refine its draft mission statement in light of the feedback and input it received from the entire team.
- The subgroups reforming into a single strategic planning team and presenting their refined draft mission statements to the entire team.
- The strategic planning team—
  - o Reviewing the refined draft mission statements.
  - o Selecting the draft mission statement that resonates most with the entire team and, if necessary, refining it.
  - o Combining, consolidating, or synthesizing the draft mission statements to create an "ideal" mission statement that resonates with the entire team.

The mission statement your strategic planning team creates will be unique to your organization. However, your planning team might find the sample mission statements listed in Figure 6.1 useful and beneficial as it drafts and refines your organization's mission statement.

These samples illustrate that some mission statements are concrete and tangible, whereas others are rather abstract, conceptual, and intangible. Although there is no general rule as to how concrete or abstract your mission statement should be, the mission statement your strategic planning team creates should resonate with your various stakeholder groups and be (1) concrete enough to provide needed focus, direction, and guidance and (2) abstract enough to permit divergent thinking and innovative action. I therefore encourage your strategic planning team to keep these points in mind while creating your organization's mission statement:

- Concrete and tangible mission statements may help your organization more clearly and concisely define acceptable behavior while limiting or narrowing its ability to—
  - o Identify trends and patterns to identify customer and client needs and expectations yet to be investigated, understood, or addressed.
  - o Analyze advances in systems, processes, and technology to identify opportunities to eliminate, create, or change the way you currently conduct business, provide services, and develop, sell, and distribute products.

Figure 6.1 Sample Mission Statements

Organization	Mission Statement
Ben & Jerry's Homemade, Inc.[a]	Ben & Jerry's is founded on and dedicated to a sustainable corporate concept of linked prosperity. Our mission consists of three interrelated parts: Product Mission: To make, distribute, and sell the finest quality all-natural ice cream and euphoric concoctions with a continued commitment to incorporating wholesome, natural ingredients and promoting business practices that respect the Earth and the environment. Economic Mission: To operate the company on a sustainable financial basis of profitable growth, increasing value for our stakeholders and expanding opportunities for development and career growth for our employees. Social Mission: To operate the company in a way that actively recognizes the central role that business plays in society by initiating innovative ways to improve the quality of life locally, nationally, and internationally.
The Corporate Executive Board Company[b]	We create revolutionary economic advantage for leaders of the world's great enterprises by enabling them to act with unparalleled intelligence and confidence. We lift their performance at key decision points and career moments by delivering insight drawn from the most powerful global executive and professional network. We enable superior outcomes by inflecting every critical decision made and important action taken by executives and professionals at the world's leading enterprises.
The Hershey Company[c]	Bringing sweet moments of Hershey happiness to the world every day. To our stakeholders, this means: Consumers—Delivering quality consumer-driven confectionery experiences for all occasions Employees—Winning with an aligned and empowered organization . . . while having fun Business Partners—Building collaborative relationships for profitable growth with our customers, suppliers, and partners Shareholders—Creating sustainable value Communities—Honoring our heritage through continued commitment to making a positive difference
Land O'Lakes, Inc.[d]	Our Mission: We are a market- and customer-driven cooperative committed to optimizing the value of our members' dairy, crop, and livestock production.

(Continued)

Figure 6.1   (Continued)

YMCA of the U.S.A.[e]	**Our Cause Defines Us**

Our Cause Defines Us

We know that lasting personal and social change comes about when we all work together. That's why, at the Y, strengthening community is our cause. Every day, we work side-by-side with our neighbors to make sure that everyone, regardless of age, income or background, has the opportunity to learn, grow, and thrive.

Our Strength Is in Community

The Y is a nonprofit like no other. That's because in 10,000 neighborhoods across the nation, we have the presence and partnerships to not just promise, but deliver, positive change.

- The Y is community centered. For nearly 160 years, we've been listening and responding to our communities.
- The Y brings people together. We connect people of all ages and backgrounds to bridge the gaps in community needs.
- The Y nurtures potential. We believe that everyone should have the opportunity to learn, grow, and thrive.
- The Y has local presence and global reach. We mobilize local communities to effect lasting, meaningful change.

Our Impact Is Felt Every Day

With a mission to put Christian principles into practice through programs that build a healthy spirit, mind, and body for all, our impact is felt when an individual makes a healthy choice, when a mentor inspires a child, and when a community comes together for the common good.

[a] *Ben and Jerry's Mission.* [Online]. (2010). South Burlington, VT: Ben and Jerry's Homemade, Inc. Available: http://www.benjerry.com/activism/mission-statement/?ref=promo

[b] *Our Corporate Mission.* [Online]. (2010). Arlington, VA: The Corporate Executive Board Company. Available: http://www.executiveboard.com/about_mission.html

[c] *Mission Statement.* [Online]. (2010). Hershey, PA: The Hershey Company. Available: http://www.thehersheycompany.com/about/

[d] *Land O'Lakes Mission.* [Online]. (2010). Arden Hills, MN: Land O'Lakes, Inc. Available: http://www.landolakesinc.com/company/philosophy/default.aspx

[e] *About Us.* [Online]. (2010). Chicago: YMCA of the U.S.A. Available: http://www.ymca.net/about-us/

- Analyze what organizations, industries, or professions similar to yours offer to explore implications for the value your organization brings to its various stakeholder groups.
- Explore the unknown, unrealized, and/or unrecognized needs and expectations of your clients or customers to determine what else your organization might do to meet or exceed those particular needs and expectations.

- ○ Think and act in a manner that is:
  - ▪ Original.
  - ▪ Inspiring.
  - ▪ Creative.
  - ▪ Resourceful.
  - ▪ Inventive.
  - ▪ Imaginative.
  - ▪ Ingenious.
  - ○ Identify, consider, and act on emerging opportunities and threats.
- • Abstract mission statements may provide less concrete direction and guidance and prove less helpful in defining acceptable and appropriate behavior while encouraging or at a minimum allowing members of your organization to—
  - ○ Explore emerging trends and patterns to identify customer and client needs and expectations yet to be investigated, understood, or addressed.
  - ○ Analyze advances to identify opportunities to eliminate, create, or change the way you currently conduct business, provide services, and develop, sell, and distribute products.
  - ○ Analyze what organizations, industries, or professions similar to yours offer to explore implications for your organization's purpose, mission and vision, and the value your organization brings to its various stakeholder groups.
  - ○ Explore the unknown, unrealized, and/or unrecognized needs and expectations of your clients or customers to determine what else your organization might do to meet or exceed those particular needs and expectations.
  - ○ Think and act in a creative and innovative manner.
  - ○ Identify, consider, and act on emerging opportunities and threats.

YOUR ORGANIZATION'S VISION STATEMENT

If your organization has a vision statement, your strategic planning team should verify its existence, review it, and discuss how it will influence strategy formulation and execution. If your organization does not have a vision statement, your planning team should create one, keeping the following information in mind.

My experience and observations suggest that organizations do not simply exist to remain static or uphold or adhere to the status quo. Rather, they aspire to change, grow, and/or develop over time; an organization's vision statement describes its desired or intended state at some point in the near or distant future. Much like an organization's mission statement, the vision statement provides focus, direction, and guidance and helps guide decisions and actions. Whereas your organization's mission statement:

- Helps guide performance and behavior with a focus on current actions, results, and outcomes, your vision statement helps ensure that actions, results, and outcomes that occur today are consistent with and supportive of what the organization wishes to become (or where it hopes to be) in the future.
- Helps you and your colleagues accomplish current goals and objectives, your vision statement helps ensure that the stream of decisions you make and the actions you take over time consistently and constantly contribute to your organization attaining the future it envisions.
- Contributes to your organization's immediate short-term success, your vision statement contributes to its long-term success.

Your vision statement describes the overarching aim of your organization as it progresses into the future. It is important that your planning team take this "intent" into consideration when establishing strategic goals and when formulating and executing your organization's strategies. If your organization does not currently have a vision statement, the strategic planning team should create one. A properly worded vision statement:

1. Resonates with all members of the organization, regardless of their position, title, level, role, or responsibility.
2. Uses words that everyone understands, from the "boardroom to the boiler room."
3. Provides a compelling vision for the future, a vision that might be described as "pulling us from the current state toward what the organization envisions for the future."
4. Is anchored in reality, in that it takes today's capabilities, strengths, weaknesses, opportunities, and threats into account.

KEY LEARNING POINT

Your vision statement provides focus, direction, and guidance and helps guide decisions and actions by describing the overarching aim of your organization as it progresses into the future.

An effective vision statement provides focus, direction, and guidance by:

- Describing the function and focus of the future organization.

- Providing boundaries within which members of the future organization will operate, potentially including—
  - Opportunities or threats they will address.
  - Needs or expectations they will fulfill.
  - Services and/or products they will provide.
  - The impression they will strive to make to their clients, customers, and community.
- Establishing expectations for how members of the future organization will behave and perform.
- Helping employees (at all levels) understand—
  - How what they do now contributes to what the organization hopes to become in the future.
  - How changes in the way they currently make decisions, behave, and act will contribute to what the organization hopes to become in the future.
- Helping customers and clients know what to expect—
  - Of the future organization, in terms of how they will be treated when speaking to or meeting with members of the organization.
  - From the future organization, in terms of the services and products they will likely receive from the organization or what needs or requirements the organization will likely fulfill.
- Sending a clear and concise message about what the organization hopes to become or where it hopes to be in the future to various stakeholders (such as board members, investors, and prospective employees).

Creating Your Organization's Vision Statement

A standard, single, best, or most effective way to create a vision statement does not exist. My experience and observations suggest that your strategic planning team members should work together to create your organization's vision statement and that the team should use an iterative process. A process your strategic planning team might find useful involves:

- Dividing the team into two or three subgroups.
- Specifying to the subgroups the timeframe within which the vision will occur (for example, "Envision what our organization will become or where it will be in five, 10, 15, or 20 years").
- Each subgroup creating a draft vision statement, taking into consideration—
  - The underlying function and focus of our future organization.
  - Opportunities or threats our future organization will strive to address.
  - Needs or expectations our future organization will strive to fulfill.

- Services our future organization will provide and/or products our future organization will produce.
- The market and/or geographic area our future organization will target.
- The impression our future organization will strive to make on our clients, customers, and community.
- How the members of our future organization will behave when speaking to or meeting with our clients and customers.
- How the members of our future organization will behave when speaking to or working with their colleagues and associates.
- In terms of how we allocate our time, effort, and money—what members of our future organization will actually attempt to accomplish on a daily basis.
- What our customers and clients should expect when speaking to or meeting with members of our future organization.
- Services and products our customers and clients are likely to receive from our future organization.
- Customer and client needs or requirements that our future organization is likely to fulfill.
- A key message about our future organization's intention that we want to emphasize to our various stakeholders.
- Values we want future employees (at all levels) to emphasize when making decisions and taking action (for example, when allocating monies when money is scarce and programs, imperatives, and initiatives must be prioritized).
• The subgroups reforming into a single strategic planning team and presenting their draft vision statements to the entire team.
• Each subgroup receiving input from and answering questions raised by the entire team.
• Each subgroup reforming to refine its draft vision statement in light of the feedback and input it received from the entire team.
• The subgroups reforming into a single strategic planning team and presenting their refined draft vision statements to the entire team.
• The strategic planning team—
  - Reviewing the refined draft vision statements.
  - Selecting the draft vision statement that resonates most with the entire team and, if necessary, refining it.
  - Combining, consolidating, or synthesizing the draft vision statements to create an "ideal" vision statement that resonates with the entire team.

The vision statement your strategic planning team creates will be unique to your organization. However, your planning team might find the sample vision statements listed in Figure 6.2 useful and beneficial as it drafts and refines your organization's vision statement.

Figure 6.2   Sample Vision Statements

Organization	Vision Statement
BASF Corporation[a]	• We are "The Chemical Company" successfully operating in all major markets. • Our customers view BASF as their partner of choice. • Our innovative products, intelligent solutions and services make us the most competent worldwide supplier in the chemical industry. • We generate a high return on assets. • We strive for sustainable development. • We welcome change as an opportunity. • We, the employees of BASF, together ensure our success.
Cummins Inc.[b]	Making people's lives better by unleashing the power of Cummins. That simple, yet ambitious, statement serves as the guiding vision for Cummins and its 28,000 employees. The company takes pride in manufacturing engines, generators, filters and related products that serve the varied needs of its customers worldwide. To do that, Cummins unleashes the power of its employees: Their energy and commitment make it possible for the company to maintain a leadership position in the markets it serves. Cummins also recognizes that with its role as a corporate leader comes a responsibility to help improve the communities in which employees work and live. It is a responsibility the Company brings to life through its actions and the activities of its employees.
Junior Achievement Worldwide[c]	The envisioned future . . . what we aspire to become. Junior Achievement maintains an active vision, front and center, on how we can have a positive impact on the lives of more students—guided by our core values: • Belief in the boundless potential of young people. • Commitment to the principles of market-based economics and entrepreneurship. • Passion for what we do and honesty, integrity, and excellence in how we do it. • Respect for the talents, creativity, perspectives, and backgrounds of all individuals. • Belief in the power of partnership and collaboration. • Conviction in the educational and motivational impact of relevant, hands-on learning.
Land O'Lakes, Inc.[d]	Our vision is to be one of the best food and agricultural companies in the world by being: • Our customer's first choice; • Our employee's first choice; • Responsible to our owners; and • A leader in our communities.

(Continued)

Figure 6.2   (Continued)

> We are committed to doing more than meeting our customers' needs. We strive to delight our customers by anticipating and exceeding their expectations through an innovative and creative workforce.
>
> We recognize employees as our most important asset and we focus on making Land O'Lakes their first choice for work. We believe in respecting diversity and in encouraging teamwork, involvement, development, and empowerment of all employees.
>
> We aim to create greater shareholder value while fulfilling our responsibilities as a cooperative.
>
> Finally, we recognize our responsibilities to the communities in which we operate. We are proactive in dedicating resources to build a better quality of life, operate in an ethical and environmentally sensitive manner, and live by our values.

[a] *Vision.* [Online]. (2010). Florham Park, NJ: BASF Corporation. Available: http://www.basf.com/group/corporate/en/about-basf/vision-values-principles/vision

[b] *Vision.* [Online]. (2010). Columbus, IN: Cummins Inc. Available: http://www.cummins.com/cmi/content.jsp?menuIndex=1&siteId=1&overviewId=2&menuId=1&langId=1033&

[c] *Who We Are.* [Online]. (2010). Colorado Springs, CO: Junior Achievement Worldwide. Available: http://www.ja.org/about/about_who_vision.shtml

[d] *Land O'Lakes Vision.* [Online]. (2010). Arden Hills, MN: Land O'Lakes, Inc. Available: http://www.landolakesinc.com/company/philosophy/default.aspx

These statements illustrate that some vision statements are rather short, whereas others are rather lengthy. Although there is no general rule as to how long your vision statement should be, the vision statement your strategic planning team creates should resonate with your various stakeholder groups and be (1) short enough for employees (at all levels) to remember when being called upon to make decisions or take action and (2) long enough to provide the needed focus, guidance, and direction.

IDENTIFYING MISSION- AND VISION-CRITICAL VALUES AND PRINCIPLES

After creating your organization's mission and vision statement, I recommend that your strategic planning team identify values and principles that, when applied, will help enable your organization to achieve its mission and attain its vision. Together, your mission, vision, values, and principles will contribute to your organization's short- and long-term success by helping the members of your organization "do the right thing for the right reason" when making decisions and taking action.

In identifying the values and principles that will help your organization achieve its mission and attain its vision, I recommend that your strategic planning team answer this fundamental question: "Given the mission and vision we now have before us, what values and principles must our decisions and actions reflect to ensure that our organization achieves its mission and attains its vision in an optimal manner?" Experience and observations suggest that your strategic planning team will most likely create (1) a bulleted list of values and principles or (2) a narrative description of values and principles that members of your organization should consider when making decisions and taking action. Either approach will yield positive results as long as the format and wording resonate with the members of your organization.

The values and principles critical to your organization's short- and long-term success will be unique to your organization. However, your planning team might find the sample values and principles listed in Figure 6.3 useful and beneficial as it discusses and decides on your organization's mission- and vision-critical values and principles.

Before beginning to formulate strategic goals and the means by which your organization will accomplish its mission and attain its vision (while taking

Figure 6.3   Sample Values and Principles

Organization	Values and/or Principles
BASF Corporation[a]	We, the employees of the BASF Group, are committed to the following values:
	Sustainable Profitable Performance Ongoing profitable performance in the sense of sustainable development is the basic requirement for all of our activities. We are committed to the interests of our customers, shareholders and employees and assume a responsibility towards society.
	Innovation for the Success of Our Customers Our business processes are oriented towards adding long-term value and competitiveness. In partnership with our customers, we help them be more successful. To accomplish this, we jointly discover business opportunities and develop products, procedures, and services that are on a high scientific and technical level.
	Safety, Health, Environmental Responsibility We act in a responsible manner and support the Responsible Care® initiatives. Economic considerations do not take priority over safety and health issues and environmental protection.
	Personal and Professional Competence We form the best team in industry by fostering group-wide the diversity of personal and professional competencies. Intercultural competence is our advantage in global competition. We encourage our employees to make use of their creativity and their potential for common success.

(Continued)

Figure 6.3　(Continued)

	Mutual Respect and Open Dialogue We treat everyone fairly and with respect. We pursue an open and trusting dialogue within our company, with our business partners and relevant groups in society. **Integrity** We act in accordance with our words and values. We comply with the laws and respect the good business practices of the countries in which we operate.
Kellogg Company[b]	Kellogg Company's values, *K Values*™, shape our culture and guide the way we run our business. In 2005, the company instituted the W.K. Kellogg Values Award, which is given annually to one individual and one team of employees who best exhibit the *K Values* in their work.

Integrity

At Kellogg Company, we act with integrity and show respect.

- Demonstrate a commitment to integrity and ethics
- Show respect for and value all individuals for their diverse backgrounds, experience, styles, approaches, and ideas
- Speak positively and supportively about team members when apart
- Listen to others for understanding
- Assume positive intent

Accountability

We are all accountable.

- Accept personal accountability for our own actions and results
- Focus on finding solutions and achieving results, rather than making excuses or placing blame
- Actively engage in discussions and support decisions once they are made
- Involve others in decisions and plans that affect them
- Keep promises and commitments made to others
- Personally commit to the success and well-being of teammates
- Improve safety and health for employees, and embrace the belief that all injuries are preventable

Passion

We are passionate about our business, our brands, and our food.

- Show pride in our brands and heritage
- Promote a positive, energizing, optimistic, and fun environment
- Serve our customers and delight our consumers through the quality of our products and services

Figure 6.3 (Continued)

- Promote and implement creative and innovative ideas and solutions
- Aggressively promote and protect our reputation

Humility

We have the humility and hunger to learn.
- Display openness and curiosity to learn from anyone, anywhere
- Solicit and provide honest feedback without regard to position
- Personally commit to continuous improvement and are willing to change
- Admit our mistakes and learn from them
- Never underestimate our competition

Simplicity

We strive for simplicity.
- Stop processes, procedures and activities that slow us down or do not add value
- Work across organizational boundaries/levels and break down internal barriers
- Deal with people and issues directly and avoid hidden agendas
- Prize results over form

Results

We love success.
- Achieve results and celebrate when we do
- Help people to be their best by providing coaching and feedback
- Work with others as a team to accomplish results and win
- Have a "can-do" attitude and drive to get the job done
- Make people feel valued and appreciated
- Make the tough calls

Land O'Lakes, Inc.[c]

The Land O'Lakes heritage is rich in rural values, family, and respect for the land. Our cooperative roots run deep. With determination and pride, we will continue our commitment to serve farmers, rural America, and our customers. Our values reflect who we are and what we firmly believe in:
- People
  We believe in people—in valuing and recognizing a workforce of diverse individuals as the key to our success.
- Performance
  We believe in setting high standards—defining clear goals and rewarding initiative that turns ideas into action and goals into reality.

(Continued)

Figure 6.3   (Continued)

- Customer Commitment
  We believe the customer is fundamental to our success—
  working together to meet their needs is the basis for all that
  we do.
- Quality
  We believe Land O'Lakes stands for quality—striving to
  make our best better.
- Integrity
  We believe in honesty—respecting each individual, fairness,
  and open communication.

  With these values as our guide, we will provide more than
  we receive and succeed both individually and as a company.

[a] *Values.* [Online]. (2010). Florham Park, NJ: BASF Corporation. Available: http://www.basf.com/group/corporate/en/about-basf/vision-values-principles/vision
[b] *Our Values.* [Online]. (2010). Battle Creek, MI: Kellogg Company. Available: http://www.kelloggcompany.com/company.aspx?id=35
[c] *Land O'Lakes Values.* [Online]. (2010). Arden Hills, MN: Land O'Lakes, Inc. Available: http://www.landolakesinc.com/company/philosophy/default.aspx

advantage of positive external forces and internal factors and addressing negative external forces and internal factors), it is important that your strategic planning team verify or define your organization's sweet spot.

YOUR ORGANIZATION'S SWEET SPOT

I consider your organization's sweet spot to be where its purpose, passion, and capabilities intersect. It is important that you define your organization's sweet spot because it will help your strategic planning team identify ways your organization might harness the energy needed to accomplish its mission and propel it toward its envisioned future.

I recommend that three factors be considered when defining an organization's sweet spot: the organization's purpose as reflected in its mission statement; the organization's passion as reflected in its vision statement; and the core capabilities that distinguish the organization from other organizations in its particular industry or profession. The diagram presented in Figure 6.4 illustrates the relationship between the organization's purpose, passion, capabilities, and sweet spot.

Defining Your Organization's Sweet Spot

Experience and observations suggest that your strategic planning team will create a rather brief description of your organization's sweet spot that (1) members of your strategic planning team should consider throughout the remainder of the strategic planning endeavor and that (2) members of your organization should then consider when making decisions and taking action. Regardless of its

Figure 6.4   The Organization's Sweet Spot

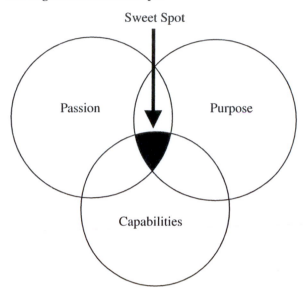

brevity, a well-articulated sweet spot will help sensitize your organization to the sources of energy needed to drive its mission and propel it toward its envisioned future.

Although your sweet spot will be unique to your organization, your planning team might find the information in Figures 6.5 and 6.6, which present potential sweet spot definitions for two sample organizations, useful and beneficial.

Figure 6.5 illustrates the kind of information your strategic planning team might consider when defining your organization's sweet spot. This information was then taken into consideration when creating Figure 6.6.

THE MEANS BY WHICH YOUR ORGANIZATION WILL ACHIEVE SUCCESS

Your strategic planning team has developed, reviewed, and refined statements summarizing your organization's strategic intent or aim. As stressed in previous chapters, strategic intent or aim alone simply is not enough. The extent to which your organization realizes its strategic intent or aim is the extent to which your organization succeeds. Although your organization might realize some level of success simply by happenstance, it is imperative that your strategic planning team identify and then your organization adopt, implement, execute, and/or deploy the means by which it will leverage or take advantage of its positive internal factors and external forces, mitigate or address its negative internal factors and external forces, realize its purpose, deliver on its value proposition, hit its sweet spot, achieve its current mission, and attain its long-term vision.

Figure 6.5   Considerations for Describing Sweet Spots

Organization	Descriptions
General Electric Company	**Why GE**[a] At GE, we are builders. It goes beyond businesses, brands and infrastructure. With four businesses and operations in over 160 countries, GE employees have an unparalleled foundation on which to build their careers, their abilities and their dreams. We offer our employees challenging, rewarding careers in dynamic businesses. Our people are the architects of the future. We sit in the front seat of history. **Innovation** From the outset, innovation has been part of GE's DNA. That means being surrounded by bright, interesting people working together on new and exciting projects. It means trying to find new and better ways of doing things. And it means enjoying a career with extraordinary opportunities and enormous potential. **Leadership and Training** We hire exceptional people and invest in their growth. GE has a culture of continuous learning, thoughtfully designed to enable employees to grow their personal capabilities and reach their full potential. We invest in your education, provide access to experienced colleagues, and give you the opportunities to work with intelligent, dedicated people, challenge yourself, and grow. **Global Business** We do business in over 160 countries, giving our employees a literal world of experience. Your opportunities at GE are defined, in part, by the emerging needs of our businesses, customers, and clients all around the world, because we go where the opportunities take us. A career at GE offers you access to some of the most exciting and dynamic challenges of your lifetime. **Integrity** Integrity is an essential component of life at GE. It is how we conduct ourselves and how we do business. It is non-negotiable. While some businesses prize results over ethics, we value both. At GE we believe that how you do something is as important as what you do. We provide you with the training and opportunities to enjoy a successful career you can be proud of, now and for the rest of your life. **IMAGINATION = INNOVATION**[b] We're determined to solve the world's biggest problems. By putting our collective imagination to work for a better future, we might get there yet. Is it possible to change the world? At GE, we are doing it one idea at a time.

Figure 6.5   (Continued)

Real Estate Investment Group[c]	**Our Mission** We strive to provide the most value to prospective home owners residing in a depressed market who have a damaged credit rating and who still grasp to the American dream of one day owning a home. **Our Vision** We will acquire a significant portion of the houses standing vacant in our target market at a preferred cost, rent, lease, and sell them to our target audience at a price point they can afford, thereby allowing them to seize upon the American dream of one day owning a home. **Our Values** We, our colleagues and associates, as well as individuals in our professional network will strive to think and behave in a manner that: • Reflects Integrity • Reflects Perseverance • Is Innovative and Creative • Is Customer-centric • Reflects Global Thinking and Local Action • Is Proper, Suitable, and Right **Our Core Capabilities** To deliver on our value proposition, we must exhibit the ability to effectively: • Purchase, manage, and sell residential properties. • Establish and manage relationships with realtors, homeowners, renters, leasers, buyers, and others involved in real estate transactions. • Manage a complex network of vendors, business owners, advisors, and consultants.

[a] *Why GE.* [Online]. (2010). Fairfield, CT: General Electric Company. Available: http://www.ge.com/careers/why_ge.html

[b] *Imagination at Work.* [Online]. (2010). Fairfield, CT: General Electric Company. Available: http://www.ge.com/innovation/archive.html

[c] Real Estate Investment Group, personal notes, 2009.

Identifying the Means by Which Your Organization Will Succeed

A standard, single, best, or most effective way to identify the means by which your organization will succeed does not exist. My experience and observations suggest that your strategic planning team members should work together to identify the means and follow a process that allows planning team members to:

1. Individually reflect on the totality of data and information they have before them and generate ideas on the various means by which your organization will

Figure 6.6   Potential Organization Sweet Spot Descriptions

Organization	Description of the Organization's Sweet Spot	
General Electric Company	Purpose	We strive to address the needs of the collective community, including the demand for global infrastructure; growing and changing demographics that need access to health care, finance, and information and entertainment; and environmental technologies.
	Passion	We are determined to solve the world's biggest problems by putting our collective imagination to work for a better future.
	Capabilities	We possess the knowledge, skills, and abilities to work collaboratively to develop and implement creative and innovative solutions to complex problems.
	Sweet Spot	Applying our collective imagination to developing and implementing creative and innovative solutions to the biggest problems facing the world.
Real Estate Investment Group	Purpose	We rent, lease, and sell residential properties to our target audience at a price point they can afford, thereby allowing them to seize upon the American dream of one day owning a home.
	Passion	We help our clients seize upon the American dream of one day owning a home.
	Capabilities	We possess the knowledge, skills, and abilities to purchase, manage, and sell residential properties to clients at a price point that they can afford.
	Sweet Spot	Owning and renting, leasing, and selling residential properties to our target audience at a price point they can afford, thereby allowing them to seize upon the American dream of one day owning a home.

leverage or take advantage of its positive internal factors and external forces, mitigate or address its negative internal factors and external forces, realize its purpose, deliver on its value proposition, hit its sweet spot, achieve its current mission, and attain its long-term vision.

2. Collectively review the ideas of other team members and as a team generate new ideas and refine existing ideas on the means by which your organization will leverage or take advantage of its positive internal factors and external forces, mitigate or address its negative internal factors and external forces, realize its purpose, deliver on its value proposition, hit its sweet spot, achieve its current mission, and attain its long-term vision.

3. While keeping the context set by your organization's mission, vision, and value proposition in mind, individually and collectively be as creative and innovative as possible; leverage, take advantage of, and/or expand upon existing products, services, markets, clients, customers, capabilities, technology, systems, process, and cultural elements while envisioning new products, services, markets, clients, customers, capabilities, technology, systems, process, values, principles, and cultural elements likely to contribute to your organization's achieving its current mission and attaining its long-term vision.

Your strategic planning team might find the following process useful and beneficial:

- Team members individually and collectively review all of the information and data they have before them.
- Team members individually brainstorm[1] ways your organization will, in essence, achieve its current mission and attain its long-term vision. Each team member—
  - Generates as many ideas as possible, without concern about whether the ideas might be considered actions, tactics, or strategies or whether they overlap or relate to each other. Again, the aim is to generate as many ideas as possible.
  - Remains silent while considering the information and data and generating ideas about how your organization will achieve its current mission and attain its long-term vision.
  - Generates ideas about how your organization will—
    - Realize its underlying nature, focus, and intent.
    - Take advantage of current and emerging external opportunities.
    - Mitigate or otherwise address current and emerging external threats.
    - Leverage or capitalize upon current and developing internal strengths.
    - Address current and developing internal weaknesses.
    - Meet or exceed client and customer needs and expectations.

- Provide services and products to the current and/or changing target client and customer population.
- Maintain or expand its target market and/or geographic area.
- Make a positive impression on your clients, customers, and community.
- Create an environment in which your employees (at all levels), clients, and customers are treated with the respect and dignity they deserve.
- Allocate its time, effort, and money on a daily basis.
- Fulfill the needs or requirements of your customers and clients.
  - Is as creative and innovative as possible, leveraging and taking advantage of existing products, services, markets, clients, customers, capabilities, technology, systems, process, values, principles, and cultural elements while envisioning new capabilities, technology, systems, process, values, principles, and cultural elements likely to contribute to your organization's achieving its current mission and attaining its long-term vision.
  - Focuses on generating as many ideas as possible; here, the aim is quantity over quality.
- Team members capture the ideas they generate on sticky notes. Each—
  - Idea must be captured on a separate sticky note.
  - Idea must be written legibly so that it can be read by others.
  - Idea must be written as a phrase or statement.
  - Phrase or statement must, at a minimum, contain a verb (action word).
- Team members process the sticky notes using an affinity diagram[2]—
  - Team members take turns to share their brainstorming results with the other members of the strategic planning team. As each team member presents his or her sticky notes, the other team members make mental notes of—but do not respond to—the nature or scope of the individual brainstorming results.
  - Each team member, after presenting his or her sticky notes to the other team members, lays his or her notes on a table or sticks them to a work surface (typically, a section of a wall covered in flip chart paper).
  - The team identifies natural themes by placing sticky notes containing ideas that are similar or connected in a group when laying them on the table or sticking them to the work surface.
  - Once all sticky notes have been presented and grouped into natural themes, the team approaches the work surface to review and refine the groupings. In reviewing the groupings, it is important that everyone understands the meaning or intent of each idea and that the ideas are properly grouped around a common theme or unifying concept. In refining the groupings, team members (1) separate an idea that does not fit into any of the existing groupings as a separate, free-standing idea and (2) if an idea fits into more than one grouping, create duplicate sticky notes and place them into the proper themes. Although

this is generally a silent exercise—to prevent individuals from assertively or aggressively advocating (1) a particular idea or (2) the placement of a sticky note into a particular group—I encourage individuals to answer questions other team members might have about the reasoning behind placing a particular sticky note in a particular group. Although some team members will find this process tedious, it is essential that it occur because the validity and credibility of subsequent decisions will rely on the sticky notes being properly sorted. Once the movement of sticky notes has ended, your strategic planning team can assume that ideas have been placed into proper groups and that each group has a unique theme or unifying concept.

- o The team reviews each group of sticky notes to identify the natural theme or unifying concept.
- o The team summarizes the natural theme or unifying concept in a concisely stated five- to seven-word description and a team member notes the description on a sticky note.
- o The team member places the sticky note (referred to as the "header card") at the top of each grouping.

• Team members review the results of the affinity diagram to ensure proper and appropriate groupings. It is essential that this review occur because the validity and credibility of subsequent decisions will rely on the sticky notes being properly sorted. Once all team members agree that the sticky notes have been properly and appropriately placed, your strategic planning team can assume that it has reached consensus on the means by which your organization will achieve its short- and long-term success.

Your strategic planning team may use the above or a similar approach to identify the means by which your organization will achieve its current mission and attain its long-term vision. In addition, the ideas your planning team generates will be unique to your organization. However, your planning team might find the ideas listed in Figure 6.7 and the resulting groupings and header cards presented in Figure 6.8 useful as it identifies the means by which your organization will achieve short- and long-term success.

Figure 6.7 illustrates the complexity of the nature and scope of ideas generated by a strategic planning team and the need for the team to organize the ideas so they are not disjointed, overlapping, and too voluminous to consider. Figure 6.8 presents many of the ideas presented in Figure 6.7 but in a more structured and organized manner.

Your strategic planning team has (1) identified the means by which your organization will achieve its short- and long-term success and (2) organized the means around common themes and unifying concepts. The team has reviewed and refined the means so they are no longer disjointed, overlapping, and too voluminous to consider. Your strategic planning team can now review the header cards and restate them as your organization's strategic goals.

Figure 6.7   Means for Achieving Organizational Success

- We continue aggressive growth in emerging markets while market growth opportunities are present.
- We use our global sourcing and development capabilities to offer our customers unique solutions.
- We organize and prioritize our product development activities to meet or exceed the needs or requirements of our customers.
- Our marketing teams enhance their understanding of the needs and expectations of our customers.
- We develop strong business relationships with our key customers to enhance our understanding of their needs and expectations.
- We maintain up-to-date information on customer needs, expectations, and requirements in our customer database.
- We eliminate small-volume, non-profitable products.
- We strive to offer products and services to consumers who value differentiation versus those who focus only on cost.
- We develop a close relationship with our customers so that our organization focuses on providing products and services customers are willing to pay for.
- We work closely with strategic customers who provide leadership within their markets.
- We lead our competition by being first to market with innovative products and industry-leading customer support.
- We reduce "time from conception to market" to 60 days and reduce in-process modifications to two days.
- We focus on international growth in Korea, China, India, and Australia.
- We increase our order fill rates and on-time delivery to exceed customer expectations.
- We strengthen our execution of customer service by incorporating related objectives and metrics in our performance management system.
- We develop strong distribution capabilities in each major market to provide efficient, cost-effective supply chains.
- We increase and improve internal communication.
- We streamline our product development process to emphasize opportunities that drive significant volume and cash flow.
- We increase our product development resources to capture more cost savings and continue to develop new products.
- We increase R&D capability to support the efficient design, manufacture, and launch of new products.
- We strengthen our organizational project management capabilities.
- We properly staff product and process development teams.
- We stop managing by geography but rather manage by product line to reduce silo thinking.
- We increase Asian revenue to $450 million to become a strong No. 2 player.
- Within 12 months of entering an emerging market, we become No. 1 or No. 2 in that particular market.
- We become No. 1 or No. 2 in every product category and No. 1 or No. 2 in every geographic area we compete in.
- We allocate resources to leverage our manufacturing efficiencies and customer service.

Figure 6.8 Organized List of Means for Achieving Organizational Success

Header Card	Means
We Will Be First to Market	• We lead our competition by being first to market with innovative products and industry-leading customer support. • We create a cross-functional team that focuses on increasing our speed to market. • We invest capital to support flexibility and speed to market goals. • We reduce "time from conception to market" to 60 days and reduce in-process modifications to two days.
We Will Exceed Customer Service Expectations	• We increase our order fill rates and on-time delivery to exceed customer expectations. • We achieve a 99 percent service level, as measured using our quarterly end-user survey. • We strengthen our execution of customer service by incorporating related objectives and metrics in our performance management system. • We develop strong distribution capabilities in each major market.
We Will Increase Personal Accountability	• We stop managing by geography but rather manage by product line to reduce silo thinking. • We divide our organization into profit centers, with each center having clearly stated objectives and metrics. • We manage product lines as profit centers, with each center having clearly stated objectives and metrics. • We firm up our performance management system so that we can hold people more accountable for their actions.
We Will Increase Our Manufacturing Flexibility	• We establish factories offering strategic, logistic cost advantages. • We build flexibility into our manufacturing processes and equipment. • We become world class in strategic supply chain management. • We become best in class in product manufacturing.
We Will Achieve Market Share Leadership	• We increase Asian revenue to $450 million to become a strong No. 2 player. • Within 12 months of entering an emerging market, we become No. 1 or No. 2 in that particular market. • We become No. 1 or No. 2 in every product category and No. 1 or No. 2 in every geographic area we compete in.

YOUR ORGANIZATION'S STRATEGIC GOALS

Your strategic planning team has identified the means by which your organization will achieve its mission and attain its long-term vision. Although it organized the means and created header cards to describe common themes and unifying concepts, it must now further refine the means by formulating your organization's strategic goals. This will add additional focus to the means and help ensure that individuals throughout your organization understand (1) what your organization aims to do to achieve its short- and long-term success and (2) what they in turn must do individually and as team members to contribute to your organization's effort.

KEY LEARNING POINT

Your organization's strategic goals add focus and help ensure that individuals throughout your organization understand (1) what your organization aims to do to achieve its short- and long-term success and (2) what they in turn must do individually and as team members to contribute to your organization's effort.

Your organization's strategic goals build on the results of all previous strategic planning activities:

- They support your organization's purpose and value proposition, which are designed to maintain and uphold your organization's reason for existence.
- They add focus to your organization's mission statement, which is designed to help guide performance and behavior with a focus on current actions, results, and outcomes.
- They support your organization's vision statement, which is designed to help ensure that the actions, results, and outcomes that occur today are consistent with and supportive of what the organization wishes to become (or where it hopes to be) in the future.
- They adhere to and further reinforce your organization's values and principles, which are designed to ensure that decisions and behavior contribute to (rather than sabotage) your organization achieving its mission and attaining its vision.
- They support your organization identifying and capitalizing on opportunities in its sweet spot, allowing your organization to harness the energy needed to accomplish its mission and propel it toward its envisioned future.

Although the purpose of goal setting is to add focus to the means, it is important for your strategic planning team to keep in mind that even more focus, detail, and specificity will be added later in the strategic planning process when it establishes concrete objectives for each of the strategic goals. My experience suggests that an organization's strategic goals are adequate when they:

- Clarify how the organization will accomplish its mission and attain its vision.
- Specify how the organization's values and principles will be exhibited and thus become "real."
- Clarify what opportunities the organization is pursuing or capitalizing upon in its "sweet spot."
- Provide boundaries within which members of the organization will make decisions and operate: for example, allowing them to decide which decisions or actions are "in" and which ones are "out."
- Establish expectations for what members of the organization are likely to direct their time, effort, and energy toward.
- Help employees (at all levels) understand how what they are being asked to do contributes to the organization's current mission and long-term vision.
- Help customers and clients know what to expect from the organization, in terms of the services and products they will receive or what needs or requirements the organization will fulfill.
- Send a clear message about how the organization plans to invest its time, energy, and money to its various stakeholders (such as board members, investors, and prospective employees).

Formulating Your Organization's Strategic Goals

A standard, single, best, or most efficient way to formulate your organization's strategic goals does not exist. Fortunately, the basis for your organization's strategic goals now exists in the form of the header cards created during the affinity diagramming. My experience and observations suggest that your strategic planning team members should work together to review and refine the header card statements and phrases; your team might find the following process useful and beneficial:

- A team member volunteers or is selected to approach the affinity diagram work surface.
- The team member reads each header card and five to six associated sticky notes.
- The team member asks a series of questions—
  - Does everyone understand the intent of this category?
  - Do I need to read additional sticky notes associated with this category?
  - How should we restate this header card so it becomes a strategic goal?
- Once all team members understand the intent of the category and, if needed, additional sticky notes associated with the category have been read, the team members work together to restate the header card.

- In restating the header cards as strategic goal statements, the planning team should ensure that the resulting goal statements—
  o Add clarity to how the organization will accomplish its mission and attain its vision.
  o Add specificity as to how the organization's values and principles will be exhibited and thus become "real."
  o Add clarity to what opportunities the organization is pursuing or capitalizing upon in its "sweet spot."
  o Provide boundaries within which members of the organization will make decisions and operate: for example, allowing them to decide which decisions or actions are "in" and which ones are "out."
  o Establish expectations for what members of the organization are likely to direct their time, effort, and energy toward.
  o Help employees (at all levels) understand how what they are being asked to do contributes to the organization's current mission and long-term vision.
  o Help customers and clients know what to expect from the organization, in terms of the services and products they will receive or what needs or requirements the organization will fulfill.
  o Send a clear message about how the organization plans to invest its time, energy, and money to its various stakeholders (such as board members, investors, and prospective employees).
- Once the strategic planning team agrees with the wording, the strategic goal statement should be noted and posted on a flip chart. Subsequent statements should be added to the flip chart.
- Once all strategic goal statements have been noted and posted, the strategic planning team can assume that it has reached consensus on the organization's strategic goals.

The strategic goals your planning team creates will be unique to your organization. However, your planning team might find the sample header cards and the associated strategic goal statements listed in Figure 6.9 useful and beneficial as it reviews the header cards and drafts your organization's strategic goals.

PRIORITIZING THE MEANS

My experience and observations consistently show that organizations seldom have adequate funding, people, or time to execute, implement, or deploy all the means by which they could achieve short- and long-term success. Strategic planning teams must therefore identify and pursue the means most likely to yield

Figure 6.9   Header Cards and Associated Strategic Goals

Header Card	Strategic Goal Statement
We Will Improve Our Management Tools	We will identify, develop, or refine the key management tools (systems, processes, procedures, and technology) necessary to be the fastest and most flexible company in our industry.
We Will Improve Internal Communication	We will adopt a communication mindset and implement a communication process that support selective and instantaneous distribution and sharing of accurate information to all of our colleagues and associates.
We Will Upgrade Staff Knowledge	We will assess the knowledge, skills, and abilities of our associates against their position requirements and provide development opportunities that align actual performance with stated performance objectives and metrics.
We Will Achieve Market Share Leadership	We will develop and refine our management, operational, and administrative systems, processes, and procedures so that we can become No. 1 or No. 2 in every product category and No. 1 or No. 2 in every geographic area we compete in.
We Will Increase Our Manufacturing Flexibility	We will develop and refine all management, operational, and administrative systems, processes, and procedures to become best in class in product manufacturing flexibility.

the greatest result and outcome. In identifying those means, planning teams (at a minimum) typically take these five factors into consideration:

- The magnitude of the impact or influence the strategic goal will have on helping the organization accomplish its overall mission and vision.
- The likelihood that the strategic goal will be achieved given the strengths, limitations, challenges, and opportunities associated with the goal.
- Whether the members at all levels of the organization are likely to consider the strategic goal to be realistic, sensible, and practical.
- The extent to which the organization can afford to execute, implement, or deploy the strategic goal considering the amount of funding, people, or time it will require.
- The extent to which the strategic goal is likely to resonate with the organization's various stakeholders, that is, whether they too are likely to consider the strategic goal to be realistic, sensitive, and practical.

Prioritizing the Means by Which Your Organization Will Succeed

A standard, single, best, or most effective way to prioritize the means by which your organization will succeed does not exist. My experience and observations suggest that your strategic planning team members should work together to identify the means and that the team should use a process that allows its members to collectively evaluate the merits of each strategic goal against the other goals, thereby allowing the team to identify the goals most likely to yield the most optimal results and outcomes. Although there are several tools your planning team might use to prioritize your organization's strategic goals, your team might find the bubble sort especially useful and beneficial.

The bubble sort[3] is a practical tool that is simple and easy to use. Do not assume that its ease of use indicates poor-quality results; although it is simple to use, your planning team—regardless of the size or complexity of your organization—will likely find that this prioritization tool produces valid and credible results. In applying the bubble sort, your planning team:

- Discusses and decides on the criterion or criteria it will use to evaluate the strategic goals. These criteria might include, but are not limited to, the following:
  - The magnitude of the impact or influence the strategic goal will have on helping the organization accomplish its overall mission and vision.
  - The likelihood that the strategic goal will be achieved given the strengths, limitations, challenges, and opportunities associated with the goal.
  - Whether the members at all levels of the organization are likely to consider the strategic goal to be realistic, sensible, and practical.
  - The extent to which the organization can afford to execute, implement, or deploy the strategic goal considering the amount of funding, people, or time it will require.
  - The extent to which the strategic goal is likely to resonate with the organization's various stakeholders: that is, whether they too are likely to consider the strategic goal to be realistic, sensitive, and practical.
- Appoints a team member to write the criterion or criteria on a flip chart and post it so that all team members can consistently apply it (or them) to each of the strategic goals.
- Appoints a team member to write each strategic goal down on a separate sticky note and then randomly place the sticky notes one above another in a vertical column on a flip chart (if necessary, the planning team extends the column by using more than one flip chart page).
- Appoints a team member to facilitate the following discussion and to:
  - Read sticky notes out loud and move sticky notes as directed.
  - Ask the planning team members, while keeping the criterion or criteria in mind, to compare the top two sticky notes to determine which is the most

important (i.e., whether it is more likely to succeed and yield the greatest result and outcome). If the lower sticky note is more important, the facilitator moves that sticky note to the top, thus positioning the more important sticky note above the less important one.

○ Repeat this paired comparison and exchange for the second and third sticky notes, then the third and fourth sticky notes, and so on until the planning team reaches the bottom of the column.

○ Repeat the process for the entire column (starting again with the top two sticky notes) if any cards are moved during the analysis.

○ Regardless of how much time it takes, apply the overall process to the entire column until no sticky notes are exchanged during a complete pass-through. Once the facilitator does not exchange any sticky notes during a complete pass-through, the sticky notes (and the list of strategic goals) are in priority order from "most" to "least" important.

KEY LEARNING POINT

Do not mistake the bubble sort's ease of use for the quality of the results it produces; although it is simple to use, your planning team—regardless of the size or complexity of your organization—will likely find that this prioritization tool produces valid and credible results.

Your strategic planning team has prioritized your organization's strategic goals from "most" to "least" important. It can now review the level of funding, the number of people, and/or the amount of time your organization has available and invest in and subsequently pursue those strategic goals most likely to yield the greatest result and outcome. Your planning team can now feel confident about these "most important" goals because they were selected in a planned and purposeful manner rather than out of happenstance. I emphasize that those teams that are not willing to invest the time to prioritize their strategic goals may find that, in some cases, a

KEY LEARNING POINT

It is important that your planning team move forward with the results of all previous discussions and decisions in mind. I therefore encourage your strategic planning team to frequently review the key findings, conclusions, and decisions previously noted on flip chart pads and posted on the walls.

strategic goal that simply happens to be "at the top of the list" or has the loudest advocate is acted upon when it unfortunately may be a less important goal (within the context of a selection criterion or selection criteria) and therefore may yield suboptimal or marginal results. If and when this happens, the organization may not realize the results or outcomes it requires and may not have adequate funding, people, or time to apply toward any of the other strategic goals.

Chapter 7

Setting Your Course of Action

As your strategic planning team develops, it is important that it do so with the results of all previous reviews, analyses, discussions, and decisions in mind. I therefore encourage your strategic planning team to frequently review the key findings, conclusions, and decisions previously noted on flip chart pads and posted on the walls. As your planning team adds specificity and detail to the means by which your organization will achieve short- and long-term success, I encourage everyone to review the flip charts and ask:

- What can, should, or must we do to act upon this particular decision?
- What are the implications for this review, analysis, conclusion, or decision in terms of our proceeding forward?
- What can, should, or must we include in our action plan to ensure that we achieve or attain the intent or imperative suggested in this noted item?
- What else might we do to help this intent or imperative come alive?

KEY LEARNING POINT

It is important that your planning team move forward with the results of all previous discussions and decisions in mind. I therefore encourage your strategic planning team to frequently review the key findings, conclusions, and decisions previously noted on flip chart pads and posted on the walls.

YOUR ORGANIZATION'S ACTION PLAN

Your strategic planning team has already made great strides in setting the stage for its—and your organization's—short- and long-term success. Your organization's strategic purpose and value proposition have been created, verified, and/or refined. Your organization's strategic intent has now been established, and the means (albeit stated in high-level terms) by which your organization will realize its intent have now been articulated. Your planning team must now augment its previous actions, results, and outcomes with some required "blocking and tackling."

For example, your team should consider the environment that exists within your organization. Regardless of your organization's purpose, value proposition, or strategic intent, it in all likelihood consists of:

- Numerous goals, objectives, metrics, initiatives, programs, and projects, some of which are competing for time, energy, resources, and/or funding.
- Numerous focal points that require time, interest, and energy from individuals who have only a certain amount of time, interest, and energy.
- Existing and ongoing strategies, tactics, and major and minor tasks that require time and attention.
- A track record of previous decisions and actions that contributed to the organization's current level of success and its current reputation within its industry, profession, and community.
- Buy-in, commitment, and enthusiasm around existing and ongoing goals, objectives, metrics, initiatives, programs, projects, strategies, tactics, tasks, and other focal points.
- An existing tempo or momentum heading in the previously established direction.

Although many of these existing and ongoing variables will likely remain intact, your strategic planning effort will impact or influence them in some way, shape, or form. Existing and ongoing goals, objectives, metrics, initiatives, programs, projects, strategies, tactics, and tasks have potentially been revised, refined, and/or otherwise modified. Others have potentially been abandoned or will no longer be a focal point because of the establishment, deployment, or implementation of new goals, objectives, metrics, initiatives, programs, projects, strategies, tactics, and tasks. In short, your strategic planning endeavor creates the need for your organization to recalibrate its attention and focus and reemphasize or redirect its effort and resources. Such recalibration and change in emphasis or direction call for a plan of action. Your organization's plan of action will help ensure adequate:

- Understanding throughout your organization about how your organization will achieve short- and long-term success.
- Consideration and thought regarding how your organization will achieve short- and long-term success.
- Attention and focus directed toward the continuing, modified, and/or newly established means by which your organization will achieve short- and long-term success.

- Allocation of money and resources to enhance the various ways your organization will achieve short- and long-term success.
- Emphasis, weight, and importance directed toward the continuing, modified, and/or newly established means by which your organization will achieve short- and long-term success.

Your organization's action plan must match prevailing assumptions, expectations, policies, and practices. Although your action plan may differ in structure and format, it will in all likelihood contain these five elements:

- Description of the strategic goal.
- Description of the means by which the organization will achieve the goal.
- The individual or individuals responsible and being held accountable for that particular goal.
- The deadline or critical timeframe for the goal's accomplishment.
- The metrics by which interim progress and ultimate success are measured.

It is important that the members of your strategic planning team keep in mind that the actions stipulated in your organization's action plan will have various degrees of detail and specificity. They (1) will come from the previously identified means and (2) will fall on a continuum ranging from:

- Comprehensive, encompassing, and inclusive strategies, to . . .
- Even more specific and concrete tactics, to . . .
- The most highly detailed tasks and subtasks.

There are no concrete rules regarding the level of specificity your organization's action plan will require or the form it will take. Regardless of its level of specificity, your action plan must provide adequate guidance and direction to produce the needed actions, progress, and short- and long-term success. My experience and observations suggest that your strategic planning team is likely to create an action plan that follows a narrative format or is laid out in a matrix. Either approach can be effective, as long as it establishes and/or illustrates the relationships among:

- The strategic goal.
- The means by which the organization will achieve the goals.
- The individual or individuals responsible and being held accountable for a particular strategic goal.
- The deadline or critical timeframe for the strategic goal's accomplishment.
- The metrics by which interim progress and ultimate success are measured.

> **KEY LEARNING POINT**
>
> Regardless of its level of specificity, your action plan must provide adequate guidance and direction to produce the needed actions, progress, and short- and long-term success.

Creating Your Organization's Action Plan

A standard, single, best, or most effective way to create an organization's action plan does not exist. My experience and observations suggest that strategic planning team members should work together to create your organization's action plan. Your planning team might find the following planning process to be useful and beneficial:

- One or more team members create a work surface using several sheets of flip chart paper.
- A team member writes the first strategic goal at the far left or very top of the work surface.
- On separate sticky notes, team members write each of the previously identified means by which the organization will achieve that particular strategic goal.
- Team members place all sticky notes (containing previously identified means by which the organization will achieve that particular goal) onto the work surface.
- Team members—
  - Place the strategic, more encompassing sticky notes directly to the right of or directly beneath the goal statement.
  - Place related but more tactical and task-oriented sticky notes directly beneath or to the right of the more strategic ones.
  - Identify other ways (tactics, major tasks, minor tasks) by which the organization will achieve that particular goal.
  - Place each sticky note at its proper location on the work surface—
    - The strategic, more encompassing, actions to the right of or directly beneath the goal statement.
    - Related but more tactical and task-oriented actions directly beneath or to the right of the more strategic ones.
    - Actions representing the greatest level of detail toward the bottom or to the right side of the work surface.
- The planning team applies the above process to each of the remaining strategic goals until each strategic goal has associated tactics, major tasks, and minor tasks.

- The strategic planning team reviews the results of the action planning process to ensure that the various means (tactics, major tasks, and minor tasks) by which the organization will achieve its strategic goals have been identified.
- For each strategic goal, the planning team—
    - Identifies the individual or individuals being held responsible for that particular goal.
    - Sets the deadline or critical timeframe for the goal's accomplishment.
    - Defines the metrics by which interim progress and ultimate success are to be measured.

The action plan your strategic planning team creates will be unique to your organization. However, your planning team might find the sample action plan presented in Figure 7.1 useful and beneficial as it drafts and refines your organization's action plan.

This figure (detailing only three strategic goals) illustrates how:

- Strategic, more encompassing, actions are inserted directly beneath the goal statement.
- Related but more tactical and task-oriented actions are inserted directly beneath the more strategic ones.

Figure 7.1   Sample Action Plan

Strategic Goal	Develop and retain the optimal talent within all disciplines to achieve our sales, professional development, and profit goals.

Tactics, Major Tasks, Minor Tasks	Evaluate our professional development needs.
	• Determine talent needs relating to our short- and long- term success.
	• Identify the actions and resources required to secure needed levels of performance.
	• Obtain benchmark and best practice data for human resources management, including recruitment, selection, orientation, performance management, evaluation, compensation, etc.
	  ○ Analyze benchmark data.
	  ○ Analyze best practice data.
	  ○ Define objectives and metrics for our organization.
	Develop or recruit the talent we need to meet our goals.
	• Determine hiring needs: what talent is best obtained by "growing" or "hiring in."
	  ○ Establish position standards to clearly define the knowledge, skills, and abilities each key position requires.
	  ○ Consistently apply the standards to all hiring decisions.

(Continued)

Figure 7.1   (Continued)

- Ensure state-of-the-art knowledge management to prevent knowledge from disappearing and/or knowledge sharing from being disrupted.
  - Ensure that our orientation, management performance, and evaluation systems encourage and reinforce the importance of knowledge attainment, retention, and sharing.
  - Conduct cross training to reinforce the importance of and support knowledge sharing.
  - Orient and train employees (at all levels) on how to attain, retain, and share knowledge.
- Assess our workforce to determine our current talent strengths and weaknesses.
  - Develop the process for inventorying talent.
  - Conduct the talent inventory assessment.
  - Identify needs that can be addressed through professional development.
- As appropriate or necessary, procure training to address professional development needs.
  - Identify reputable vendors.
  - Identify training programs that address predefined needs and expectations.
- As appropriate or necessary, develop training to address professional development needs.
  - Design curriculum.
  - Identify objectives and evaluation criteria and methods.
  - Identify trainers.
  - Develop training materials.
- Conduct training.
  - Internal training: conduct train-the-trainer sessions and advertise and conduct training sessions.
  - External training: advertise external training opportunities and select and sponsor attendees.

Retain and nurture the talent we already have in place to meet our strategic goals.

- Assess our work environment.
  - Review retention and turnover data to identify challenges and opportunities.
  - Conduct and review exit interview data to identify challenges and opportunities.
  - Use an organizational practice or employee opinion survey to measure the satisfaction of employees (at all levels).
- Create a leadership development plan for each supervisor, manager, and executive.
  - Analyze benchmark and best practice data.
  - Incorporate findings into the development plan.

Figure 7.1   (Continued)

- Create a professional development plan for each employee.
  - Analyze benchmark and best practice data.
  - Incorporate findings into the development plan.
- Conduct a compensation analysis.
  - Analyze benchmark and best practice data.
  - Incorporate findings into our compensation system.
  - Consistently apply the compensation system throughout the organization.
- Strengthen the performance management and evaluation systems.
  - Analyze benchmark and best practice data.
  - Incorporate findings into our performance management and evaluation system.
  - Consistently apply the performance management and evaluation system throughout the organization.
- Establish a formal reward and recognition system.
  - Analyze benchmark and best practice data.
  - Design a reward and recognition system that reflects best-in-class and best practice data.
  - Develop and share information about the reward and recognition system throughout the organization.
  - Introduce and/or reinforce the importance of reward and recognition in all milestone events.
  - Introduce and then consistently apply the reward and recognition system throughout the organization.
- Enhance communication within and throughout the organization.
  - Develop and conduct interpersonal communication courses for all employees.
  - Develop and conduct communication courses for supervisors, managers, and executives.
  - Introduce and/or reinforce the importance of effective interpersonal communication in all milestone events.
  - Introduce and/or reinforce the importance of effective interpersonal communication in all orientation and assimilation activities.

Responsible Party or Parties	John Doe
Deadline or Critical Timeframe	Eighteen months from today's date.
Metric(s)	• Retention rate, to be determined following review of the current data. • Employee satisfaction level, to be determined following review of the current data.

(Continued)

157

Figure 7.1 (Continued)

	• Extent to which we achieve our sales, professional development, and profit goals versus the organization's current performance.
Strategic Goal	Supplier partners provide innovative solutions that allow us to exceed customer expectations and requirements.

Tactics, Major Tasks, Minor Tasks	Define terms, conditions, and stipulations pertaining to customer relationships and partners.
	• Establish terms, conditions, and stipulations by customer and customer requirements. Factor in:
	  ○ Cost, quality, and response time.
	  ○ Variables relating to R&D, retooling, and technical support.
	  ○ Delivery terms and conditions.
	  ○ Payment terms and conditions.
	Define and identify supplier partners based on predefined partnership criteria.
	Develop supplier partnerships.
	• Benchmark best-in-class companies in our industry and in adjacent industries.
	• Incorporate best-in-class objectives and metrics into our supplier relationship policies and procedures.
	• Incorporate best-in-class features into our supplier relationship practices by developing:
	  ○ Standardized formulation and manufacturing processes.
	  ○ Strategic partnerships with tooling companies.
	  ○ Regional partnerships with strategic suppliers.
	  ○ A separate remanufacture/resale business.

Responsible Party or Parties	Jane Doe
Deadline or Critical Timeframe	Twelve months from today's date.
Metric(s)	• Flexibility of our manufacturing process versus best-in-class competitor. • Price of our Category 1 products versus competitor prices. • Quality as is reported through our end-user survey. • Timeliness and accuracy of our delivery as is reported through our end-user survey.
Strategic Goal	Reduce manufacturing waste to match or exceed best-in-class.
Tactics, Major Tasks, Minor Tasks	• Identify and appoint quality improvement director. • Procure or develop and sponsor or conduct quality improvement training.

Figure 7.1   (Continued)

- Monitor and manage manufacturing quality.
  - Establish and manage against manufacturing quality metrics (scrap, rework, corrections, and reconciliations):
    - Identify the champion and team lead(s).
    - Define team members.
    - Define the type of waste we will strive to reduce.
    - Define starting and target points for waste reduction (as a dollar amount, percentage, or amount of time).
    - Develop and consistently implement a quality improvement action plan.
  - Manage material-handling and information-sharing variables:
    - Benchmark best-in-class companies in our industry and in adjacent industries.
    - Incorporate best-in-class objectives and metrics into our material-handling process and our information-sharing efforts.
    - Incorporate best-in-class features into our material-handling process and information-sharing efforts.
  - Eliminate nonproductive associate assignments:
    - Benchmark best-in-class companies in our industry and in adjacent industries.
    - Incorporate best-in-class objectives and metrics into our performance management and employee assignment process.
    - Incorporate best-in-class features into our employee performance management and assignment process.
  - Strengthen inventory control:
    - Benchmark best-in-class companies in our industry and in adjacent industries.
    - Incorporate best-in-class objectives and metrics into our inventory control process.
    - Incorporate best-in-class features into our inventory control plans and practices.

Responsible Party or Parties	Jane Smith
Deadline or Critical Timeframe	Twelve months from today's date.
Metric(s)	• Scrap less than 2.5 percent of gross manufactured product. • Rework orders 25 percent less than the industry norm. • Ensure that cost of poor quality is less than 5 percent of industry mean.

- The more tactical and task-oriented actions generally provide the greatest level of detail.
- One or more individuals are listed as being responsible for each particular strategic goal.
- A deadline or critical timeframe is established for each strategic goal.
- Metrics (by which interim progress and ultimate success are to be measured) are established for each strategic goal.

The sample in Figure 7.1 also illustrates how the action plan created during the planning session is the beginning—rather than the end—of your strategic planning and strategy execution journey. Figure 7.1 reinforces several important points relating to strategic management:

- Tactics, major tasks, and/or minor tasks identified during the strategic planning session will likely need to be refined; for example, new tactics may need to be added, and some of the existing tactics may need to be reworded, completely modified, or deleted.
- Critical dates or timeframes set during the strategic planning session will likely need to be strengthened; for example, dates for specific tactics, major tasks, and/or minor tasks may need to be added to ensure that adequate funds, time, and resources are available and to increase the likelihood of proper sequencing of actions, activities, and results.
- Metrics established during the strategic planning session may need to be further defined following additional research or analysis or augmented to provide additional direction and guidance to individuals or teams responsible for implementing specific tactics, major tasks, and/or minor tasks.
- Responsible parties identified during the strategic planning session will likely need to be changed (if, for example, they cannot, for whatever reason, devote enough time and attention to the strategic goal) or augmented (if, for example, some of the tactics, major tasks, or minor tasks require additional direction, guidance, or support).

YOUR ORGANIZATION'S CONTINGENCY PLAN

Your strategic planning team has—in a planned, purposeful, and structured way—identified the means by which your organization will strive to achieve short- and long-term success:

- Your organization's mission, vision, and value proposition have been verified or established.
- The values that will guide decisions and actions have been verified or defined.
- Strategic goals and the means by which they will be achieved—along with associated responsible parties, critical dates or timeframes, and metrics—have been established.

Unfortunately, unexpected and/or unanticipated obstacles, impediments, and barriers will undoubtedly surface as your organization implements its strategic plan. If left unaddressed, these challenges may significantly impede your organization's ability to deliver on its value proposition, fulfill its mission, or attain its vision. It is therefore important that your strategic planning team supplement its action plan with a contingency plan.

A contingency plan identifies actions your organization will take to quickly and effectively address unexpected or unanticipated impediments, obstacles, or barriers.[1] It is therefore important that your strategic planning team members keep in mind that the:

- Challenges they include in your contingency plan must relate to the previously identified tactics, major tasks, and minor tasks.
- Countermeasures (e.g., what your organization will do to avoid, reduce, mitigate, or otherwise address the impediments, obstacles, or barriers) they recommend must be realistic and doable.

My experience and observations suggest that your strategic planning team is likely to create a contingency plan that follows a narrative format or is laid out in a matrix. Either approach can be effective, as long as it establishes and/or illustrates the relationship between the challenge(s) and recommended countermeasure(s).

KEY LEARNING POINT

Your contingency plan must establish and/or illustrate the relationship between the challenges your organization is likely to face and the actions it can take to neutralize those impediments, obstacles, and barriers if and when they materialize.

Creating Your Organization's Contingency Plan

A standard, single, best, or most effective way to create an organization's contingency plan does not exist. My experience and observations suggest that strategic planning team members should work together to create your organization's contingency plan. Your planning team might find the following contingency planning process to be useful and beneficial:

- A team member volunteers to facilitate this process; he or she reads your organization's first strategic goal (and to the extent needed, the associated tactics, major tasks, and minor tasks) out loud to the entire team.
- The facilitator writes the first strategic goal at the top of a sheet of flip chart paper.

- Team members brainstorm challenges (impediments, obstacles, or barriers) likely to adversely impact the organization's achieving that particular goal.
- The facilitator lists the challenges on the flip chart paper.
- Team members review the list of challenges and identify the two to three challenges most likely to occur, given the prevailing conditions and circumstances.
- The facilitator highlights each of the two to three challenges on the flip chart paper.
- For each of the two or three challenges, team members brainstorm the means by which the organization might avoid, reduce, mitigate, or otherwise address the impediment, obstacle, or barrier.
- The facilitator lists the means on flip chart paper.
- The team reviews the various means by which the organization might avoid, reduce, mitigate, or otherwise address each challenge and selects the most realistic and doable one, which becomes the countermeasure the organization will use if or when that particular challenge surfaces.

Figure 7.2   Sample Contingency Plan

Impediments/Barriers/Obstacles	Countermeasures (** Recommended Countermeasure)
Budgetary constraints threaten a particular strategic goal.	• ** Build out the strategic plan to include cost estimates and create a protected line item in the annual budget dedicated to each strategic goal. • More effectively monitor and manage the annual budget. • More effectively practice "exception to the rule" management.
People cannot invest the needed time to a particular strategic goal because they are already devoting their time to other programs and initiatives.	• ** Establish "mission-critical priorities" and share information (in a variety of ways, using a variety of forums) on what must start, stop, and continue (done by senior-level leadership). • Encourage employees (all levels) to use existing time management tools. • Review and modify the policies and procedures to reinforce the importance of effective time management.
Key employees with mission-critical knowledge, skills, and abilities leave our company.	• ** Create and execute a broad-based strategy for acquiring, developing, and retaining our talent. • Develop and implement a succession plan. • Develop and implement a mentor program.

- The facilitator highlights the recommended countermeasure on the flip chart paper.
- The strategic planning team applies this process to each challenge until it has identified the most realistic and doable countermeasure for each impediment, obstacle, or barrier.

The contingency plan your strategic planning team creates will be unique to your organization. However, your planning team might find the sample contingency plan presented in Figure 7.2 useful and beneficial as it drafts and refines your organization's contingency plan.

The figure presents a list of actions an organization might take to quickly and effectively address unexpected or unanticipated impediments, obstacles, or barriers. It also illustrates how challenges outlined in a contingency plan relate to previously identified tactics, major tasks, and minor tasks, and how recommended countermeasures must be realistic and doable.

ENSURING EXECUTION THROUGHOUT THE ENTIRE ORGANIZATION

Even though strategic planning teams typically agree with the adage "communicate and then communicate some more, all the time realizing that you cannot communicate too often," they generally fail to adequately communicate the organization's newly created or updated strategic plan throughout the organization. I therefore recommend that your team consider creating a supplemental communication plan.

The communication plan will facilitate awareness and understanding by helping you manage and coordinate the wide variety of communications that must occur to support strategy execution throughout the entire organization. Although communication plans may differ in content and format, it is important that your strategic planning team take initial steps to identify the:

- Key messages needing to be shared with various stakeholder groups.
- Situations, events, and opportunities in which messages are to be transmitted.
- Media, vehicles, and mechanisms through which the key messages are to be delivered.
- Individuals responsible for delivering those key messages, along with critical dates and success measures.

This communication framework will help ensure that your leaders, executives, managers, and supervisors provide relevant, accurate, and consistent information to the members of your organization and its various key stakeholder groups. On this front, I recommend that select members of your organization's strategic planning team:

- Develop materials to guide and support communication pertaining to your organization's strategic plan.

- Encourage and reinforce the importance of relevant, accurate, and consistent information being communicated throughout the organization.
- Support the delivery of relevant, accurate, and consistent information throughout the organization.
- Verify the delivery of messages and the distribution of communication materials.
- Monitor implementation of the communication plan.
- Measure the progress and overall effectiveness of the communication strategy.
- Monitor feedback and ensure that appropriate follow-up actions are taken.

Your strategic planning team should keep these principles in mind when creating and implementing your organization's supplemental communication plan:

- It is important that formal and informal leaders communicate often and use words everyone understands.
- Be sure to give everyone the "big picture" so they understand how all of the elements (e.g., mission, vision, value proposition, strategic goals, tactics, etc.) relate to each other.
- Include a "top-down" component to your organization's communication effort, to reinforce to employees (at all levels) that key leaders buy into and support the newly created or modified strategic plan.
- Communicate critical dates and timeframes and then share information on progress being made so that employees (at all levels) quickly realize that changes resulting from the strategic plan are doable and achievable.
- Help every level of the organization understand what will remain the same and what will change as a result of the newly created or modified strategic plan.

The adoption and execution of a supplemental communication plan will help ensure the successful execution of your organization's newly created or modified strategic plan. I recommend that your communication plan include a communication matrix and that the matrix contain the following information:

- A discrete, sequential number assigned to each communiqué, to be inserted into the communication calendar.
- The individual, level, or position responsible for sending the communiqué.
- The audience receiving the communiqué.
- The situation or event in which the communiqué will be shared.
- The media or vehicle(s) used to transmit the communiqué.
- Key message(s) or content to be emphasized or included in the communiqué.
- The frequency or critical date of the communiqué.
- Success measure(s), for use in determining the effectiveness of the communiqué.

Although the communication matrix your strategic planning team creates will be unique to your organization, your planning team might find the sample matrix presented in Figure 7.3 (which provides information on two communiqués) to be useful and beneficial.

This matrix (1) illustrates how the communication plan created during the planning session represents the beginning—rather than the end—of your communication endeavor and (2) reflects an opportunity for your strategic planning team to solicit ideas, suggestions, and recommendations from all members of your organization on how to "package" information related to strategic planning so it is likely to be considered and subsequently acted upon.

KEY LEARNING POINT

The communication plan you create during the strategic planning session represents the beginning—rather than the end—of your communication endeavor. Seek out and take advantage of opportunities to solicit ideas, suggestions, and recommendations from others on how to further "package" strategic planning–related information.

Figure 7.3   Sample Communication Matrix

	Consideration	Related Information
Communiqué 1	Responsible party	Leadership team.
	Target audience	All members of the organization.
	Situation or event	Specially held town hall meeting.
	Media or vehicle	Presentation and handouts.
	Key message(s)	• Information on the strategic planning session, the participants involved, the process followed, and key results and outcomes. • How the strategic plan will benefit the organization and help it accomplish its mission and attain its vision. • The organization's newly stated mission, vision, value proposition, values, and strategic goals. • How all members of the organization will play an important role in helping the organization achieve short- and long-term success.

(Continued)

Figure 7.3 (Continued)

	Frequency or critical date	Within five business days of the last day of the strategic planning session.

	Success measure(s)	• When asked, members of the organization will—in their own words—be able to describe:
		  ○ The purpose and key results and outcomes of the strategic planning session.
		  ○ How the strategic plan will benefit the organization and help it accomplish its mission and attain its vision.
		  ○ The organization's mission and vision.

Communiqué 2	Responsible party	Leadership team.
	Target audience	All members of the organization.
	Situation or event	Monthly publication.
	Media or vehicle	Organization-wide newsletter published monthly.
	Key message(s)	• The organization's strategic goals and high-level action plan showcasing key tactics, critical dates or timeframes, and responsible parties. • Highly visible strategy, process, technology, people, or cultural changes associated with the newly created strategic plan. • Opportunities all members of the organization will have to further contribute to, support, and otherwise assist with refining and executing the strategic plan. • The most significant impact the strategic plan will have on employee roles and responsibilities, in terms of what they are being asked to do on a daily basis.
	Frequency or critical date	First newsletter that follows the conclusion of the strategic planning session.
	Success measure(s)	• When asked, members of the organization will—in their own words—be able to describe: ○ The organization's strategic goals and high-level action plan.

Figure 7.3   (Continued)

            ○ From their perspective, the most significant changes associated with the strategic plan.

            ○ Opportunities they will have to further contribute to, support, and otherwise assist with refining and executing the strategic plan.

            ○ The most significant impact the strategic plan will have on what they are being asked to do on a daily basis.

I recommend that your communication plan also include a communication calendar, a summary of key messages you should initially communicate and reinforce, and principles that will guide your organization's communication effort:

- The communication calendar should—at a minimum—contain the following information—
  - Days, weeks, or months covered in the calendar period.
  - Numbered communiqués to send or share during the calendar period.
  - Numbered communiqués to send or share each day, week, or month throughout the calendar period.
- The summary should—at a minimum—highlight messages your leaders, executives, managers, and supervisors should initially communicate and reinforce—
  - Key messages to initially communicate and reinforce will vary from organization to organization.
  - As is reflected in the sample communication matrix, your initial key messages might include—
    - A summary of what has recently transpired, current events, and near-future events pertaining to your newly created or modified strategic plan.
    - A description of how the newly created or modified strategic plan will benefit your organization and enhance the quality of its services and products.
    - Your organization's (1) mission, vision, value proposition, and values, (2) strategic goals and associated tactics, major tasks, and minor tasks, and (3) action plan, including critical dates or timeframes, responsible parties, and metrics.

- A summary of strategy, process, technology, people, or cultural changes associated with the newly created or modified strategic plan and a description of the resources and support assigned to facilitate the associated changes.

- A brief description of opportunities all members of your organization will have to further contribute to, support, and otherwise assist with refining and executing your organization's strategic plan.

- A description of the impact the newly created or modified strategic plan will have on the roles and responsibilities of employees at all levels, in terms of what they are being asked to do on a daily basis and the important role they will play in your organization's short- and long-term success.

- The principles should—at a minimum—confirm and further reinforce your organization's values—

  - Your organization, given its culture and practices, may wish to emphasize (or deemphasize) certain communication principles.

  - The communication principles that guide your strategic planning communication effort might include—

    - It is important that formal and informal leaders communicate often and use words everyone understands.

    - Be sure to give everyone the "big picture" so they understand how all of the elements (e.g., mission, vision, value proposition, strategic goals, tactics, etc.) relate to each other.

    - Include a "top-down" component to your organization's communication effort to reinforce to employees (at all levels) that key leaders buy into and support the newly created or modified strategic plan.

    - Communicate critical dates and timeframes and then share information on progress being made so that employees (at all levels) quickly realize that changes resulting from the strategic plan are doable and achievable.

    - Help every level of the organization understand what will remain the same and what will change as a result of the newly created or modified strategic plan.

Ensuring Employee Understanding and Buy-in

Experience and observations suggest that your strategic planning team may need to further augment your organization's strategic plan to help increase levels of employee awareness, understanding, buy-in, and advocacy. I therefore recommend that your team consider creating a supplemental change management plan.

Newly created and modified strategic plans typically drive change throughout the organization. For example, your strategic plan may include new or modified strategies, tactics, major tasks, and minor tasks that require your organization to (1) transform its services to meet or exceed customer and client needs, expectations, and requirements or (2) adopt new technology and processes to maintain or reduce costs while maintaining or increasing the value of services provided to clients and internal customers. Such change requires an organization to develop new policies, adopt new practices, capitalize on new technologies, and implement new work processes. To succeed, existing work methods and traditional mindsets must change.

Recognizing the importance of such changes and how they typically impact the organization's culture, policies, procedures, and practices, your planning team should consider incorporating change management into the strategic planning effort rather than leaving it to chance. On this front, I recommend (1) that your planning team take initial steps to create a supplemental change management plan and (2) that select members of the planning team subsequently work with your organization's leadership, stakeholders, and operational and functional leaders to:

1. Explore the nature and magnitude of change associated with the newly created or modified strategic plan.
2. Assess the state of your organization's capacity (for change) and capabilities.
3. Identify challenges, obstacles, or impediments (e.g., your leadership team's inability to manage strategically or a history of failed change efforts) likely to impede your organization's progress and success.
4. Develop and implement actions that take advantage of your organizational strengths, address your organizational challenges, and accelerate organization-wide change.
5. Investigate and implement ways to optimize the rewards of—and minimize challenges associated with—new strategies, work processes, and technology associated with your strategic plan.
6. Monitor and manage behavior and performance associated with and therefore impacting changes associated with your strategic plan.
7. Encourage and reinforce behavior that produces desired results.
8. Monitor progress, share lessons learned, and when necessary address unexpected challenges.

The supplemental change management plan will augment your organization's strategic plan by specifying:

- Goals for setting the stage for, introducing, and reinforcing organizational changes related to the strategic plan.
- Specific actions your organization will take to achieve each of the change goals.
- Individuals responsible for the change-related actions.
- Critical dates or timeframes by which the change-related actions should occur.

I recommend that your strategic planning team keep the following principles in mind as it (1) takes initial steps to develop your organization's supplemental change management plan and (2) subsequently helps your organization accelerate change related to the strategic plan:

- It is critical that your organization's leadership team—
  o Involve key stakeholders in identifying ways to facilitate the adoption of new strategies, methods of work, and technology.
  o Help articulate and actively support the change vision.
  o Craft and send tailored messages to address change-related issues and concerns.
  o Support the adoption of processes and systems that emphasize and support appropriate behavior.
  o Seek out and capitalize on opportunities to personally acknowledge and reinforce appropriate behavior.
- Because resistance by employees (at all levels), if not adequately addressed, may impede progress and overall success—
  o To decrease resistance, you must increase awareness of the "why" and "how" of needed change.
  o To further decrease resistance, you must decrease everyone's fear of the unknown by assuring them that the needed changes are doable and by providing needed assistance and support.
- Communication informs, professional development enables, and incentives encourage employees (at all levels) to adopt new ways of thinking and acting.
- Change-related activities must—
  o Occur throughout the overall effort and not be viewed as isolated actions or events.
  o Become part of, rather than remain separate from, the way your leaders lead and managers manage.
  o Be viewed by everyone as being integral to your organization's success rather than an add-on.
- Employees typically want to hear messages about change from two people: their formal or informal leader and their immediate supervisor.

The supplemental change management plan your strategic planning team creates will be unique to your organization. However, your planning team might find the partial and incomplete supplemental change management plan presented in Figure 7.4 to be useful and beneficial.

This sample (1) illustrates how the change management plan created during the planning session represents the beginning—rather than the end—of your change

Figure 7.4   Sample Supplemental Change Management Plan

Goal: Determine the nature and magnitude of change associated with the newly created or modified strategic plan.

Actions	• Conduct a change review session involving a cross section of the organization.
	• Share results of the change review session with members of the organization—
	  ○ Seek out comments pertaining to the completeness, accuracy, and credibility of the results.
	  ○ Obtain recommendations for improvement.
	• Once the results are vetted and refined, post on the strategic planning Web site.

Responsible Party or Parties	Select member(s) of the strategic planning team.
Critical Date or Timeframe	Within two weeks of the conclusion of the strategic planning session.

Goal: Determine the organization's capacity (for change) and capabilities.

Actions	• Conduct a capacity/capability review session involving a cross section of the organization.
	• Obtain and review information about the organization's current capacity (for change) and capabilities.
	• Interview key stakeholders; obtain their perceptions about the organization's products and services.
	• Share results of the review session, data analysis, and key stakeholder interviews with members of the organization—
	  ○ Seek out comments pertaining to the completeness, accuracy, and credibility of the results.
	  ○ Obtain recommendations for improvement.
	• Once the results are vetted and refined, post on the strategic planning Web site.

Responsible Party or Parties	Select member(s) of the strategic planning team.
Critical Date or Timeframe	Within two weeks of the conclusion of the strategic planning session.

Goal: Identify challenges, obstacles, or impediments likely to impede the organization's progress and success.

Actions	• Summarize key findings of the change and capacity/capability review sessions.
	• Have select members of the strategic planning team meet to:
	  ○ Review the key findings.
	  ○ Analyze and discuss implications.

(Continued)

Figure 7.4   (Continued)

	○ Identify challenges, obstacles, or impediments most likely to impede the organization's progress and success.
	• Share results of the session with the strategic planning team—
	  ○ Seek out comments pertaining to the completeness, accuracy, and credibility of the results.
	  ○ Obtain recommendations for improvement.
	• Once the results are vetted and refined, post on the strategic planning Web site.

Responsible Party or Parties	Select member(s) of the strategic planning team.
Critical Date or Timeframe	Within three weeks of the conclusion of the strategic planning session.

management endeavor and (2) reflects an opportunity for your strategic planning team to solicit ideas, suggestions, and recommendations from employees (at all levels) on what your organization can do to ensure organization-wide understanding, buy-in, and commitment.

KEY LEARNING POINT

The change management plan you create during the planning session represents the beginning—rather than the end—of your change management endeavor. Seek out and take advantage of opportunities to solicit ideas, suggestions, and recommendations from others on what your organization can do to ensure wide-scale understanding, buy-in, and commitment.

ENSURING CONTINUOUS IMPROVEMENT

Your strategic planning team has taken steps—both during and following the strategic planning session—to ensure your organization's short- and long-term success. While these actions will likely yield positive results and outcomes, it is important that your organization strive to enhance and further improve:

• Its next strategic planning endeavor to help ensure increasingly more effective and efficient strategy formulation.

• The way it deploys and implements its strategies to help ensure increasingly more effective and efficient execution.

Your strategic planning team members must recognize that "continuous improvement" involves what the term suggests: continuous improvement. It is therefore important for team members to monitor the process and deliverables throughout the strategic planning session, identify opportunities for enhancement and improvement, and when feasible, take advantage of those opportunities (e.g., "course correct") while this year's session is still under way. Opportunities and their associated solutions that are not dealt with at this time should be noted so that they can be considered and applied when planning and conducting your next planning session.

It is equally important for your strategic planning team members to recognize that continuous improvement extends beyond the strategic planning session to immediate next steps, short-term follow-up actions, and then subsequent follow-on actions. In striving to further enhance and improve your performance throughout the strategy formulation and execution journey, I recommend that your strategic planning team take advantage of the continuous improvement (CI) methodologies, tools, and techniques used in your organization. If your organization does not adhere to a certain CI framework, model, or process, your strategic planning team might consider the following five-step continuous improvement framework,[2] which students and clients typically consider useful and beneficial:

- Step 1. Determine how we are doing—
  - Select members of the strategic planning team meet to conduct a strategy review.
  - Team members review the goals, actions, timeframes and critical dates, and metrics stipulated in the action plan.
  - Team members review progress to date to determine the extent to which (1) progress has been made and/or (2) the strategic goals and associated tactics, major tasks, and minor tasks have been accomplished.
- Step 2. Determine if we should improve—
  - For tactics, major tasks, and minor tasks that have experienced optimal execution, the team members identify and note potential lessons learned and best practices.
  - For each marginal or suboptimal gain or achievement, team members analyze its impact on the predefined metrics and the organization's short- and long-term success to determine whether to invest resources, time, and energy to improve performance.
- Step 3. Determine how we should improve—
  - As appropriate, the team members further—
    - Analyze the gap between the actual progress or accomplishment and the desired or required performance.
    - Explore underlying factors or factors contributing to the performance gap.

- Solicit ideas from other employees (at all levels) on how to effectively and efficiently close the performance gap.
- Identify and select the solution(s) most likely to lead to optimal execution.
- Incorporate solution(s) into the organization's action and/or contingency plan, assigning a responsible party, a critical date or timeframe, and metrics.

- Step 4. Apply and then determine the effectiveness of the improvement—
  - Tactics, major tasks, and minor tasks are implemented according to the action plan.
  - The responsible party monitors and notes progress and accomplishment.
- Step 5. Determine how we should continuously improve—
  - The person responsible for the remedial action(s) shares the results and outcomes in accordance with the organization's action plan.
  - Actions, situations, and circumstances contributing to optimal results and outcomes are explored; lessons learned and best practices are identified.
  - Lessons learned and best practices are shared throughout the organization and are applied to the organization's ongoing continuous improvement effort.
  - The five-step continuous improvement framework is applied to marginal and suboptimal results and outcomes.

KEY LEARNING POINT

In striving to further enhance and improve performance throughout the strategy formulation and execution journey, your planning team should take advantage of continuous improvement (CI) methodologies, tools, and techniques in use in your organization.

MOVING FORWARD WITH STRATEGIC PLANNING

The remainder of this book presents information, tools, techniques, and resources readers can use to increase the likelihood of effective and efficient strategic planning and optimal strategic planning results and outcomes, as well as further explore strategic thinking and planning and strategy formulation and execution.

Chapter 8

Strategic Planning Knowledge, Skills, and Abilities

The previous chapters provided guidance, information, tools, and techniques your strategic planning team considered and applied as it:

- Developed a strategic plan to help your organization accomplish its mission and attain its vision.
- Created a contingency plan to help your organization address unexpected and unanticipated challenges.
- Explored and decided on what your organization will do to ensure constant and consistent execution throughout the entire organization.
- Investigated and decided how your organization will help ensure that everyone has the needed levels of awareness, understanding, buy-in, commitment, and advocacy.
- Took steps to continuously improve its next strategic planning session to help ensure increasingly more effective and efficient strategy formulation.
- Identified ways to strengthen the way your organization implements its strategies to help ensure increasingly more effective and efficient execution.

To further enhance your strategy formulation and execution and to increase the likelihood of optimal short- and long-term success, it is important that your organization strengthen its strategic planning, strategy formulation, and strategy execution capabilities. To help ensure that your employees (at all levels) possess the needed planning capabilities and to help "frame" the associated knowledge, skills, and abilities, I recommend that your organization help its employees become capable of planning, preparing for, leading, facilitating, participating in, and following up on strategy formulation and execution.

KEY LEARNING POINT

It is important that your organization develop a cadre of employees capable of planning, preparing for, leading, facilitating, participating in, and following up on strategy formulation and execution.

More specifically, optimal strategy formulation and execution require a team of individuals capable of:

- Setting the stage for strategic planning by—
  - Helping leaders make credible decisions about whether to proceed with strategic planning.
  - Properly setting the stage for a successful strategic planning endeavor.
  - Adequately raising everyone's interest in participating in or otherwise contributing to strategy formulation and execution.
- Planning to plan by—
  - Designing or selecting a credible strategic planning framework, model, or process.
  - Identifying the components to be included in the resulting strategic plan.
- Preparing for strategic planning by—
  - Helping leaders decide when to conduct the strategic planning session.
  - Properly selecting individuals to participate in the process.
  - Ensuring that needed information, data, facilities, equipment, and supplies are available throughout the strategic planning session.
- Analyzing the current state and envisioning the future by—
  - Examining and/or refining the organization's value proposition.
  - Exploring the organization's internal strengths and weaknesses.
  - Investigating the organization's external opportunities and threats.
  - Verifying, modifying, or creating the organization's mission and vision.
- Formulating or refining the organization's values, strategic goals, and the means through which the organization will achieve short- and long-term success by—
  - Exploring, verifying, or clarifying your organization's values.
  - Determining, verifying, or clarifying your organization's sweet spot.
  - Reviewing, modifying, or developing your organization's strategic goals.
  - Identifying the means through which your organization will accomplish its mission and attain its vision.

- Action planning for short- and long-term success by—
  - Helping translate strategic goals into specific and concrete tactics, major tasks, and minor tasks.
  - Exploring obstacles, barriers, and impediments most likely to interfere with subsequent execution and identifying viable ways of resolving such unexpected and unanticipated occurrences.
- Successfully executing strategies by—
  - Taking steps to ensure subsequent execution throughout the entire organization.
  - Identifying ways of ensuring that everyone has the needed levels of awareness, understanding, buy-in, commitment, and advocacy.
- Striving to continuously improve by—
  - Seeking and capitalizing on ways to continuously improve your strategic planning session to help ensure optimal results and outcomes.
  - Taking steps to improve the way your organization executes strategy to help ensure increasingly more effective and efficient performance.

The above actions combine to yield optimal strategy formulation and execution; such actions reflect members of the organization capable of effectively functioning as strategic leader, manager, facilitator, coach, and/or participant.

KEY LEARNING POINT

It is important that your organization develop employees (at all levels) who are capable of functioning as a strategic leader, manager, facilitator, and coach.

THE STRATEGIC LEADER

In *The Manager as Leader*, Michael Venn (my coauthor) and I describe various roles that leaders play, including crafting strategy, developing people, and supporting them in their work. Although we describe a number of roles, the one most relevant to this book is the role of the strategic leader.

As your strategic planning team witnesses and experiences when conducting the SWOT analysis, the strategic leader must maintain both an internal and external view. The strategic leader strives to understand:

- External forces influencing his or her industry, competition, and the reality of doing business in today's turbulent business environment.
- Internal factors impacting his or her organization's ability to achieve short- and long-term success.

The strategic leader recognizes (and emphasizes) the importance of strategy formulation and execution. He or she must clearly communicate the organization's value proposition to its stakeholder groups and involve as many members of the organization as possible in creating the organization's mission and vision. The strategic leader must then help his or her followers (i.e., all members of the organization) work together and function as a team to accomplish the mission and attain the vision. Strategic leaders have a multifaceted focus: they work with members of the organization to create and communicate a compelling mission (the "what") and vision (the "where") and then work with them to formulate a path (the "how") to success. Strategic leaders:

- Keep an eye on the competition, suppliers, and distributors.
- Consider the multitude of external forces and internal factors impacting the organization's ability to accomplish its mission and attain its vision.
- Learn as much as they can about their particular industry and adjacent industries, as well as trends pertaining to business technology, systems, and processes.
- Strive to reinvent their industry instead of trying to simply remain in it.
- Accept input from a variety of other sources, including colleges, universities, research institutes, think tanks, luminaries, and thought leaders.
- Intentionally strive to see things from a different perspective.
- Communicate clearly with others and involve others in strategy formulation and execution.
- Stress the importance of—
  - Everyone working together to do the right things for the right reasons.
  - People recognizing and adhering to previously established boundaries.
  - The organization moving forward rather than remaining static or becoming complacent.
  - All members of the organization moving forward together.
  - Team members recognizing and working together to mitigate, reduce, or avoid the hazards of the path forward.
- Help all stakeholders know what to expect from the organization, in terms of its value proposition, services, and products.
- Help others focus on the overall mission and vision rather than on the day-to-day challenges and crises.[1]

MANAGING STRATEGICALLY

There is a fundamental difference between leadership and management. Whereas leaders strive to influence followers to perform at exemplary levels, managers strive to effectively and efficiently plan, organize, staff, direct, coordinate, report, budget for,[2] and evaluate organizational functions, systems, and processes. Experience and observations suggest that effective strategic managers also take steps to ensure efficient and effective implementation of the organization's strategies, tactics, major tasks, and minor tasks; ensure that the organization's teams perform in a way that produces optimal results and outcomes; and ensure that organizational integration, coordination, incentives, and controls set the stage for optimal individual performance.

To help ensure efficient and effective implementation of your tactics, major tasks, and minor tasks, individuals responsible for managing organizational functions, systems, and processes should:

- Build out the strategic plan to include cost estimates and to create a protected line item in the annual budget dedicated to each strategic goal.
- Establish "mission-critical" priorities and share information (in a variety of ways, using a variety of forums) on what must start, stop, and continue.
- Develop sound project plans containing defined objectives, responsible parties, critical dates, and metrics to augment the action plan.
- Work with other members of the organization to build out the communication and change management plans to include specific, multifaceted actions to increase understanding, buy-in, commitment, and advocacy of the strategic plan.
- Take steps to ensure that organizational systems and processes (e.g., performance management, employee performance evaluation, and salary administration, etc.) reinforce decisions and behaviors critical to strategy execution.
- Manage organizational systems and processes to properly recognize, reward, and reinforce decisions and behaviors contributing to the organization's short- and long-term success.
- Create and execute a strategy for acquiring, developing, and retaining talented individuals who possess the knowledge, skills, and abilities critical to strategy execution.
- Take steps to continuously improve the effectiveness and efficiency of "mission-critical" functions, systems, and processes.
- Conduct monthly report-outs to showcase progress being made, successes being achieved, lessons being learned, and best practices needing to be communicated throughout the organization.
- Monitor external forces and internal factors, identify challenges and opportunities, and take steps to address the challenges and take advantage of the opportunities.

To ensure that the organization's teams perform in a way that produces optimal results and outcomes, individuals responsible for managing organizational functions, systems, and processes should work with the team leader(s) to:

- Establish or clarify—
  ○ The purpose or reason for the team's existence.
  ○ How the team will contribute to the organization's short- and long-term success.

○ Goals the team is expected to achieve and ground rules it will employ to ensure efficient and effective performance and optimal success.

○ Critical dates and metrics designed to further guide team focus and tempo.

• Form or develop a team of individuals with the knowledge, skills, and abilities required to achieve the team's goals—

○ Assess team members to ensure they possess the required knowledge, skills, and abilities.

○ As needed, acquire required capabilities and/or develop the existing team members.

• Establish and communicate team and team member expectations, and monitor effort, behavior, and performance to ensure that team actions and activities—

○ Are conducted in an efficient and effective manner.

○ Follow the ground rules.

○ Reflect individual and team effort and contribute to individual and team accomplishment.

○ Directly or indirectly contribute to the organization's short- and long-term success.

• Establish, modify, or refine processes, tools, and techniques that team members will use to ensure efficient and effective performance and optimal success—

○ Develop the processes, tools, and techniques.

○ Orient team members to the purpose and proper administration, implementation, or conduct of each process, tool, and technique.

○ Take steps to ensure that team members know how to properly administer, implement, or conduct each process, tool, and technique.

○ Monitor performance and, as appropriate, reinforce and reward or provide corrective feedback.

• Manage team and individual team member performance, results, and outcomes to ensure optimal short- and long-term success—

○ Recognize and reward exemplary team and individual team member performance.

○ Take steps to correct inappropriate behavior and to enhance or improve suboptimal performance.

○ Identify lessons learned and best practices and share them throughout the organization.

○ Take steps to continuously improve team processes, tools, and techniques.

To ensure that organizational integration, coordination, incentives, and controls set the stage for optimal individual performance, individuals responsible for managing functions, systems, and processes should work with functional leaders and system and process owners to ensure that—

- Employees at all levels—
  - Receive accurate and timely information about changes relating to the newly developed or modified strategic plan.
  - Understand how they are expected to contribute to the organization's short- and long-term success.
  - Possess the knowledge, skills, and abilities to effectively and efficiently contribute to the organization's short- and long-term success.
  - Receive information about lessons learned and best practices.
  - Are briefed on behavioral changes needing to occur as soon as the need for such change is known.
  - Receive accurate information and proper guidance and direction from their supervisors and colleagues.
  - Are recognized and rewarded for exemplary behavior, receive corrective feedback for inappropriate behavior, and receive the guidance, direction, and support needed to enhance or improve suboptimal performance.
- Organizational components and elements key to the organization's short- and long-term success are in place—
  - Systems, processes, and technology critical to the organization's success have been acquired, developed, or implemented.
  - People possessing capabilities critical to the organization's success are being employed and retained.
  - Cultural attributes conducive to optimal behavior and performance are recognized, emphasized, celebrated, and reinforced.
- The organization's action, communication, and change management plans emphasize and reinforce—
  - Behaviors, actions, and activities critical to the organization's short- and long-term success.
  - Changes in focus, behavior, performance, and tempo relating to the organization's newly created or modified strategic plan.
  - The means by which the organization will address current and emerging external threats and internal weaknesses and take advantage of or capitalize on internal strengths and external opportunities.
  - The organization's value proposition and its newly developed or modified mission, vision, sweet spot, and values.
  - The organization's strategic goals and how they translate into tactics, major tasks, and minor tasks.

- How members of the organization will work together in a coordinated and integrated way to accomplish the organization's mission and attain its vision.

- How the organization will monitor the external environment to identify changing trends likely to impact the organization's mission and vision.

- How the organization will learn about changing customer and client needs and expectations.

- How the organization will nurture and further develop its network of suppliers and distributors.

SERVING AS THE FACILITATOR OR COACH

The strategic planning framework, model, or process your organization adopts will require certain capabilities and behaviors on the part of the individuals guiding and directing your strategic planning effort. To help ensure optimal strategy formulation and execution, it is important that one or more individuals function as your organization's strategy facilitator and coach.

Functioning as a Facilitator

The facilitator will provide consultation and advice on your strategic planning framework, model, or process and on the tools and techniques likely to prove useful throughout the strategic planning effort. Throughout the strategic planning session, the facilitator guides, directs, and supports the planning team's behavior and performance.

More specifically, the individual serving as your facilitator will help your strategic planning team:

- Plan, structure, and conduct efficient and productive meetings.
- Creatively, effectively, and efficiently generate ideas.
- Identify, analyze, and visually display factors related to an issue (including interrelationships, contributions, and dependencies).
- Come to a consensus on symptoms and root causes.
- Display and record factors that contribute to and otherwise impact decisions so that decision streams can be duplicated and decisions can be audited.
- Record and display the sequence of events in a process so that they can be analyzed and (if appropriate) improved upon.
- Analyze existing and emerging conditions, to identify factors likely to contribute to or impede adoption, deployment, or implementation.
- Identify and analyze—
  - Impediments and obstacles so that realistic countermeasures can be identified, deployed, and implemented.

- Interrelationships that exist between mission-critical issues so that optimal solutions can be identified and prioritized.
- Come to a consensus on the—
  - Utility and viability of solutions.
  - Adoption or sequencing of solutions, given prevailing challenges and available resources.
- Structure follow-on actions so they are likely to occur on time and on budget and yield desired results.
- Efficiently and effectively lead, manage, or personally contribute to the successful implementation of the newly created or modified strategic plan by working together—
  - And with other members of the organization to minimize competing activities.
  - To come to a consensus on how to move forward.
  - To prioritize issues needing to be addressed and actions needing to be taken.
  - To manage disagreement, conflict, and resistance to change.
  - And with colleagues, supervisors, managers, and leaders to overcome silos of doubt and disagreement.
  - To garner needed or additional buy-in and commitment throughout the organization.

The individual serving as your facilitator must be capable of directing, guiding, and supporting the strategic planning session in such a way that allows your planning team to:

- Capitalize on the insights, knowledge, and expertise of its team members.
- Explore factors contributing to the current state and pressures pulling and pushing the organization to a differing future state.
- Investigate alternate futures, future paths, and solutions to existing and emerging challenges and opportunities.
- Take advantage of diverse perspectives and divergent viewpoints.
- Properly handle disagreement and manage conflict.

Such actions help create the environment in which strategic planning team members will be more likely to buy into, contribute to, and advocate to others the importance of supporting the organization's newly created or modified mission, vision, values, strategic goals, tactics, major tasks, and minor tasks. Such actions also help planning team members address issues, draw needed conclusions, and make decisions they consider to be worthwhile and credible. The facilitator's contribution extends well beyond the strategic planning session. Facilitators typically support subsequent strategy execution by helping the organization address mission-critical issues; bring divergent viewpoints, perspectives, and ideas to consensus;

establish project teams; help build out the action plan; reengineer business systems and processes; and capitalize on continuous improvement opportunities.

My experience and observations suggest that facilitators are typically responsible for developing certain documents related to strategic planning. For example, your facilitator might be asked to develop:

- The strategic planning session agenda, including the objectives, process, pre-work assignments, and overview of the session tools, techniques, and deliverables.
- A meeting summary showcasing the process followed and key results and outcomes, which can be used to "audit" decisions made during the planning session.
- Associated work documents, such as the strategic plan, action plan, contingency plan, communication plan, and change management plan.

Functioning as a Coach

The individual serving as your strategy coach will provide personalized guidance and advice to select members of your organization on a broad slate of topics ranging from personal ethics to project management. Such guidance and advice are frequently provided one-on-one and in private; over time, coaches typically develop a close and trusting relationship with the individuals they coach. The coach's role differs from the role of the facilitator in the nature and scope of the advice the coach provides, the relationship the coach forms with his or her client, and the manner in which the advice is provided. Throughout the strategic planning endeavor, the coach guides, advises on, and otherwise supports key team member behavior and performance.

More specifically, the individual serving as your strategy coach will help select team members:

- Gain a better understanding of—and insights pertaining to—the demands and challenges being placed on them.
- Crystallize their understanding of the principles, systems, processes, tools, and techniques that will guide future performance.
- Analyze and gain a better understanding of current dynamics within their various stakeholder groups and executive or management team.
- Learn about how they prefer to—
  - Relate to and influence the situations and circumstances they encounter.
  - Analyze information, make decisions, manage disagreement, and manage conflict.
- Learn how to more effectively—
  - Relate to and influence the situations and circumstances they encounter.
  - Analyze information, make decisions, manage disagreement, and manage conflict.

- Learn how to more efficiently and effectively lead, manage, or personally contribute to the successful implementation of newly created or modified strategic plans by—
  ○ Working with others to minimize competing activities.
  ○ Helping individuals come to a consensus on how to move forward.
  ○ Prioritizing issues needing to be addressed and actions needing to be taken.
  ○ Managing disagreement, conflict, and resistance to change.
  ○ Working with colleagues, supervisors, managers, and leaders to overcome silos of doubt and disagreement.
  ○ Taking steps to garner needed or additional buy-in and commitment throughout the organization.
- Create personal development plans designed to enhance problem solving, decision making, and interpersonal communication with fellow team members and key stakeholders.

The individual serving as your strategy coach must be capable of:

- Interviewing key stakeholders to gain insight into existing issues, pressures confronting the select team member (i.e., the individual receiving coaching) and team, and the group and personal dynamics currently impacting the team.
- Interviewing an adequate number of team members to gain a solid understanding of the dynamics currently at play within the team and to—
  ○ Solicit information on perceptions and opinions of the way the team currently functions.
  ○ Gain a better understanding of underlying assumptions and expectations.
  ○ Learn more about the challenges the team currently faces and the extent to which the team is leveraging its strengths and capabilities to address those challenges.
- Administering a psychological inventory when appropriate and needed to identify factors contributing to, and "blind spots" associated with, how the select team member prefers to (and therefore how he or she typically) communicates, makes decisions, manages change, and manages conflict.
- Providing guidance and advice to allow the select team member to—
  ○ Further explore and better understand his or her personal (and the team's) preferences.
  ○ Develop, and as appropriate, refine his or her personal development plan.
  ○ Monitor the execution of the personal development plan.
  ○ Address and/or capitalize upon unanticipated results and outcomes.
  ○ Modify and update his or her personal development plan.

My experience and observations suggest that coaches are typically responsible for developing work documents to support the coaching process. For example, your strategy coach may need to:

- Document the results of the stakeholder and team interviews—
  - Summarize the notes taken during the stakeholder and team interviews.
  - Share key findings and conclusions with the select team member.
  - Results will contribute to the—
    - Issues discussed and topics explored throughout the coaching sessions.
    - Means the select team member will use to enhance his or her behavior and strengthen his or her performance.
- Report the results of the psychological inventory—
  - Showcase factors contributing to, and "blind spots" associated with, the select team member's preferences for communicating, making decisions, and managing change and conflict.
  - Highlight ways the select team member can bring more balance to his or her personality, more effectively capitalize on the strengths of his or her personality, and/or more effectively use facets of his or her personality in certain situations.
- Help the select team member create a personal development plan to—
  - Minimize, reduce, or mitigate "blind spots" associated with the select team member's preferences for communicating, making decisions, managing change, and managing conflict.
  - Bring more balance to the select team member's personality.
  - Leverage or take advantage of the strengths of the select team member's personality and to more effectively apply them in certain situations.
- Work with the select team member to create and maintain a coaching schedule—
  - Sequence and schedule the sessions to ensure optimal impact.
  - Schedule a combination of face-to-face meetings and telephone conversations.

EVERYONE PARTICIPATING IN STRATEGIC PLANNING

Along with the unique or special capabilities associated with serving as a strategic leader, manager, facilitator, or coach, it is important that everyone contributing to your strategic planning effort be capable of and willing to:

- Analyze and act on relatively—
  - Little information.
  - Complex information.

- Make sound decisions.
- Take reasonable risks.
- Ask insightful questions and contribute divergent viewpoints.
- Communicate with others and express opinions and ideas in a way that does not upset others.
- Work with individuals—
  - With unfamiliar skill sets.
  - From other cultures.
  - From other geographic regions.
- Work in an environment in which a structured framework is applied.
- Exhibit a well-rounded orientation, viewpoint, and perspective.
- Manage disagreement and resolve conflict in an efficient and effective manner.

Such knowledge, skills, and abilities will enhance your strategy formulation and execution and increase the likelihood of optimal short- and long-term success. Building on the principles cited in the previous chapter, it is important that your organization recognize that room for personal improvement always exists and that organizationally, there are always ample opportunities for continuous improvement. It is therefore important that your organization take steps to continuously strengthen its strategic planning, strategy formulation, and strategy execution capabilities.

Although it is unlikely that a majority of any organization's employees possess the knowledge, skills, and abilities to plan, prepare for, lead, facilitate, participate in, and follow up on strategy formulation and execution, it is important that your organization:

- Adopt a strategic planning framework, model, or process to provide needed structure.
- Assign roles such as strategic leader, manager, facilitator, and coach to provide needed guidance and direction to the strategic planning effort.
- Utilize management and planning methodologies, tools, and techniques to help support effective and efficient performance and ensure optimal results and outcomes.

It is also important that everyone participating in your organization's strategic planning effort recognize that the combined strategic planning framework, roles, and tools contribute to—but do not necessarily ensure—optimal performance, results, and outcomes. My experience and observations reinforce the importance of all participants recognizing how each individual's effort, involvement, and input directly or indirectly contribute to or impede performance, results, and outcomes. Such realization spotlights the critical role that each and every member of the organization plays in strategy formulation and execution and the impact (either positive or negative) that one person might have on the strategic planning team's or organization's short- and long-term success.

It is therefore important for you to reconsider an important point made in an earlier chapter. If, for example, you realize that your organization's strategic planning process requires you to think strategically and you are naturally a tactical thinker, keep in mind that all is not lost. You may find that the strategic planning process is a bit frustrating and that forcing yourself to think strategically feels a bit awkward and perhaps takes you a little more time than it does for others. Nevertheless, I encourage you to strive to think strategically anyway and to act on the assumption that (1) the positive result of your effort will outweigh the associated discomfort and (2) as you "flex your strategic thinking muscle," it will become less challenging, you will begin to feel less awkward, and it will eventually require less effort and time. Such exemplary effort will allow you to provide positive input, force you to deal with discomfort in an appropriate way, and compel you to explore tools and techniques likely to help you address personal blind spots and biases and contribute to your organization's strategic planning effort.

Chapter 9

Ensuring Optimal Execution

By this point, the members of your strategic planning team have carefully analyzed volumes of data and information; considered a myriad of factors, topics, and issues; reflected on your organization's purpose and reason for existence; factored conclusions drawn on all of the above into the development, refinement, or verification of your organization's mission, vision, sweet spot, and values; and identified the means by which your organization will achieve short- and long-term success. Your organization now has:

- A strategic plan to help it accomplish its mission and attain its vision.
- A contingency plan to help it address unexpected and unanticipated challenges.
- Supplemental communication and change management plans to help ensure—
  - Constant and consistent enterprise-wide strategy execution.
  - Possession by everyone of the needed levels of awareness, understanding, buy-in, commitment, and advocacy.
- Continuous improvement tactics in place to help—
  - Ensure increasingly more effective and efficient strategy formulation.
  - Further strengthen the way it implements strategies to ensure increasingly more effective and efficient execution.
- Tactics in place to help—
  - Strengthen its overall strategic planning, strategy formulation, and strategy execution capabilities.
  - Create a cadre of employees capable of—

- Planning, preparing for, leading, supporting, participating in, and following up on strategy formulation and execution.
- Effectively functioning as strategic leader, manager, facilitator, coach, and/ or participant.

To further ensure optimal strategy execution and increase the likelihood of optimal short- and long-term success, my experience and observations suggest that your organization should set the stage for success by identifying and utilizing an executive sponsor; manage natural biases and blind spots by developing and utilizing a balanced scorecard; and strengthen commitment and advocacy by properly managing its various key stakeholders.

KEY LEARNING POINT

It is important that your organization set the stage for success by identifying and utilizing an executive sponsor, manage natural biases and blind spots by developing and utilizing a balanced scorecard, and strengthen commitment and advocacy by properly managing its various key stakeholders.

IDENTIFYING AND UTILIZING AN EXECUTIVE SPONSOR

Prior to exploring the importance of identifying and utilizing an executive sponsor, I encourage you to consider the organizational environment within which you plan to introduce and subsequently implement your newly developed or modified strategic plan. Does it consist of or contain:

- Numerous goals, objectives, metrics, initiatives, programs, and projects, some of which are competing for time, energy, resources, and/or funding?
- Numerous focal points that require time, interest, and energy from individuals who have only a certain amount of time, interest, and energy?
- Existing and ongoing strategies, tactics, and major and minor tasks that require everyone's time and attention?
- A stream of previous decisions and actions that contributed to the organization's current level of success and its current reputation within its industry, profession, and community?
- Enthusiasm around existing and ongoing goals, objectives, metrics, initiatives, programs, projects, strategies, tactics, tasks, and other focal points?
- An existing tempo or momentum heading in the previously established direction?

If such variables do exist, they will impact or influence the introduction and implementation of your organization's newly developed or modified strategic plan in some way, shape, or form. The degree to which such variables adversely impact or influence your newly developed or modified strategic plan will depend largely on the nature, scope, and magnitude of change associated with the strategic plan; impact may be rather severe if your strategic plan includes a new or different mission, a new vision, and new strategic goals, major tactics, and minor tactics; involves the adoption, deployment, installation, or execution of new technology, systems, or processes; and/or requires organizational members to change their focus and tempo.

How important is it that you identify and utilize an executive sponsor? My experience and observations lead me to believe that an executive sponsor will increase the likelihood of your achieving optimal short- and long-term success to the same extent that (1) such variables exist within your organization and (2) your newly developed or modified strategic plan requires the members of your organization to change the way they think, behave, and perform. In short, your strategic planning endeavor creates the need for your organization to recalibrate its attention and focus and reemphasize or redirect its effort and resources. Such recalibration and change in emphasis or direction create the need for identifying and utilizing an executive sponsor.

The individual serving as your executive sponsor will help set the stage for your short- and long-term success in several important ways. He or she will help individuals responsible for leading and managing your strategy execution make credible decisions and take reasonable and responsible action—within the context of prevailing cultural norms and organizational assumptions and expectations—and thus establish credibility. Your executive sponsor—a person in a position to formally and informally influence the perspectives, decisions, behavior, and performance of others—will help reduce, mitigate, and otherwise nullify the adverse impact that competing priorities, conflicting initiatives, and organizational politics have on the newly developed or modified strategic plan. Your sponsor will also take steps to address significant resource, budgetary, and other challenges, obstacles, and barriers that may impede strategy execution; share lessons learned and best practices; and recognize and reinforce efforts and actions contributing to—and otherwise promote—successful execution throughout the organization. More specifically, the individual serving as your executive sponsor will:

- Personally advocate the importance of the newly developed or modified strategic plan (and its associated strategic goals, tactics, major tasks, and minor tasks) to leaders, executives, managers, and supervisors.
- Emphasize the strategic plan's importance when discussing general issues, topics, and subjects with—
  - Internal stakeholders and external constituents.
  - Network members (e.g., suppliers and distributors).
- Advocate the importance of modifying technology, systems, and processes to support and reinforce behaviors that are important to the organization's short- and long-term success.

- Personally model new ways of thinking, behaving, and performing that are important to the organization achieving its mission and attaining its vision.
- Encourage leaders, executives, managers, and supervisors to, in turn, model behaviors that are essential to the organization's short- and long-term success.
- Encourage operational and functional leaders and system and process owners to work in a planned, purposeful, coordinated, and unified manner to ensure optimal strategy execution.
- Facilitate the establishment of needed internal and external relationships, partnerships, and alliances to help ensure optimal strategy execution.
- Encourage leaders and executives to incorporate strategic plan–related objectives and metrics into their systems and processes (e.g., the performance management system and employee evaluation process).
- While encouraging other leaders and executives to do the same, personally monitor progress and take steps to—
  - Address impediments, obstacles, and barriers.
  - Share lessons learned and duplicate best practices throughout the organization.
- While encouraging all other members of the organization to do the same, personally strive to continuously improve the way the organization formulates and executes strategy.
- Work with other leaders and executives to manage disagreement, resolve conflict, and manage crises relating to strategy formulation and execution.

DEVELOPING AND USING A BALANCED SCORECARD

Your strategic planning team has approached strategic planning in a deliberate and purposeful way; a strategic planning framework, model, or process has guided the planning team's focus and energy; and management and planning methodologies, tools, and techniques have strengthened the analyses the team conducted, the conclusions it drew, and the decisions it made. In short, your strategic planning team has taken major steps to ensure optimal strategy formulation and execution by reducing, avoiding, or mitigating natural biases and blind spots otherwise likely to impact or influence the planning team's performance and deliverables.

As your organization strives to translate its strategic goals into concrete actions, it is important that your employees (at all levels, especially leaders, executives, managers, and supervisors):

- Focus their time, attention, and resources on the multitude of factors—rather than the one or two that for whatever reason resonate with your leaders or stakeholders—driving your organization's short- and long-term success.
- Take steps to ensure that divisions, departments, and units work in a coordinated and integrated manner to achieve system-wide success, rather than success that

is limited to isolated areas and/or has little or no impact on helping the organization achieve its mission and attain its vision.

- Produce results and outcomes—
  - Likely to be valued by your customers, clients, and surrounding community.
  - In such a way that will benefit your internal stakeholders and external constituents.
- Monitor enterprise-wide performance, results, and outcomes to identify and communicate lessons learned and duplicate best practices throughout the organization.

Your Organization's Balanced Scorecard

Kaplan and Norton[1] published an important book some time ago that emphasizes the importance of organizations clarifying their mission, vision, and strategy; linking strategic objectives to concrete actions and measures; aligning and coordinating strategic initiatives and programs; and identifying and sharing lessons learned throughout the organization. To help ensure optimal performance, results, and outcomes, they encourage organizations to develop a "balanced scorecard" of realistic and meaningful objectives and metrics to help employees (at all levels) focus their attention, direct their performance, and ensure continuous improvement.

To ensure optimal organizational success, Kaplan and Norton emphasize that employee performance, results, and outcomes must impact internal and external stakeholder groups in a positive way. To help ensure such positive impact, they stress the importance of assessing organization performance from two separate and distinct perspectives:

- From an external perspective—
  - How clients or customers perceive an organization's services and products.
  - How shareholders perceive an organization's financial success.
- From an internal perspective—
  - Issues (such as technology, systems, or processes) in which an organization must excel.
  - Areas (such as learning or innovation) in which an organization must improve and/or by which it will strengthen its products or services.

Kaplan and Norton stress the importance of establishing objectives and metrics relating to:

- Financial performance—
  - Growth.
  - Income.
  - Earnings.

- ○ Revenue.
- ○ Profitability.
- ○ Return on assets.
- ○ Return on investment.
- • Customer expectations and requirements—
  - ○ Price of services or products.
  - ○ Extent to which services and products meet or exceed customer and client expectations and requirements.
  - ○ Product performance.
  - ○ Timeliness of service delivery or product availability.
- • Internal technology, systems, and processes—
  - ○ Quality of distributed products and delivered services.
  - ○ Cost of poor quality (e.g., rework).
  - ○ Time to—
    - ▪ Recognize and address new and changing customer or client expectations and requirements.
    - ▪ Respond to a customer or client request.
    - ▪ Design, manufacture, distribute, sell, or ship a new product.
    - ▪ Design, develop, sell, and deliver a new service.
  - ○ Ease of system modification, change-out, or expansion.
  - ○ Degree to which product and service specifications are met without wasted time, energy, or effort.
- • Innovation, learning, and development—
  - ○ Extent to which employees (at all levels) develop their knowledge, skills, and abilities.
  - ○ Extent to which the organization—
    - ▪ Strives to continuously improve its systems and processes.
    - ▪ Develops new products and services to meet customer and client expectations and requirements.
  - ○ Change, creativity, and/or innovation that occurs throughout the organization.

Such broad-based and multifaceted objectives and metrics help employees (at all levels) understand the multitude of factors, decisions, and actions contributing to optimal organizational performance, results, and outcomes and help ensure that employees (at all levels) direct sufficient focus, time, and effort toward them.

Conversations with numerous leaders, executives, and graduate students suggest that public- and private-sector, profit and nonprofit, and small, medium, and large organizations have embraced the balanced scorecard and now use it to help ensure clarity, alignment, direction, coordination, progress, achievement, and continuous improvement. I therefore recommend that your strategic planning team take advantage of this valuable tool and use it to help ensure optimal strategy execution.

Creating Your Organization's Balanced Scorecard

When working together to create your organization's balanced scorecard, the members of your planning team should apply the principles and practices they used throughout the strategic planning session. With those principles and practices in mind, your strategic planning team might find the following process to be useful and beneficial when developing your organization's balanced scorecard:

- Members of the planning team meet to develop your balanced scorecard.
- A team member volunteers to facilitate this process; he or she initially posts four sets of flip chart paper on a wall surface and writes—
  - "Financial Performance" on the first flip chart sheet and leaves the next sheet blank.
  - "Customer Expectations and Requirements" on the third flip chart sheet and leaves the next sheet blank.
  - "Internal Technology, Systems, and Processes" on the fifth flip chart sheet and leaves the next sheet blank.
  - "Innovation, Learning, and Development" on the seventh flip chart sheet and leaves the last sheet blank.
- The facilitator reads your organization's first strategic goal and its associated tactics, major tasks, and minor tasks out loud to the other planning team members.
- The team decides whether the first strategic goal relates to financial performance; customer expectations and requirements; internal technology, systems, and processes; or innovation, learning, and development.
- The facilitator writes the strategic goal at the top of the sheet of flip chart paper containing the appropriate heading.
- The team members repeat the process until they have decided on all of your organization's strategic goals and the facilitator has added each strategic goal to the sheets of flip chart paper containing the appropriate headings.
- The team should review the results to ensure that all four perspectives contain one or more strategic goals. Such coverage will help ensure that your employees (at all levels)—
  - Focus their time, attention, and resources on the multitude of factors—rather than the one or two that, for whatever reason, resonate with your leaders or stakeholders—driving your organization's short- and long-term success.

- ○ Take steps to ensure that divisions, departments, and units work in a coordinated and integrated manner to achieve system-wide success, rather than success limited to isolated areas and/or having little or no impact on the organization achieving its mission and attaining its vision.
- ○ Produce results and outcomes—
  - ▪ Likely to be valued by your customers, clients, and surrounding community.
  - ▪ In such a way that will benefit your internal stakeholders and external constituents.
- ○ Monitor enterprise-wide performance, results, and outcomes to identify and communicate lessons learned and duplicate best practices throughout the organization.
- • Once your planning team has ensured adequate coverage, the facilitator reads the first strategic goal listed on the first flip chart sheet, along with its tactics, major tasks, and minor tasks.
- • Team members brainstorm objectives and metrics for that particular goal. Experience and observations suggest that your team will brainstorm and decide on the objectives and then brainstorm and decide on the metrics or decide on the objectives and metrics at roughly the same time. Your planning team should follow the approach it believes works best.
- • As your team agrees on each objective and metric, the facilitator writes it on the blank sheet of flip chart paper next to the strategic goal. Once objectives and metrics are listed for each strategic goal, the facilitator and planning team direct their attention to the next stated strategic goal.
- • Your team members repeat the process until they have established objectives and metrics for all of your organization's strategic goals.
- • Your planning team is not expected to develop "x" number of objectives and metrics for each strategic goal. However, it should review the overall results to ensure that each strategic goal contains an adequate number of objectives and metrics so that critical success factors are put into place to drive and enable your organization's short- and long-term success.
- • Once your planning team is comfortable with the results of its effort, it should:
  - ○ Share the draft balanced scorecard with the remainder of the strategic planning team and other internal stakeholders.
  - ○ Solicit feedback from other planning team members and internal stakeholders on—
    - ▪ The appropriateness of the strategic goal(s) assigned to each category (or perspective).
    - ▪ The adequacy of the objectives and metrics assigned to each strategic goal.
  - ○ Incorporate the refined balanced scorecard into your organization's action plan.

The balanced scorecard your strategic planning team creates will be unique to your organization. Nevertheless, your planning team might find the sample balanced scorecard presented in Figure 9.1 useful and beneficial as it drafts and refines your organization's contingency plan.

This figure presents the four perspectives typically included in an organization's balanced scorecard, along with the strategic goals associated with the four

Figure 9.1   Sample Balanced Scorecard

Scorecard Category/Perspective	Strategic Goals, Objectives, and Metrics

Financial Performance	• Strategic Goal: improve our financial performance to match or exceed 95 percent of the companies in the intermodal transportation industry.
	• Objectives:
	  ○ Increase shareholder value by 7 percent.
	  ○ Decrease costs by 9 percent.
	  ○ Increase revenue by 3 percent.
	• Metrics:
	  ○ Shareholder value increases 7 percent or more.
	  ○ Costs decrease 9 percent or more.
	  ○ Revenue increases 3 percent or more.

Customer Expectations	• Strategic Goal: our customer service is ranked No. 1 in the intermodal transport industry.
	• Objectives:
	  ○ Increase overall customer satisfaction scores 4.5 percent.
	  ○ Increase satisfaction scores of our strategic customers 4 percent.
	  ○ Increase market share 9 percent.
	• Metrics:
	  ○ Overall customer satisfaction scores increase 4.5 percent or more.
	  ○ Strategic customer satisfaction scores increase 4 percent or more.
	  ○ Market share increases 9 percent or more.

Internal Technology, Systems, and Processes	• Strategic Goal: the speed of our intermodal transport process is ranked as one of the top three in North America.
	• Objectives:
	  ○ Fully deploy our new intermodal integration and coordination system.
	  ○ Fully implement our new shipment schedule package.
	  ○ Conduct transport audits to assess system-wide quality and efficiency.

(Continued)

Figure 9.1   (Continued)

	• Metrics:
	  ○ The new intermodal integration and coordination system is deployed and fully operational throughout the entire enterprise.
	  ○ The new shipment schedule package is deployed and fully operational throughout the entire enterprise.
	  ○ The quarterly transport audit score across all client categories exceeds 9.5.

Innovation, Learning, and Development	• Strategic Goal: our workforce possesses the capabilities to make our customer service rank No. 1 in the intermodal industry.
	• Objectives:
	  ○ Conduct capability assessment to determine current state and identify opportunities for improvement.
	  ○ Determine the capability gap that currently exists and identify ways to address it.
	  ○ Modify the employee development, executive development, and management development programs to address prevailing development needs.
	  ○ Conduct employee development, executive development, and management development programs that strengthen knowledge, skills, and abilities.
	• Metrics:
	  ○ The organization-wide capability assessment is conducted.
	  ○ The capability assessment is conducted; results are analyzed and shared with all members of the organization.
	  ○ The employee, executive, and management development programs are strengthened to address prevailing development needs.
	  ○ The Training and Organizational Development Department conducts employee development, executive development, and management development programs that strengthen knowledge, skills, and abilities.
	  ○ The average score on the training effectiveness surveys completed at the end of each development program exceeds 4.75 on the 5.0-point scale.
	  ○ Our quarterly training effectiveness index exceeds 9.5 on the 10.0-point scale.

perspectives. It also illustrates objectives and metrics your planning team might create for each of the strategic goals.

MANAGING YOUR KEY STAKEHOLDERS

To further ensure optimal strategy execution and increase the likelihood of optimal short- and long-term success, my experience and observations suggest that an organization should strengthen commitment and advocacy by properly managing its various key stakeholders.

An organization's short- and long-term success requires the input, contribution, assistance, and support of everyone within the organization. While leaders, executives, managers, and supervisors have the authority to ask all members of the organization to share ideas, make decisions, and behave and perform in a manner that is consistent with and supportive of the organization's mission, vision, and values, key stakeholders are individuals within an organization who—regardless of their position, role, or title—are capable of substantially contributing to the organization's success and/or to influencing, persuading, or inducing others to exert above-average levels of effort, exhibit ideal behavior, and behave and perform in exemplary ways.

Your Organization's Key Stakeholders

Your key stakeholders are important because they personally and through others will impact your organization's ability to achieve its newly developed, refined, or verified mission. More specifically, they will influence the:

- Degree to which your methodologies, tools, and techniques are deployed, utilized, or implemented according to a design, instruction, or specification, a central element of your organization's efficient operation.
- Sharing of creative ideas, suggestions, and recommendations, an important part of designing, developing, and providing innovative products and services.
- Perspectives, attitudes, and inclinations of individuals to answer questions and respond to requests for support or assistance, which are important to meeting or exceeding the expectations of customers or clients.

Your stakeholders may or may not exert tremendous personal effort, display ideal behavior, or perform in an exemplary manner. They may or may not choose to influence, persuade, or induce others to exert above-average levels of effort, exhibit ideal behavior, or behave and perform in exemplary ways. Optimal execution of your organization's newly created or updated strategic plan relies on your key stakeholders' personal contribution and/or positive influence, persuasion, or inducement. It is therefore important that your strategic planning team (1) determine the likelihood that your key stakeholders will (personally and/or through others) exert above-average levels of effort, exhibit ideal behavior, and perform in exemplary ways to support your organization's strategic plan, and (2) take steps to reposition those key stakeholders who are unlikely to (personally and/or through others) contribute to its optimal implementation.

Managing Your Organization's Key Stakeholders

When working together to manage your organization's key stakeholders, the members of your planning team should apply the principles and practices they used throughout the strategic planning session. With those principles and practices in mind, your strategic planning team might find the following process to be useful and beneficial when analyzing and taking steps to ensure the input, contribution, assistance, and support of your organization's key stakeholders:

- Members of the planning team meet to determine how to solidify the input, contribution, assistance, and support of your organization's key stakeholders.
- A team member volunteers to facilitate this process; he or she initially posts six overlapping sheets of flip chart paper on a wall surface and creates a matrix that contains two major headers, "Key Stakeholder" and "Interest Level."
- The facilitator:
  - Writes "Key Stakeholder" at the top of the first flip chart sheet.
  - Writes "Interest Level" at the top of the flip chart sheet located at the center of the remaining blank sheets of flip chart paper.
  - Underneath the "Interest Level" heading, writes the following five sub-headings spaced equally apart: "Resist," "Neutral," "Accept," "Support," and "Advocate."
- The facilitator describes a key stakeholder as someone in your organization who—regardless of position, role, or title—is personally capable of greatly contributing to your organization's success and/or to influencing, persuading, or inducing others to exert above-average levels of effort, exhibit ideal behavior, and behave and perform in exemplary ways.
- The team works together to identify your organization's key stakeholders.
- The facilitator writes the names of the key stakeholders on the flip chart sheet containing the "Stakeholder" heading.
- The facilitator defines the five interest level categories—
  - Resist: the stakeholder is against or opposes what is required or expected.
  - Neutral: the stakeholder neither opposes nor does what is required or expected.
  - Accept: the stakeholder does what is minimally required or expected.
  - Support: the stakeholder will personally go above and beyond what is required or expected.
  - Advocate: the stakeholder will influence, persuade, or induce others to go above and beyond what is required or expected.
- For the first stakeholder, the—
  - Team members discuss and decide on the amount of interest the stakeholder must have to contribute (personally and/or through others) to your strategic plan's optimal execution.
  - Facilitator writes "D" or "Desired" under the "Resist," "Neutral," "Accept," "Support," or "Advocate" heading.

- ○ Team members discuss and decide on the amount of interest the stakeholder is likely to currently possess.
- ○ Facilitator writes "C" or "Current" under the "Resist," "Neutral," "Accept," "Support," or "Advocate" heading.
- The team members repeat the process until they have analyzed all of your organization's key stakeholders and have decided on each stakeholder's desired and current interest level.
- The planning team members review the results and identify stakeholders who are positioned between the desired and current interest levels. The more space between the two levels, the greater the need for actions to be taken to reposition the stakeholder so that he or she possesses the needed (the "D" or "Desired") level of interest.
- The facilitator highlights each stakeholder who needs to be repositioned as well as his or her current and desired interest levels.
- For each stakeholder needing to be repositioned, the planning team members—
  - ○ Analyze the magnitude of repositioning that needs to occur (e.g., "although currently resistant, we need this stakeholder to become an advocate").
  - ○ Determine actions the strategic planning team can take to reposition the stakeholder from the current to the desired interest level, taking his or her personal values, personality, personal style, and personal preferences into consideration.
- For each action, the planning team identifies a responsible party and sets a critical date or timeframe.
- The facilitator adds the actions, responsible parties, and critical dates and timeframes to the flip chart sheets and develops a document summarizing the planning team's process and results.
- Once your planning team is comfortable with the summary, it should—
  - ○ Share the draft document with the remainder of the strategic planning team.
  - ○ Solicit feedback from other planning team members on—
    - ▪ Whether the list of key stakeholders is appropriate and whether it should be narrowed or broadened.
    - ▪ The accuracy of the interest level assessment.
    - ▪ The adequacy of the recommended actions, responsible parties, and critical dates and timeframes.
  - ○ Incorporate suggestions and recommendations into the summary document.
- Once the summary document is in its final form, the strategic planning team should work with the responsible parties and take steps to ensure that needed actions occur within the specified timeframes.

Figure 9.2 Action Items for Stakeholder Management

Stakeholder	Objective, Action, Responsible Party, and Critical Date

C. Smith	• Objective: reposition from Neutral to Support.
	• Actions:
	  ○ Meet in C. Smith's office.
	  ○ Stress how the tactics, major tasks, and minor tasks will position the organization for optimal business success.
	  ○ Share a copy of last month's industry newsletter, highlighting changes occurring throughout our industry.
	  ○ Use business reasoning and logic when describing purpose, benefits, and implications.
	• Responsible Party: C. Able
	• Critical Date or Timeframe: within five business days.

D. Jones	• Objective: reposition from Resist to Accept.
	• Actions:
	  ○ Have a breakfast, lunch, or dinner meeting with D. Jones.
	  ○ Stress how our new business practices will impact members of the organization in a positive way.
	  ○ Be personable in your interaction.
	  ○ Focus on the assistance and support that will be available to help all employees succeed.
	• Responsible Party: B. Smyth
	• Critical Date or Timeframe: within five business days.

E. Peabody	• Objective: reposition from Resist to Neutral.
	• Actions:
	  ○ Discuss while exercising with E. Peabody before work.
	  ○ Be passionate and excited about the coming changes.
	  ○ Stress how the tactics, major tasks, and minor tasks will be less challenging than those encountered during the Wilson crisis.
	  ○ Focus on your personal excitement and commitment to helping make these changes work.
	  ○ Stress how we will one day share this story with our children, nieces, or nephews.
	• Responsible Party: V. Long
	• Critical Date or Timeframe: within five business days.

F. Goode	• Objective: reposition from Accept to Advocate.
	• Actions:
	  ○ Meet in F. Goode's office.
	  ○ Stress how changes we are making will position the organization for optimal business success.
	  ○ Use business reasoning and logic when describing purpose, benefits, and implications.
	  ○ Be sure to mention that thought leaders at the U of I School of Business are excited about the changes we are making within our organization.

Figure 9.2   (Continued)

	• Responsible Party: D. Roseman • Critical Date or Timeframe: within 10 business days.

J. Poste	• Objective: reposition from Accept to Support.
	• Actions:
	  ◦ Have lunch with J. Poste.
	  ◦ Stress how our new business practices will impact our strategic customers in a positive way.
	  ◦ Be personable in your interaction.
	  ◦ Focus on training programs being offered to help employees succeed.
	  ◦ Mention that we will be using social networking systems to update employees on progress and overall success.
	• Responsible Party: D. Litaker
	• Critical Date or Timeframe: within 10 business days.

M. Sides	• Objective: reposition from Support to Advocate.
	• Actions:
	  ◦ Discuss while walking around the courtyard with M. Sides after lunch.
	  ◦ Be passionate and excited about the coming changes.
	  ◦ Stress how the challenges we now face are less challenging than those encountered during the Wilson crisis.
	  ◦ Focus on your personal optimism and confidence.
	  ◦ Stress how our new products will be the most innovative in our industry.
	• Responsible Party: E. Thompson
	• Critical Date or Timeframe: within 10 business days.

The process your strategic planning team uses and the documents it creates to help manage your key stakeholders will be unique to your organization. However, your planning team might find the sample stakeholder-related action items presented in Figure 9.2 useful and beneficial as it analyzes and identifies ways to reposition your organization's key stakeholders.

This figure illustrates how your strategic planning team might summarize actions that need to occur to reposition your organization's key stakeholders. It also illustrates how those actions will differ from person to person to match the particular stakeholder's personal values, personality, personal style, and personal preferences.

Your planning team's effort to manage your organization's key stakeholders does not end once steps have been taken to "position" the key stakeholders to substantially contribute to your organization's success and/or to influence, persuade, or induce others to exert above-average levels of effort, exhibit ideal behavior, and behave and perform in exemplary ways. Rather, it is important that planning team members periodically meet to reassess the current and desired interest levels of your key stakeholders and, as needed, take action to reposition key stakeholders to strengthen buy-in and commitment.

Chapter 10

Planning Methodologies, Tools, and Techniques

While laying the groundwork for strategic planning and as you work with others to prepare for, carry out, and follow up on your strategic planning session, I encourage you to apply the methodologies, tools, and techniques introduced throughout this book. They are designed to help you move forward on your strategic planning journey in an efficient and effective way and to reduce, avoid, or mitigate the obstacles, impediments, and barriers you are likely to face along the way.

The methodologies, tools, and techniques described and applied throughout this book are reproduced on the following pages. While additional information about when you should use these methodologies, tools, and techniques is provided elsewhere in this book, this chapter provides guidance, instructions, and directions on how to derive the most benefit from their use. While exploring strategic planning, when preparing to launch your planning effort, while undertaking your journey, and as you strive to continuously improve, I encourage you to review the methodologies, tools, and techniques illustrated in Samples of Application 10.1 to 10.9, determine their utility, and apply them when useful and beneficial.

PROCESS FOR CREATING A MISSION STATEMENT

Your strategic planning team members should work together to create your organization's mission statement; a useful process for doing this involves:

- Dividing the team into two or three subgroups.
- Having each subgroup create a draft mission statement, taking these questions into consideration—
  - What are the underlying nature, focus, and intent of our organization?

Sample of Application 10.1

SAMPLE BILLFORD OR WALLET REMINDER CARD

Why Us?

- Although we have been successful, we undoubtedly could be much more successful.
- Strategic planning supports our focus on continuous improvement.
- Strategic planning will help us clarify our thinking, focus our effort and actions, and do all that is needed to ensure short- and long-term future success.

Why Strategic Planning?

- It will allow us to take a multitude of factors into consideration when we decide on our future.
- It will help us make decisions about how our systems, technology, processes, people, and technology will contribute to our future success.
- When it comes to meeting the needs of our clients, strategic planning will help us "do the right things for the right reasons."

Why Now?

- We have historically been challenged—and are being increasingly challenged—when it comes to having adequate money or resources.
- We have previously gone about our business in a rather piecemeal, happenstance way. Strategic planning will provide some much-needed direction as well as the structure we need to be more focused regarding future decisions and actions.
- Added direction and focus will benefit us, our colleagues, and our clients.

Sample of Application 10.2

SAMPLE AWARENESS-RAISING E-MAIL OR MEMORANDUM

Date: Today's date
To: Members of our leadership team
From: A. B. Smith

Subject: Results of Research on Strategic Planning

I have completed researching the topic of strategic planning. I have reviewed books written by noted authors and have considered their advice and comments within the context of our organization. Although we feel that we have achieved a certain level of success during our three years of existence, we as a leadership team feel confident we can do better. My research suggests that strategic planning is one tool likely to prove useful as we strive to continuously improve and set the stage for even higher levels of short- and long-term future success!

Advantages of Strategic Planning

A strategic plan, in short, serves as a roadmap to an organization's future. Strategic planning is not new; applications in the public and private sectors have proven time and again that the strategic planning process adds structure to an organization's planning efforts and helps ensure proper analysis, adequate strategy formulation, and successful execution. The strategic planning session (or series of sessions) serves as a forum; it gives members of the organization the opportunity to think strategically and to exercise their "strategic management muscle." Strategic planning requires members of an organization to:

- Consider prevailing and emerging external forces and internal factors.
- Evaluate what they currently do, where they currently are (for example, within the competitive landscape), and where they hope to be or what they hope to become.
- Consider alternate futures, various strategic intents and goals, and different means for realizing the intent and achieving the goals.
- Recognize resource limitations (including facilities, equipment, supplies, time information, money, and capabilities).
- Recognize uncertainty and therefore formulate contingencies.
- Select and prioritize options so that whatever future actions they take are likely to yield results and outcomes consistent with and supportive of the organization's mission and vision.

Advantages to Our Organization

As you know, we have been reflecting on how we function as a leadership team. Within the context of those discussions and based on what I have learned about strategic planning, I sincerely believe that embarking on a strategic planning effort will benefit our organization in these ways:

- The personal biases of a handful of people will no longer overly influence our organization's focus.
- Decisions impacting the organization's success will become more credible in our eyes and in the eyes of our people.
- The decisions we make in the future will no longer occur in a vacuum, but rather within the context of a clearly defined mission and articulated future.
- We as a leadership team will be more confident that the decisions our executives make pertaining to our systems, processes, technology, and people contribute to the organization's success rather than the success of a particular division, department, or unit.
- We will stop making decisions pertaining to the services and products we offer to our clients in a vacuum; rather, we will include a stakeholder representative in our process or consider stakeholder input obtained through interviews or surveys.

Next Steps

I encourage you to give some personal thought to this issue and to perhaps explore the topics of strategic thinking, strategic planning, and strategic management. I ask that we devote a portion of our next "Friday Leadership Team Meeting" to the topic of strategic planning, with the objective of deciding whether embarking on a strategic planning effort is likely to benefit our organization, our people, and our clients.

For More Information

Numerous articles, books, and white papers have been written on the topic of strategic planning, and I am confident that a review of the trade journals you typically read will yield quite a few articles on this topic. I found the following three books to be of immense value in my personal learning:

- Hrebiniak, Lawrence G. 2005. *Making Strategy Work*. Upper Saddle River, NJ: Wharton School Publishing.
- Mintzberg, Henry, Joseph Lampel, and Bruce Ahlstrand. 2008. *Strategy Safari: A Guided Tour through the Wilds of Strategic Management*. New York: The Free Press.
- Kim, W. Chan, and Renee Mauborgne. 2005. *Blue Ocean Strategy*. Boston: Harvard Business School Press.

Sample of Application 10.3

ADDRESSING CHALLENGES TO STRATEGIC PLANNING

If you discover that . . .	Consider . . .
Senior leadership does not consider strategic planning to be important to your organization's future.	• Arrange for your leader and/or leadership team to meet with or speak to strategic planning thought leaders (researchers, authors, and icons of your particular industry or profession). • Send key members of your leadership team to strategic planning workshops or sessions sponsored by respected institutes, colleges, universities, think tanks, or consultancies. • Share additional information with the leader and/or leadership team during private meetings. • Brief the leader and/or leadership team during normally scheduled business meetings. • Seek out information about the experience that board members have pertaining to strategic planning and share the information with the leader and/or leadership team. • Share articles on strategic planning from professional journals to which the leader and/or leadership team subscribe. • Share white papers on strategic planning from professional associations to which the leader and/or leadership team belong.
Executives and managers do not understand strategic management or do not consider strategic planning to be an important part of strategic management.	• Arrange for key executives or managers to speak with a strategic planning thought leader in a respected college or university. • Arrange for key executives or managers to speak with their counterparts in similar (but noncompeting) organizations that recently tackled strategic planning. • Share additional information with executives and managers who are held in exceptionally high regard by their fellow executives and managers. • Share additional information with executives and managers during normally scheduled executive and management team meetings. • Find out from your organization's training department (if it has one) if it has any materials or courses on strategic planning; if so, share the materials or information with the executives and managers or ask the training department to offer a special briefing or offer the briefing during a normally scheduled executive or management team meeting.

- Share articles on strategic planning from professional journals, emphasizing to the executives and managers that the articles are from professional journals to which the leader and/or leadership team subscribe.
- Share white papers on strategic planning from professional associations, emphasizing to the executives and managers that the papers are from professional associations to which the leader and/or leadership team belong.
- If your organization's leaders and/or leadership team recognize the importance of strategic planning and agree to advocate strategy formulation and execution, ask the leader or select members of the leadership team to meet with the executives or managers to emphasize to them the importance of strategic planning to the organization and why it is important that executives and managers commit personal and team member time and energy to the strategic planning endeavor.

Supervisors do not consider strategic planning to contribute to organizational performance or continuous improvement.	• Arrange for key supervisors (e.g., in a core area of the organization, from one of the larger stakeholder groups, or a supervisor who is held in exceptionally high regard by superiors, colleagues, and direct reports) to speak with a strategic planning thought leader in a respected college or university. • Arrange for key supervisors to speak with their counterparts in similar (but noncompeting) organizations that recently tackled strategic planning. • Using a variety of means and forums, share additional information with those supervisors held in exceptionally high regard by their fellow supervisors and through direct reports. • Share additional information with all supervisors during normally scheduled meetings. • Find out from your organization's training department (if it has one) if it has any materials or courses on strategic planning; if so, share the materials or information with supervisors or ask the training department to offer a special workshop. • Share articles on strategic planning from professional journals, emphasizing to the supervisors that the articles are from professional journals to which the leadership, executive, or management team subscribe.

	• Share white papers on strategic planning from professional associations, emphasizing to the supervisors that the papers are from professional associations to which the leadership, executive, or management team belong.
	• If your organization's leadership team recognizes the importance of strategic planning and agrees to advocate strategy formulation and execution, ask a select member of the leadership team, accompanied by one or more executives or managers, to meet with the supervisors to emphasize to them the importance of strategic planning to the organization and why it is important that they commit personal and team member time and energy to the strategic planning endeavor.
Members of your organization do not recognize the importance of strategic planning to the organization's— and thus to their personal—success.	• Conduct informational meetings or sessions throughout the organization.
	• If your organization has a cafeteria or formal break areas, set up information desks when a large portion of the organization is likely to see and most likely to approach individuals staffing the desks.
	• Share additional information with key members (i.e., the informal leaders) of your organization who are held in exceptionally high regard by their superiors, colleagues, associates, and/or direct reports.
	• Share additional information with members of your organization during normally scheduled "all-hands" meetings.
	• Find out from your organization's training department (if it has one) if it has any materials or courses on strategic planning; if so, include materials or information in normally scheduled or "special circumstance" newsletters.
	• Find out from your organization's training department if it has any materials or courses on strategic planning; if so, ask them to offer special or additional sessions and/or showcase the information and materials during normally scheduled business programs or business meetings.
	• Share articles on strategic planning from professional journals to which a large segment of your organization subscribe.

- Share white papers on strategic planning from professional associations to which a large segment of your organization belong.
- If your organization's leaders and/or leadership team recognize the importance of strategic planning and agree to advocate strategy formulation and execution, ask the leader or members of the leadership team, accompanied by select executives, managers, and supervisors, to conduct special meetings (perhaps an all-hands meeting or a series of department or division meetings) to emphasize to everyone the importance of strategic planning to the organization and why it is important for everyone to personally commit to supporting and assisting with the strategic planning endeavor.

Members of your organization do not understand what strategy formulation entails in terms of the concepts and principles that typically contribute to successful strategy formulation and execution.	<ul><li>Add books on strategic planning and professional journals containing articles on strategic planning to your organization's library. If your organization does not have a library, purchase a bookcase and place it (and the relevant reading material) in an area that many of your leaders, executives, managers, supervisors, and individual contributors are likely to visit.</li><li>Distribute a reading list of materials on and about strategic planning throughout your organization and make it easy for everyone to borrow books or journals containing information on strategic planning.</li><li>Send representatives to public courses or workshops on strategic planning.</li><li>Conduct informational meetings or sessions throughout the organization.</li><li>If your organization has a cafeteria or formal break areas, set up information desks when a large portion of the organization is likely to see and most likely to approach individuals staffing the desks.</li><li>Share additional information with key members (i.e., the informal leaders) of your organization who are held in exceptionally high regard by their superiors, colleagues, associates, and/or through direct reports.</li><li>Share additional information with members of your organization during normally scheduled "all-hands" meetings.</li></ul>

- Find out from your organization's training department (if it has one) if it has any materials or courses on strategic planning; if so, include materials or information in normally scheduled or "special circumstance" newsletters.
- Find out from your organization's training department if it has any materials or courses on strategic planning; if so, ask them to offer special or additional sessions and/or showcase the information and materials during normally scheduled business programs or business meetings.
- Share articles on strategic planning from professional journals to which a large segment of your organization subscribe.
- Share white papers on strategic planning from professional associations to which a large segment of your organization belong.
- If your organization's leaders and/or leadership team recognize the importance of strategic planning and agree to advocate strategy formulation and execution, ask the leader or members of the leadership team, accompanied by select executives, managers, and supervisors, to conduct special meetings (perhaps an all-hands meeting or a series of department or division meetings) to emphasize to everyone the importance of strategic planning to the organization and why it is important for everyone to personally commit to supporting and assisting with the strategic planning endeavor.

Members of your organization do not possess tools and techniques likely to prove useful in formulating strategy, preparing the organization for execution, and implementing and deploying the resulting strategic plan.	• Add books on strategic planning models, frameworks, approaches, principles, tools, and techniques to your organization's library. Add professional journals containing articles on strategic planning models, frameworks, approaches, principles, tools, and techniques to your organization's library. If your organization does not have a library, purchase a bookcase and place it (and the relevant reading material) in an area that a large segment of your leaders, executives, managers, supervisors, and individual contributors are likely to visit.

- Distribute a reading list of materials on and about strategic planning models, frameworks, approaches, principles, tools, and techniques throughout your organization and make it easy for everyone to borrow books or journals containing information on strategic planning.
- Send representatives to public courses or workshops on strategic planning models, frameworks, approaches, principles, tools, and techniques.
- Conduct informational meetings or sessions on strategic planning models, frameworks, approaches, principles, tools, and techniques throughout the organization.
- If your organization has a cafeteria or formal break areas, set up information desks (showcasing sample strategic planning models, frameworks, approaches, principles, tools, and techniques) when a large portion of the organization is likely to see and most likely to approach individuals staffing the desks.

Sample of Application 10.4

TEMPLATE FOR STRATEGIC PLANNING SESSION PARTICIPANT MATRIXS

Name	Will Provide Access to Intel or Specialty Knowledge	Will Help Identify Forces and Factors Impacting Our Ability to Succeed	Will Help Set the Stage for Effective and Efficient Execution	Will Help Identify Impediments and Associated Counterme asures	Will Help Us Continuously Improve

Note: Insert each participant's name and indicate key contribution(s) by placing a ■ in the appropriate cell(s).

Sample of Application 10.5

SAMPLE PARTICIPANT NOTIFICATION E-MAIL OR MEMORANDUM

Date: Today's date
To: Dale Litaker
From: A. B. Smith

Subject: Invitation to Participate in Strategic Planning

This correspondence follows up the briefing I gave to the executive team last month and the face-to-face meeting you and I had last week. As you know, we are about to embark on a strategic planning endeavor that will initially involve a five-day meeting being conducted October 15–19 at the Ridgeway Conference Center. The accompanying agenda provides detailed information on the focus of the week, issues the planning team will address, topics of discussion, and decisions we plan to make throughout the meeting. As you and I concluded last week, although this meeting and subsequent actions will require an investment of time and effort on everyone's part, strategic planning is a natural continuation of all we have previously done to achieve our current level of success and will undoubtedly prove useful as we strive to continuously improve and set the stage for even greater short- and long-term future success.

You are being asked to participate in the upcoming strategic planning session; we believe your input will be invaluable and that you will prove especially helpful in helping the planning team:

- Understand the people, processes, and technological capabilities that would allow us to accelerate our design–build process.

- Analyze and interpret information and data pertaining to our internal strengths and weaknesses and external threats and opportunities.

- Recognize and address factors impacting our ability to deliver quality products and services to our customers in a timely and cost-effective manner.

Meeting Specifications

Dates: October 15–19

Place: Ridgeway Conference Center, Pine Tree Meeting Room

Breakfast: 6:30 A.M. continental breakfast will be set up in the meeting room

Meeting Start Time: 7:00 A.M.

Lunch: 12:00 P.M.–1:30 P.M. (to allow you to check e-mails and voice mails)

Finish Time: 7:00 P.M.

Needed Equipment and Supplies: Bring your laptop; all other materials will be provided.

To Prepare

We encourage you to give some personal thought to strategic planning as it relates to our organization and to strategic thinking, strategic planning, and strategic management in general. Between now and the strategic planning session, we ask that you:

- Review the strategic planning handouts I distributed during last month's executive briefing.
- Review the "Strategic Imperative" memorandum Dave Conlin sent last week.
- Review last December's "Year in Review" document.
- Review the quarterly report from the last 12 months.
- Consider and come prepared to discuss the following—
  - Factors relating to systems, processes, technology, people, and culture our organization should eliminate, create, or change.
  - Feedback, information, and any other type of input you have received from your key stakeholders.
  - Information or data you have on whether our clients or customers are likely to purchase our services and products because our services and products meet or exceed their needs and expectations.
  - Information or data you have pertaining to the quality, cost, and availability of our products and services and whether our products and services meet or exceed our client and customer requirements on these three important fronts.
  - Factors impacting our organization's ability to act on its value proposition to ensure, for example, that manufacturing, transportation, and distribution costs and the price of our services and products will allow (1) our clients and customers to purchase them and (2) our organization to realize needed profit.

For More Information

For general information on strategic planning, we recommend that you review the trade journals you typically read to find articles on this topic. I found the following three books to be of immense value in my personal learning:

- Hrebiniak, Lawrence G. 2005. *Making Strategy Work*. Upper Saddle River, NJ: Wharton School Publishing.

- Mintzberg, Henry, Joseph Lampel, and Bruce Ahlstrand. 2008. *Strategy Safari: A Guided Tour through the Wilds of Strategic Management.* New York: The Free Press.
- Kim, W. Chan, and Renee Mauborgne. 2005. *Blue Ocean Strategy.* Boston: Harvard Business School Press.

Contact me at IC123-4 if you would like to meet to discuss anything relating to this memo or to participating in our upcoming strategic planning session. We look forward to seeing you at 7:30 A.M. on October 15!

Sample of Application 10.6

SAMPLE STRATEGIC PLANNING TEAM INTERVIEW QUESTIONS

1. As we strive to build on the success of last year's strategic planning effort, what would you like to see changed or included in this year's strategic planning session?

2. Factors such as board of director expectations, recent critical events, needs and expectations of your business groups, and corporate-wide initiatives carrying over into next year create the context for this year's strategic planning session. From your viewpoint, what other factors are helping "set the stage" for this year's session?

3. This year's strategic planning session involves planning team members gathering and presenting information that will allow you to analyze areas such as internal strengths and weaknesses, external opportunities and threats, your leveraging capabilities, your focus on quality and customers, current trends relating to your market growth, your exit strategies, and challenges associated with globalization. What other factors/areas do you think should be included in your analysis? Presenters: how much time will it take you to share this information during the strategic planning session?

4. We plan to structure the strategic planning session so you can discuss issues and information pertaining to human resources, information technology, finance, and the global supply chain. What other factors/issues do you think should be included in this discussion?

5. The strategic planning session gives the planning team the opportunity to enjoy time together and to "decompress" with some social/recreational activity. From your viewpoint, what is the optimal amount of time (for example, a half-day, a full day) in a four-day session that should be spent on such activities?

Sample of Application 10.7

SAMPLE STRATEGIC PLANNING SESSION AGENDA

Strategic Planning Session

Date of Session

Location of Session

———

Meeting Objectives

- Gain a better understanding of factors contributing to, and "blind spots" associated with, the leadership team's ability to communicate, make decisions, manage change, and manage conflict.
- Gain a better understanding of the leadership team's underlying assumptions, expectations, guiding principles, and values.
- Develop a purpose statement for our division that dovetails off of the corporate mission statement by drawing on various perspectives and capitalizing on differing viewpoints.
- Develop strategies for our division that are consistent with, and supportive of, the 11 strategies currently in place for the corporation.
- Issue a management and planning pocket guide to each leadership team member and give them an opportunity to apply several management and planning tools in a safe, nonthreatening environment.

Meeting Pre-work

- Identify three "teaming" challenges we face as a leadership team and be prepared to share them with the team along with how we might address the challenges.
- Within the context of our corporate mission statement, think about the key features of a mission statement for our division and come prepared to discuss your ideas with the team.
- Review the 11 strategies currently in place for the corporation and come fully prepared to factor them into our conversations.
- Bring a copy of the corporate executive handbook with you to the session.

Daily Agenda

Time	Topic	Process/Action/Tool	Result
Day 1			
8:00–8:15	• Meeting overview	• Share meeting objectives	• Purpose of meeting is understood

		• Establish meeting ground rules	• Boundaries within which the meeting will proceed are clarified
8:15–9:15	• Team warm-up activities	• Leadership team tackles the "matrix" • Leadership team reviews information pertaining to high-performing teams • Leadership team creates its "rules of engagement"	• Leadership team members recognize the strengths of the group and mitigate the group's "blind spots" • Leadership team members adopt rules of engagement, in part to address or mitigate blind spots and capitalize on strengths

9:15–1:00 (includes break)	• Personality: a key factor
	• Complete individual and team worksheets
		• Introduce personality and how it contributes to individual and team success
		• Review personality report
		• Review and process:
		  ○ Team dynamics process
		  ○ Team individual worksheet
		  ○ Team dynamics worksheet
		  ○ Team demographics sheet
		  ○ Team scale
			• Increased awareness of how one's personality impacts one's thinking and behavior
			• Increased awareness of how one's personality impacts other individuals and the team
			• Increased awareness of personal strengths and blind spots
			• Increased awareness of team strengths and blind spots
			• A plan for capitalizing on the strengths and minimizing the blind spots

Day 2

8:00–8:15	• Review results of Day 1	• Conduct a "gallery walk" of flip charts • Participants comment on key insights	• Recognition of learnings, for incorporation in the Day 2 proceedings

8:15–12:00	• Leadership team develops its purpose statement	• Review information pertaining to purpose statements • Review the corporate mission statement • Leadership team members discuss their purpose • Following a structured process, leadership team members work together to develop a purpose statement	• A purpose statement that (1) describes the division's purpose, (2) is consistent with what corporate is asking the division to do, and (3) will resonate with key stakeholders, as well as the expanded management team
12:00–1:00	Lunch		
1:00–5:00 (includes break)	• The leadership team develops its strategies	• Review the 11 strategies currently in place for the corporation • Review information shared when leadership team members discussed their purpose • Review the purpose statement developed earlier in the day, discuss implications • Following a structured process, team members work together to develop division strategies	• Strategies are identified that (1) describe at a high level how the division will achieve its purpose, (2) are consistent with and supportive of the corporate strategies, and (3) are feasible and doable
Day 3			
8:00–8:15	• Review results of Day 2	• Conduct a "gallery walk" of flip charts • Participants comment on key insights	• Recognition of learnings, for incorporation in the Day 3 proceedings

Time			
8:15–10:30	• Identify information needing to be shared about the strategic planning session and deliverables	• Participants develop a communications matrix • Participants conduct a stakeholder analysis and, if needed, an influence plan	• A completed communications matrix • A completed stakeholder analysis • If needed, a completed influence plan
10:30–12:30 (includes break)	• Identify potential obstacles and develop feasible countermeasures	• Using a contingency matrix, participants identify obstacles and develop countermeasures	• A completed contingency matrix
12:30–1:00	• Action items and next steps	• Identify actions needing to be taken to support the team's effort (responsible parties, critical dates, success measures) • Agree on immediate next steps	• Action items are agreed upon • Next steps are identified and agreed upon

Sample of Application 10.8

SAMPLE LEADER'S GUIDE

Strategic Planning Session Leader's Guide

Day 1 Preparation

- Check with conference center to see if anyone has called to cancel
- Check voice mails and e-mails to see if anyone has called to cancel
- Arrive at meeting room at 5:30
- Verify that primary conference room is set up as planned
  - ○ Set up as a U
  - ○ Table for audiovisual equipment

- ○ Table for handout materials
- ○ Space for team-building exercise
- ○ Wall space available for flip charts
- Verify that breakout rooms are available and set up as planned
  - ○ Breakout rooms are reserved (4)
  - ○ Rectangular table in each room
- Verify that equipment and supplies are available in the primary conference room
  - ○ Audiovisual equipment: projector and screen
  - ○ Flip chart easels (2)
  - ○ Flip chart pads (8)
  - ○ Markers for flip charts (6 sets)
  - ○ 3 × 5 note cards (24)
  - ○ Felt markers for note cards (24)
  - ○ Masking tape (4 rolls)
- Verify that equipment and supplies are available in each breakout room
  - ○ Flip chart easel
  - ○ Flip chart pads (2)
  - ○ Markers for flip charts (1 set)
  - ○ 3 × 5 note cards (1 pack)
  - ○ Felt markers for note cards (1)
  - ○ Masking tape (1 roll)
- Check to make sure equipment works properly
- Check to make sure handout materials and participant notebooks are available and organized
- Welcome participants as they arrive
  - ○ Answer questions
  - ○ Address concerns

Kick-off Session

- Thirty-minute session
- Chairman and CEO shares a few comments (15 minutes)
- Describe overall intent of session
- Describe role of facilitator
- Walk through the agenda—highlight topical areas, questions being answered, and issues being addressed

- Point out session objectives being addressed today
- Develop ground rules
  - Capture on flip chart
  - Post in room
  - Refer to as necessary throughout the session

Identify SWOTs (Strengths, Weaknesses, Opportunities, and Threats)

- Monitor emotions closely and respond appropriately and decisively
- Four-hour session
- Participants remain in one large group
- Describe purpose of the SWOT analysis and talk about "pushes"
- Provide definitions of SWOTs
- List headings on flip chart; work through SWOTs in a structured manner
- Capture input on flip charts; number pages; post in room

Further Develop the Corporate Vision for 2020

- Warning! Two-hour session
- Describe purpose of the visioning exercise and talk about "pulls"
- Break group out into two teams
- Hand out visioning exercise guide
- Facilitator monitors status or progress of both teams
- As slides are shown, the facilitator captures key points on flip charts
- Consolidate the results of the visioning exercise and SWOT analysis; identify key pushes and pulls
- Monitor emotions closely and respond appropriately and decisively
- Warning! Ninety-minute session
- Facilitator leads 30- to 45-minute consolidation or synthesis of vision
- Facilitator sets up multivoting exercise (refer to resource material)
- Participants vote; votes are tabulated; key pushes and pulls are noted on a separate flip chart sheet
  - Prepare work surface for vote tabulation
  - Highlight patterns of agreement and disagreement
  - Link SWOT results and items to the various facets of the vision
  - Identify points unique to the corporation from a competitive standpoint:
    - Weaknesses to address
    - Strengths to exploit

Define Key Strategic Issues Relating to the 2020 Vision and SWOTs

- Monitor emotions closely and respond appropriately and decisively
- Three-hour session
- Refer to and review preread materials
  - Discuss the pros and cons of various strategic options (one-half to one hour); capture results on flip charts
    - Ensure we are discussing pros and cons in the following areas/categories
      - Growth opportunity
      - Synergies of combination
      - Shareholders
      - Operations
      - People and organization
      - Processes
      - Business cycles
  - Review the pros and cons of each strategy in relation to our vision and our SWOTs. How do our SWOTs or vision impact the direction we go? (15 minutes)
  - Discuss how each strategy fits in with our 2020 strategic imperatives. Does one strategy or the other lend itself better to those imperatives? (30 minutes)
  - Even if we reach consensus (or if we don't), is there a need to have an external party provide us with pros and cons of strategies and/or recommendations from a shareholder value point of view? (15 minutes)
  - Discuss next steps or action plans to take away from this meeting (15 minutes)
- Monitor emotions closely and respond appropriately and decisively

Conclude Day 1

- Insights from today's session.
- Framework being used, process being followed, and tools being applied: are there opportunities for improvement?
- Individual and team behavior against the preestablished ground rules: are there opportunities for improvement?
- Review the focus of day; describe how to prepare, organize, and/or set up for Day 2

Sample of Application 10.9

SAMPLE ORGANIZATION-WIDE LAUNCH NOTIFICATION

Strategic Planning Launch Notification E-mail or Memorandum

Date: Today's date

To: All organizational members

From: A member of the leadership team

Subject: Launch of Our Strategic Planning Endeavor

This correspondence supplements the information we have previously shared with you regarding embarking on a strategic planning endeavor. An important milestone for us will be the initial five-day strategic planning session being held on October 15–19 at the Ridgeway Conference Center.

The session will allow our strategic planning team to:

- Review strengths, weaknesses, opportunities, and threats impacting our ability to provide our services and products to our customers.

- Analyze the market and competitive forces to understand how they are impacting our ability to provide services and products to our customers.

- Develop mission and vision statements for our organization, to help us focus on what's important when making decisions and taking action.

- Identify corporate values that will help ensure our short- and long-term success, to be factored into our performance management system.

- Given the existing environmental conditions, our mission, vision, and values, and the results of the market and competitive analysis, further refine our value proposition.

- Identify the means (i.e., the strategies) by which we will accomplish our short-term mission and attain our long-term vision.

- Create an action plan for moving forward, identifying related actions, responsible parties, and critical dates for each strategy.

We have taken steps to involve as many members of our organization as possible in this meeting. Even if you may not be participating in this meeting as a member of the strategic planning team, you will be asked to review and comment on the results of the meeting; your input and contribution are vital to our effort, and we look forward to involving you in this endeavor in the coming weeks and months. In addition to involving individuals from throughout our organization, we have solicited information from our customers to be used during the session. This information will help ensure that our analysis is not overly internally focused and that resulting decisions and actions are in our customers'—and thus, our—best interest.

We are very excited about our strategic planning effort in general and the upcoming strategic planning session in particular; although this meeting and subsequent actions will require an investment of time and effort on everyone's part, strategic planning is a natural continuation of all we have previously done to achieve our current level of success and will undoubtedly prove useful as we strive to continuously improve and set the stage for even greater short- and long-term future success.

For More Information

For general information on strategic planning, we recommend that you drop by the corporate library and review the articles we have collected on this topic. If you are interested in learning more, consider checking out one of the following books we currently have available in the library:

- Hrebiniak, Lawrence G. 2005. *Making Strategy Work*. Upper Saddle River, NJ: Wharton School Publishing.
- Mintzberg, Henry, Joseph Lampel, and Bruce Ahlstrand. 2008. *Strategy Safari: A Guided Tour through the Wilds of Strategic Management*. New York: The Free Press.
- Kim, W. Chan, and Renee Mauborgne. 2005. *Blue Ocean Strategy*. Boston: Harvard Business School Press.

If you have questions about the upcoming strategic planning session or how you might contribute and share input, contact me at IC123-4 and I will gladly share additional information with you or let you know how you might be able to assist in this important effort.

- What opportunities or threats does our organization strive to address?
- What needs or expectations does our organization strive to fulfill?
- What services does our organization provide and/or what products does our organization produce?
- What market and/or geographic area does our organization target?
- What impression do we hope our organization makes on our clients, customers, and community?
- How do we expect the members of our organization to behave when speaking to or meeting with our clients and customers?
- How do we expect the members of our organization to behave when speaking to or working with their colleagues and associates?

- o In terms of how we allocate our time, effort, and money, what are we actually attempting to accomplish on a daily basis?
- o What should our customers and clients expect when speaking to or meeting with members of the organization?
- o What services and products are our customers and clients likely to receive from our organization?
- o What customer and client needs or requirements is our organization likely to fulfill?
- o What message about our organization's intention do we want to emphasize to our various stakeholders (board members, investors, and prospective employees)?
- o What values do we want employees (at all levels) to emphasize when making decisions and taking action (for example, when allocating monies when money is scarce and when programs, imperatives, and initiatives must be prioritized)?
- The subgroups reforming into a single strategic planning team and presenting their draft mission statements to the entire team.
- Each subgroup receiving input from and answering questions raised by the entire team.
- Each subgroup reforming to refine its draft mission statement in light of the feedback and input it received from the entire team.
- The subgroups reforming into a single strategic planning team and presenting their refined draft mission statements to the entire team.
- The strategic planning team—
  - o Reviewing the refined draft mission statements.
  - o Selecting the draft mission statement that resonates most with the entire team and, if necessary, refining it.
  - o Combining, consolidating, or synthesizing the draft mission statements to create an "ideal" mission statement that resonates with the entire team.

PROCESS FOR CREATING A VISION STATEMENT

Your strategic planning team members should work together to create your organization's vision statement; a process your strategic planning team might find useful involves:

- Dividing the team into two or three subgroups.
- Specifying to the subgroups the timeframe within which the vision will occur (for example, "Envision what our organization will become or where it will be in five, 10, 15, or 20 years").
- Each subgroup creating a draft vision statement, taking these topics into consideration—
  - o The underlying function and focus of our future organization.

- ○ Opportunities or threats our future organization will strive to address.
- ○ Needs or expectations our future organization will strive to fulfill.
- ○ Services our future organization will provide and/or products our future organization will produce.
- ○ The market and/or geographic area our future organization will target.
- ○ The impression our future organization will strive to make on our clients, customers, and community.
- ○ How the members of our future organization will behave when speaking to or meeting with our clients and customers.
- ○ How the members of our future organization will behave when speaking to or working with their colleagues and associates.
- ○ In terms of how we allocate our time, effort, and money, what members of our future organization will actually attempt to accomplish on a daily basis.
- ○ What our customers and clients should expect when speaking to or meeting with members of our future organization.
- ○ Services and products our customers and clients are likely to receive from our future organization.
- ○ Customer and client needs or requirements that our future organization is likely to fulfill.
- ○ A key message about our future organization's intention that we want to emphasize to our various stakeholders.
- ○ Values we want future employees (at all levels) to emphasize when making decisions and taking action (for example, when allocating monies when money is scarce and programs, imperatives, and initiatives must be prioritized).
- The subgroups reforming into a single strategic planning team and presenting their draft vision statements to the entire team.
- Each subgroup receiving input from and answering questions raised by the entire team.
- Each subgroup reforming to refine its draft vision statement in light of the feedback and input it received from the entire team.
- The subgroups reforming into a single strategic planning team and presenting their refined draft vision statements to the entire team.
- The strategic planning team—
  - ○ Reviewing the refined draft vision statements.
  - ○ Selecting the draft vision statement that resonates most with the entire team and, if necessary, refining it.

- Combining, consolidating, or synthesizing the draft vision statements to create an "ideal" vision statement that resonates with the entire team.

PROCESS FOR IDENTIFYING YOUR STRATEGIES

Planning team members should work together to identify the means by which your organization will achieve short- and long-term success; a process your strategic planning team might find useful involves the following steps:

- Team members individually and collectively review all of the information and data they have before them.
- Team members individually brainstorm ways your organization will, in essence, achieve its current mission and attain its long-term vision. Each team member—
  - Generates as many ideas as possible, without concern about whether the ideas might be considered actions, tactics, or strategies or whether they overlap or relate to each other. Again, the aim is to generate as many ideas as possible.
  - Remains silent while considering the information and data and while generating ideas about how your organization will achieve its current mission and attain its long-term vision.
  - Generates ideas about how your organization will—
    - Realize its underlying nature, focus, and intent.
    - Take advantage of current and emerging external opportunities.
    - Mitigate or otherwise address current and emerging external threats.
    - Leverage or capitalize upon current and developing internal strengths.
    - Address current and developing internal weaknesses.
    - Meet or exceed client and customer needs and expectations.
    - Provide services and products to the current and/or changing target client and customer population.
    - Maintain or expand its target market and/or geographic area.
    - Make a positive impression on your clients, customers, and community.
    - Create an environment in which your employees (at all levels), clients, and customers are treated with the respect and dignity they deserve.
    - Allocate its time, effort, and money on a daily basis.
    - Fulfill the needs or requirements of your customers and clients.
  - Is as creative and innovative as possible, leveraging and taking advantage of existing products, services, markets, clients, customers, capabilities, technology, systems, process, values, principles, and cultural elements while envisioning

new capabilities, technology, systems, process, values, principles, and cultural elements likely to contribute to your organization's achieving its current mission and attaining its long-term vision.

- ○ Focuses on generating as many ideas as possible; here, the aim is quantity over quality.
- Team members capture the ideas they generate on sticky notes. Each—
  - ○ Idea must be captured on a separate sticky note.
  - ○ Idea must be written legibly so it can be read by others.
  - ○ Idea must be written as a phrase or statement.
  - ○ Phrase or statement must, at a minimum, contain a verb (action word).
- Team members process the sticky notes using an affinity diagram—
  - ○ Team members take turns to share their brainstorming results with the other members of the strategic planning team. As each team member presents his or her sticky notes, the other team members make mental notes of—but do not respond to—the nature or scope of the individual brainstorming results.
  - ○ Each team member, after presenting his or her sticky notes to the other team members, lays his or her notes on a table or sticks them to a work surface (typically, a section of a wall covered in flip chart paper).
  - ○ The team identifies natural themes by placing sticky notes containing ideas that are similar or connected in a group when laying them on the table or sticking them to the work surface.
  - ○ Once all sticky notes have been presented and grouped into natural themes, the team approaches the work surface to review and refine the groupings. In reviewing the groupings, it is important that everyone understands the meaning or intent of each idea and that the ideas are properly grouped around a common theme or unifying concept. In refining the groupings, (1) separate an idea that does not fit into any of the existing groupings as a separate, free-standing idea and (2) if an idea fits into more than one grouping, create duplicate sticky notes and place them into the proper themes. Although this is generally a silent exercise (to prevent individuals from assertively or aggressively advocating (1) a particular idea or (2) the placement of a sticky note into a particular group), I encourage individuals to answer questions other team members might have about the reasoning behind placing a particular sticky note in a particular group. Some team members will find this to be a tedious process, but it is essential that it occur because the validity and credibility of subsequent decisions will rely on the sticky notes being properly sorted. Once the movement of sticky notes has ended, your strategic planning team can assume that ideas have been placed into proper groups and that each group has a unique theme or unifying concept.
  - ○ The team reviews each group of sticky notes to identify the natural theme or unifying concept.

- The team summarizes the natural theme or unifying concept in a concisely stated five- to seven-word description and a team member notes the description on a sticky note.
- The team member places the sticky note (referred to as the "header card") at the top of each grouping.
- Team members review the results of the affinity diagram to ensure proper and appropriate groupings. It is essential that this review occur because the validity and credibility of subsequent decisions will rely on the sticky notes being properly sorted. Once all team members agree that the sticky notes have been properly and appropriately placed, your strategic planning team can assume it has reached consensus as to the means by which your organization will achieve its short- and long-term success.

PROCESS FOR FORMULATING YOUR STRATEGIC GOALS

The basis for your organization's strategic goals materializes in the form of the header cards created during the affinity diagramming. Your team members might find the following process useful and beneficial as they review and refine the header cards:

- A team member volunteers or is selected to approach the affinity diagram work surface.
- The team member reads each header card and five to six associated sticky notes.
- The team member asks a series of questions—
  - Does everyone understand the intent of this category?
  - Do I need to read additional sticky notes associated with this category?
  - How should we restate this header card so it becomes a strategic goal?
- Once all team members understand the intent of the category and, if needed, additional sticky notes associated with the category have been read, the team members work together to restate the header card.
- In restating the header cards as strategic goal statements, the planning team should ensure the resulting goal statements—
  - Add clarity to how the organization will accomplish its mission and attain its vision.
  - Add specificity as to how the organization's values and principles will be exhibited and thus become "real."
  - Add clarity to what opportunities the organization is pursuing or capitalizing upon in its "sweet spot."

- Provide boundaries within which members of the organization will make decisions and operate; for example, allowing them to decide which decisions or actions are "in" and which ones are "out."
- Establish expectations for what members of the organization are likely to direct their time, effort, and energy toward.
- Help employees (at all levels) understand how what they are being asked to do contributes to the organization's current mission and long-term vision.
- Help customers and clients know what to expect from the organization, in terms of the services and products they will receive or what needs or requirements the organization will fulfill.
- Send a clear message about how the organization plans to invest its time, energy, and money to its various stakeholders (such as board members, investors, and prospective employees).

- Once the strategic planning team agrees with the wording, the strategic goal statement should be noted and posted on a flip chart. Subsequent statements should be added to the flip chart.
- Once all strategic goal statements have been noted and posted, the strategic planning team can assume that it has reached consensus on the organization's strategic goals.

PRIORITIZING THE MEANS BY WHICH YOU WILL ACHIEVE SUCCESS

Your strategic planning team should evaluate the merits of each strategic goal against the other goals, thereby identifying the goals most likely to yield the most optimal results and outcomes. On this front, your team might find the bubble sort especially useful and beneficial; in applying the bubble sort, your strategic planning team:

- Discusses and decides on the criterion or criteria it will use to evaluate the strategic goals. Criteria might include, but are not limited to, the following:
  - The magnitude of the impact or influence the strategic goal will have on the organization accomplishing its overall mission and vision.
  - The likelihood that the strategic goal will be achieved, given the strengths, limitations, challenges, and opportunities associated with the goal.
  - Whether the members (at all levels) of the organization are likely to consider the strategic goal to be realistic, sensible, and practical.
  - The extent to which the organization can afford to execute, implement, or deploy the strategic goal because of the amount of funding, people, or time it will require.
  - The extent to which the strategic goal is likely to resonate with the organization's various stakeholders: that is, whether they too are likely to consider the strategic goal to be realistic, sensitive, and practical.

- Appoints a team member to write the criterion or criteria on a flip chart and post it so that all team members can consistently apply it (or them) to each of the strategic goals.
- Appoints a team member to write each strategic goal down on a separate sticky note and then randomly place the sticky notes one above another in a vertical column on a flip chart (if necessary, the planning team extends the column by using more than one flip chart page).
- Appoints a team member to facilitate the following discussion and to:
  - Read sticky notes out loud and move sticky notes as directed.
  - Ask the planning team members, while keeping the criterion or criteria in mind, to compare the top two sticky notes to determine which is the most important (i.e., it is more likely to succeed and yield the greatest result and outcome). If the lower sticky note is more important, the facilitator exchanges the positions of the notes. This results in the more important sticky note being positioned above the less important one.
  - Repeat this paired comparison and exchange for the second and third sticky notes, then the third and fourth sticky notes, and so on until the planning team reaches the bottom of the column.
  - Repeat the process for the entire column (starting again with the top two sticky notes) if any cards are moved during the analysis.
  - Regardless of how much time it takes, apply the overall process to the entire column until no sticky notes are exchanged during a complete pass-through. Once the facilitator does not exchange any sticky notes during a complete pass-through, the sticky notes (and the list of strategic goals) are in priority order from "most" to "least" important.

CREATING YOUR ACTION PLAN

Your strategic planning team members should work together to create your organization's action plan; your team might find the following action planning process to be useful and beneficial:

- One or more team members create a work surface using several sheets of flip chart paper.
- A team member writes the first strategic goal at the far left or very top of the work surface.
- On separate sticky notes, team members write each of the previously identified means by which the organization will achieve that particular strategic goal.
- Team members place all sticky notes (containing previously identified means by which the organization will achieve that particular goal) onto the work surface.

- Team members—
  - Place the strategic, more encompassing sticky notes directly to the right of or directly beneath the goal statement.
  - Place related but more tactical and task-oriented sticky notes directly beneath or to the right of the more strategic ones.
  - Identify other ways (tactics, major tasks, and minor tasks) by which the organization will achieve that particular goal.
  - Place each sticky note at its proper location on the work surface—
    - The strategic, more encompassing actions to the right of or directly beneath the goal statement.
    - Related but more tactical and task-oriented actions directly beneath or to the right of the more strategic ones.
    - Actions posted toward the bottom or to the right side of the work surface represent the greatest level of detail.
- The planning team applies the above process to each of the remaining strategic goals until each strategic goal has associated tactics, major tasks, and minor tasks.
- The strategic planning team reviews the results of the action planning process to ensure that the various means (tactics, major tasks, and minor tasks) by which the organization will achieve its strategic goals have been identified.
- For each strategic goal, the planning team—
  - Identifies the individual or individuals being held responsible for that particular goal.
  - Sets the deadline or critical timeframe for the goal's accomplishment.
  - Defines the metrics by which interim progress and ultimate success are to be measured.

CREATING YOUR CONTINGENCY PLAN

Your strategic planning team members should work together to create your organization's contingency plan. Your planning team might find the following contingency planning process to be useful and beneficial:

- A team member volunteers to facilitate this process; he or she reads your organization's first strategic goal (and to the extent needed, the associated tactics, major tasks, and minor tasks) out loud to the entire team.
- The facilitator writes the first strategic goal at the top of a sheet of flip chart paper.
- Team members brainstorm challenges (impediments, obstacles, or barriers) likely to adversely impact the organization's achieving that particular goal.
- The facilitator lists the challenges on the flip chart paper.

- Team members review the list of challenges and identify the two to three challenges most likely to occur, given the prevailing conditions and circumstances.
- The facilitator highlights each of the two to three challenges on the flip chart paper.
- For each of the two to three challenges, team members brainstorm the means by which the organization might avoid, reduce, mitigate, or otherwise address the impediment, obstacle, or barrier.
- The facilitator lists the means on flip chart paper.
- The team reviews the various means by which the organization might avoid, reduce, mitigate, or otherwise address each challenge and selects the most realistic and doable one, which becomes the countermeasure the organization will utilize if or when that particular challenge surfaces.
- The facilitator highlights the recommended countermeasure on the flip chart paper.
- The strategic planning team applies this process to each challenge until it has identified the most realistic and doable countermeasure for each impediment, obstacle, or barrier (see Samples of Application 10.10 and 10.11).

Sample of Application 10.10

COMMUNICATION MATRIX TEMPLATES

	Consideration	Related information
Communiqué 1	Responsible party	
	Target audience	
	Situation or event	
	Media or vehicle	
	Key message(s)	
	Frequency or critical date	
	Success measure(s)	
Communiqué 2	Responsible party	
	Target audience	
	Situation or event	
	Media or vehicle	
	Key message(s)	
	Frequency or critical date	
	Success measure(s)	

CHANGE MANAGEMENT PLAN TEMPLATES

Goal: Determine the nature and magnitude of change associated with the newly created or modified strategic plan.

Actions	
Responsible party or parties	
Critical date or timeframe	

Goal: Determine the organization's capacity (for change) and capabilities.

Actions	
Responsible party or parties	
Critical date or timeframe	

Goal: Identify challenges, obstacles, or impediments likely to impede the organization's progress and success.

Actions	
Responsible party or parties	
Critical date or timeframe	

Goal: Develop and implement actions that take advantage of your organizational strengths, address your organizational challenges, and accelerate organization-wide change.

Actions	
Responsible party or parties	
Critical date or timeframe	

Goal: Investigate and implement ways to optimize the rewards of new strategies, work processes, and technology associated with your strategic plan.

Actions	
Responsible party or parties	
Critical date or timeframe	

Goal: Monitor and manage behavior and performance associated with and thus impacting changes associated with your strategic plan.

Actions	
Responsible party or parties	
Critical date or timeframe	

Goal: Encourage and reinforce behavior that produces desired results.

Actions	
Responsible party or parties	
Critical date or timeframe	

Goal: Monitor progress, share lessons learned, and when necessary address unexpected challenges.

Actions	
Responsible party or parties	
Critical date or timeframe	

FIVE-STEP CONTINUOUS IMPROVEMENT FRAMEWORK

If your organization does not adhere to a certain continuous improvement framework, model, or process, your planning team might find the following five-step continuous improvement framework to be useful and beneficial:

- Step 1. Determine how we are doing—
  - Select members of the strategic planning team meet to conduct a strategy review.
  - Team members review the goals, actions, timeframes and critical dates, and metrics stipulated in the action plan.
  - Team members review progress to date to determine the extent to which (1) progress has been made and/or (2) the strategic goals and associated tactics, major tasks, and minor tasks have been accomplished.
- Step 2. Determine if we should improve—
  - For tactics, major tasks, and minor tasks that have experienced optimal execution, the team members identify and note potential lessons learned and best practices.
  - For each marginal or suboptimal gain or achievement, team members analyze its impact on the predefined metrics and the organization's short- and long-term success to determine whether to invest resources, time, and energy to improve performance.
- Step 3. Determine how we should improve—
  - As appropriate, the team members further—
    - Analyze the gap between the actual progress or accomplishment and the desired or required performance.
    - Explore underlying factors or factors contributing to the performance gap.
  - Solicit ideas from other employees (at all levels) on how to effectively and efficiently close the performance gap.
  - Identify and select the solution(s) most likely to lead to optimal execution.
  - Incorporate solution(s) into the organization's action and/or contingency plan, assigning a responsible party, a critical date or timeframe, and metrics.
- Step 4. Apply and then determine the effectiveness of the improvement—
  - Tactics, major tasks, and minor tasks are implemented according to the action plan.
  - The responsible party monitors and notes progress and accomplishment.
- Step 5. Determine how we should continuously improve—
  - The person responsible for the remedial action(s) shares the results and outcomes in accordance with the organization's action plan.
  - Actions, situations, and circumstances contributing to optimal results and outcomes are explored; lessons learned and best practices are identified.

- ○ Lessons learned and best practices are shared throughout the organization and are applied to the organization's ongoing continuous improvement effort.
- ○ The five-step continuous improvement framework is applied to marginal and suboptimal results and outcomes.

READINESS ASSESSMENT CONSIDERATIONS

It is important that your organization manage (1) factors likely to contribute to or impede effective and efficient execution of your organization's strategic plan and (2) variables likely to impact (in a positive or negative way) your organization's short- and long-term success. This suggests that your readiness assessment should focus on:

- Attitudes relating to changes associated with the newly developed or modified strategic plan, specifically, about the—
  - ○ Changes impacting the employee in a positive, neutral, or negative way.
  - ○ Employee possessing the knowledge, skills, and abilities to think, behave, and perform in the newly expected way.
  - ○ Likelihood of the strategic plan–related changes taking place.
- Views pertaining to whether employees (at all levels) have accurate information about the newly developed or modified strategic plan and how the plan impacts—
  - ○ How they are expected to contribute to the organization's short- and long-term success.
  - ○ What they will be asked to do on a daily basis.
  - ○ The emphasis they place on quality, customer service, product innovation, and process efficiency.
- Views pertaining to whether employees (at all levels) and their colleagues support the changes associated with the newly developed or modified strategic plan and the likelihood that they will contribute to their execution, implementation, or deployment.
- Perceptions about whether organizational components (divisions, departments, and units) are likely to work together to produce the change associated with the newly developed or modified strategic plan.
- Views about whether division, department, and unit executives and managers are likely to work together to produce the change associated with the newly developed or modified strategic plan.
- Attitudes about whether the organizational elements (technology, systems, and processes) necessary to drive and support strategic plan–related change are in place.

- Views about whether the organization's senior leaders believe in, commit to, and are likely to invest in the needed time, resources, and money to support the change associated with the newly developed or modified strategic plan.

- Perceptions about whether the organization's executives, managers, and supervisors are likely to manage and supervise in a manner that drives and supports organization-wide change associated with the newly developed or modified strategic plan.

- Views about whether the purpose, importance, and details of the changes associated with the newly developed or modified strategic plan have been adequately, consistently, and accurately communicated.

- Perceptions about whether the organization as a whole will achieve its newly developed, modified, or verified mission and/or attain its newly developed, modified, or verified vision.

SPOT SURVEY CONSIDERATIONS

It is important for your organization to recognize and respond to developing or rapidly materializing (1) factors likely to contribute to or impede effective and efficient execution of your organization's strategic plan and (2) variables likely to impact (in a positive or negative way) your organization's short- and long-term success. This suggests that your spot survey should focus on variables similar or identical to the ones evaluated in your readiness survey:

- Attitudes relating to changes occurring during strategy execution, specifically, about the—
  - Changes impacting the employee in a positive, neutral, or negative way.
  - Employee thinking, behaving, and performing in the newly expected way.
  - Progress associated with the strategic plan–related changes taking place.
- Views pertaining to whether employees (at all levels) have accurate information about the strategic plan and how strategy execution has impacted—
  - How they contribute to the organization's short- and long-term success.
  - What they are being asked to do on a daily basis.
  - The emphasis they now place on quality, customer service, product innovation, and process efficiency.
- Views pertaining to whether employees (at all levels) and their colleagues support the changes occurring during strategy execution and the extent to which they are supporting strategy execution, implementation, or deployment.
- Perceptions about the extent to which organizational components (divisions, departments, and units) are working together to produce strategic plan–related change.

- Views about the extent to which division, department, and unit executives and managers are working together to produce strategic plan–related change.
- Attitudes about the extent to which the organizational elements (technology, systems, and processes) necessary to drive and support strategic plan–related change are in place.
- Views about the extent to which the organization's leaders have invested needed time, resources, and money to support strategic plan–related change.
- Perceptions about the extent to which the organization's executives, managers, and supervisors are managing and supervising in a manner that drives and supports strategic plan–related change.
- Views about the extent to which information about progress, lessons learned, and best practices is being consistently and accurately communicated.
- Perceptions about the extent to which the organization as a whole is achieving its mission.
- Views about the extent to which the organization is identifying and acting on opportunities for continuous improvement.

STRATEGY REVIEW SESSION GUIDANCE

It is important for your strategic planning team, working closely with your organization's leaders, to conduct periodic strategy review sessions to:

- Determine how your organization is doing—
  - Review the goals, actions, timeframes and critical dates, and metrics stipulated in the action plan.
  - Review progress to date to determine the extent to which (1) general progress has been made and/or (2) the strategic goals and associated tactics, major tasks, and minor tasks have been accomplished.
  - Review specific actions and activities stemming from previous strategy review sessions to determine the extent to which (1) progress has been made and/or (2) the strategic goals and associated tactics, major tasks, and minor tasks have been accomplished.
- Determine if your organization should—
  - For tactics, major tasks, and minor tasks that are experiencing optimal execution, identify and note potential lessons learned and best practices.
  - For each marginal or suboptimal gain or achievement, analyze its impact on the metrics outlined in the action plan and the organization's short- and long-term success to determine whether to invest resources, time, and energy to improve performance.
- Determine how your organization should improve—
  - As appropriate, further—

- ■ Analyze the gap between the actual progress or accomplishment and the desired or required performance.

- ■ Explore the underlying factors or factors contributing to the performance gap.

- ○ Solicit ideas from other employees (at all levels) on how to effectively and efficiently close the performance gap.

- ○ Identify and select the solution(s) most likely to lead to optimal execution.

- ○ Incorporate solution(s) into the organization's action and/or contingency plan, assigning a responsible party, a critical date or timeframe, and metrics.

- Determine how your organization should continuously improve—

  - ○ Review previously enacted remedial actions; determine how to consolidate gains and replicate positive results and outcomes.

  - ○ Explore actions, situations, and circumstances contributing to optimal results and outcomes; identify lessons learned to share and best practices to replicate throughout the organization.

  - ○ Determine how to incorporate exemplary methodologies, processes, tools, and techniques into the organization's ongoing continuous improvement effort.

  - ○ Assign select marginal and suboptimal performance issues to one or more response teams; each response team applies the organization's continuous improvement framework, model, or process to those issues.

MOVING FORWARD WITH STRATEGIC PLANNING

While exploring strategic planning, preparing to launch your planning effort, undertaking your journey, and striving to continuously improve, I encourage you to review the above methodologies, tools, and techniques, determine their utility, and when useful and beneficial apply them. To augment these important aids, I encourage you to review the resources listed in the Appendix and investigate the ones most likely to contribute to your personal growth and development.

Chapter 11

Ensuring Effective and Efficient Execution

The members of your planning team have applied a slate of methodologies, tools, and techniques to formulate strategy and to set the stage for effective organization-wide strategy execution. My experience and observations suggest that your organization should take steps before, during, and throughout the strategic planning effort to further ensure effective and efficient strategy execution and increase the likelihood of optimal short- and long-term success. On this front, I recommend that your strategic planning team conduct:

- A readiness assessment prior to initiating strategy execution to determine whether success is likely and, if not, what additional actions must occur to properly set the stage for success.
- A series of spot surveys during strategy execution to identify changing needs, expectations, and requirements, lessons learned and best practices, and pockets of resistance (to address) and commitment (to leverage).
- Periodic strategy review sessions to—
    - Identify changing external opportunities and threats and internal strengths and weaknesses.
    - Identify ways to take advantage of factors impacting the organization in a positive way and to address factors impacting it in a negative way.
    - Determine progress being made on all fronts and identify ways to leverage the achievement and reduce, avoid, or mitigate barriers, obstacles, and impediments.
    - Identify lessons learned to share and best practices to replicate throughout the organization.

○ Identify opportunities for enhancement and improvement and—

■ When feasible, take advantage of those opportunities (e.g., "course correct") while execution is under way.

■ As appropriate, note opportunities and their associated solutions to apply to your organization's next planning session or during its next planning cycle.

KEY LEARNING POINT

To further ensure effective and efficient strategy execution and to increase the likelihood of optimal short- and long-term success, it is important that your strategic planning team conduct a readiness assessment prior to initiating strategy execution, a series of spot surveys during strategy execution, and periodic strategy review sessions.

CONDUCTING A READINESS ASSESSMENT

Before exploring the importance of conducting a readiness assessment, I encourage you to once again consider the organizational environment within which you plan to implement your newly developed or modified strategic plan. Does it consist of or contain:

• Numerous goals, objectives, metrics, initiatives, programs, and projects, some of which are competing for time, energy, resources, and/or funding?

• Numerous focal points that require time, interest, and energy from individuals who have only a certain amount of time, interest, and energy?

• Existing and ongoing strategies, tactics, or major and minor tasks that require everyone's time and attention?

• Enthusiasm around existing and ongoing goals, objectives, metrics, initiatives, programs, projects, strategies, tactics, tasks, and other focal points?

• Effort and energy being exerted toward the previously established direction?

If such variables do exist, they will impact or influence the implementation of your organization's newly developed or modified strategic plan. The degree to which such variables adversely impact or influence your newly developed or modified strategic plan will depend largely on the nature, scope, and magnitude of change associated with the strategic plan; the impact may be rather severe if your strategic plan includes a new or different mission or vision or new strategic goals, major tactics, and minor tactics; involves the adoption, deployment, installation, or execution of new technology, systems, or processes; and/or requires organizational members to change their focus and tempo.

How important is it that you conduct a readiness assessment? My experience and observations lead me to believe that conducting and acting on the results of a readiness assessment will increase the likelihood of your achieving optimal short- and long-term success to the same extent that (1) such variables exist within your organization and (2) your newly developed or modified strategic plan requires the members of your organization to change the way they think, behave, and perform. In short, your strategic planning endeavor creates the need for your organization to recalibrate its attention and focus and reemphasize or redirect its effort and resources. Such recalibration and change in emphasis or direction creates the need for you to conduct and act on the results of a readiness assessment.

Actions resulting from a readiness assessment will help your organization set the stage for your short- and long-term success in several important ways. The individuals responsible for leading and managing your strategy execution will have the information they need to make credible decisions and take reasonable and responsible action—within the context of the existing situation, conditions, and circumstances—and thus establish or reinforce their personal credibility. Your executive sponsor will have the information he or she needs to help reduce, mitigate, and otherwise nullify the adverse impact that competing priorities, conflicting initiatives, and organizational politics have on the newly developed or modified strategic plan. The leaders of your organization will have the information they need to address significant resource, budgetary, and other challenges, obstacles, and barriers that may impede strategy execution; and to strengthen systems and processes to encourage, recognize, and reinforce efforts and actions required to achieve successful execution throughout the organization. All members of your organization will have the information they need to make decisions about the purpose and importance of changes associated with the newly developed or modified strategic plan and about how they can contribute to your organization's short- and long-term success.

YOUR ORGANIZATION'S READINESS

For your organization to effectively and efficiently translate its strategic goals into concrete actions, a multitude of organizational environmental factors must be in place to induce and support:

- Employees (at all levels) throughout your organization—
  - To focus their time, attention, and resources on the multitude of decisions and actions that will contribute to your organization's short- and long-term success.
  - To strive to continuously improve systems, processes, the nature and scope of their personal contribution, and their team's ability to deliver on its value proposition.
- Divisions, departments, and units working—
  - In a coordinated and integrated manner to achieve system-wide success.
  - Together to produce results and outcomes likely to be valued by your customers, clients, and surrounding community.

YOUR ORGANIZATION'S READINESS ASSESSMENT

Your organization's readiness assessment evaluates the willingness and ability of employees (at all levels) to adopt and adhere to changes associated with your organization's newly developed or modified strategic plan. Your strategic planning team will use readiness assessment results when identifying issues to be considered, challenges to be addressed, and strengths and opportunities to be leveraged or taken advantage of. Your organization's readiness assessment will focus on (1) factors likely to contribute to or impede effective and efficient execution of your organization's strategic plan and (2) variables likely to impact (in a positive or negative way) your organization's short- and long-term success. My experience and observations suggest that your readiness assessment may focus on:

- Attitudes relating to changes associated with the newly developed or modified strategic plan, specifically, about the—
  ○ Changes impacting the employee in a positive, neutral, or negative way.
  ○ Employee possessing the knowledge, skills, and abilities to think, behave, and perform in the newly expected way.
  ○ Likelihood of the strategic plan–related changes taking place.
- Views pertaining to whether employees (at all levels) have accurate information about the newly developed or modified strategic plan and how the plan impacts—
  ○ How they are expected to contribute to the organization's short- and long-term success.
  ○ What they will be asked to do on a daily basis.
  ○ The emphasis they place on quality, customer service, product innovation, and process efficiency.
- Views pertaining to whether employees (at all levels) and their colleagues support the changes associated with the newly developed or modified strategic plan and the likelihood that they will contribute to their execution, implementation, or deployment.
- Perceptions about whether organizational components (divisions, departments, and units) are likely to work together to produce the change associated with the newly developed or modified strategic plan.
- Views about whether division, department, and unit executives and managers are likely to work together to produce the change associated with the newly developed or modified strategic plan.
- Attitudes about whether organizational elements (technology, systems, and processes) necessary to drive and support strategic plan–related change are in place.

- Views about whether the organization's senior leaders believe in, commit to, and are likely to invest needed time, resources, and money to support the changes associated with the newly developed or modified strategic plan.
- Perceptions about whether the organization's executives, managers, and supervisors are likely to manage and supervise in a manner that drives and supports organization-wide changes associated with the newly developed or modified strategic plan.
- Views about whether the purpose, importance, and details of the changes associated with the newly developed or modified strategic plan have been adequately, consistently, and accurately communicated.
- Perceptions about whether the organization as a whole will achieve its newly developed, modified, or verified mission and/or attain its newly developed, modified, or verified vision.

CONDUCTING YOUR ORGANIZATION'S READINESS ASSESSMENT

A branch of the military, when preparing to execute changes associated with its strategic plan, recognized the importance of engaging employees and obtaining their views, attitudes, and perceptions on their willingness and ability to adopt and adhere to changes associated with the organization's strategic plan; issues to consider, challenges to address, and strengths and opportunities to leverage or take advantage of before, during, and throughout the organization's strategy execution; factors likely to contribute to or impede effective and efficient execution of the organization's strategic plan; and the multitude of variables likely to impact (in a positive or negative way) the organization's short- and long-term success.

The military conducted an organizational readiness assessment to:

- Solicit views on the importance of the planned change and its impact on employees (at all levels) and their colleagues.
- Obtain feedback on organizational elements and components likely to impact strategy execution and the organization's ability to achieve its mission and attain its vision.
- Gather information on the effectiveness of previous communiqués and identify opportunities to strengthen communication throughout the entire organization and within select divisions, departments, and units.
- Ask questions about the existing level of buy-in, ownership, and commitment for changes associated with the organization's strategic plan.
- Obtain feedback on the effectiveness and efficiency of technology, systems, and processes key to the organization's short- and long-term success.
- Gather information on strengths needing to be leveraged and weaknesses needing to be addressed prior to strategy execution.

- Identify silos of leadership, executive, management, and supervisor—
  - Excellence to leverage before, during, and throughout strategy execution.
  - Weakness or resistance to reduce before, during, and throughout strategy execution.
- Solicit suggestions and recommendations to apply toward the organization's continuous improvement efforts.
- Obtain baseline information against which future strategic decisions and actions might be assessed.

All uniformed and civilian members of the military impacted by this particular strategic plan were asked to complete the readiness assessment. For this particular readiness assessment, respondents were asked to provide information pertaining to these demographic variables:

- Position (uniformed or civilian) held within the organization.
- Level (executive, manager, supervisor, or individual contributor) within the organization.
- Length of service with the organization.
- Division, department, or unit in which the respondent is assigned.

The organization tracked response rates so that (1) gaps in levels of understanding, buy-in, and commitment could be identified and addressed and (2) lessons learned could be identified, leveraged, and capitalized upon.

The team administering the readiness assessment analyzed and summarized the results and shared participant statistics and assessment results with the strategic planning team. The data across the demographic categories revealed that employees (at all positions, levels, divisions, departments, or units) in general shared consistent views but that there were some differences in opinion across certain positions, levels, and divisions. The planning team believed that this information reflected positively on the organization's culture and management practices but identified opportunities to strengthen information being shared throughout the organization and within the various positions, levels, and divisions.

Given the complexity of military organizations and the multitude of factors impacting their employees' (whether uniformed or civilian) ability to succeed, it was essential that the strategic planning team take readiness assessment information into consideration. Figure 11.1 presents actions the strategic planning team decided to take to further prepare the organization for strategy execution. Please note that some information was omitted from Figure 11.1 and that some of the information was modified to protect sensitive and/or confidential material.

Figure 11.1 presents the kind of information that is typically obtained in a readiness assessment, although this briefing was designed to be delivered in three

Figure 11.1   Results of Organization Readiness Assessment

Readiness Assessment Findings, Conclusions, and Recommendations

We are planning to undertake wide-scale change relating to our recently modified strategic plan. Taking on such enterprise-wide change in a planned and purposeful manner requires us to first understand our organization's readiness for change. Such understanding allows us to:

- Identify existing enablers and impediments to change.
- Capitalize on the enablers of change.
- Take steps to counter the impediments of change.

This briefing provides an analysis of the results of the readiness assessment completed by 5,280 members (about 92 percent) of our organization. Select members of the planning team reviewed the assessment results and respectfully provide draft conclusions and recommendations for your review and consideration. NOTE: Assessment results are detailed in the accompanying document; this briefing only summarizes the conclusions and recommendations.

Conclusions, based on the analysis of the findings:

- In general, there is an adequate level of support for this change within our organization.
- There is a prevailing desire within and throughout our organization for more concrete information about the need for and purpose of changes associated with our recently modified strategic plan.
- There is a prevailing perception that senior-level leaders and executives currently have a more accurate understanding about the need for and purpose of changes associated with our strategic plan.
- There is a perception that manager and supervisor decisions and actions in AOR 3 are not currently aligned and that systems to adequately support the new ways of doing things are not currently in place.
- There is a belief that the buy-in and commitment of uniformed officers exceed those of civilian executives and managers.

Recommendations, based on the analysis of the conclusions:

- Confirm and strengthen alignment among the organization's leaders in general and AOR 3 leaders in particular.
- Take planned and purposeful steps to ensure organization-wide alignment.
- Take concrete steps to cascade information throughout the organization, focusing on managers, supervisors, and sole contributors.
- Share detailed information about the purpose, nature, and scope of changes associated with the strategic plan with civilian executives and managers.
- Develop and execute a comprehensive organization-wide communication strategy.

(Continued)

Figure 11.1   (Continued)

- Target and then begin modifying support systems and processes to support and/or reinforce the strategic plan–related changes.

- Monitor decisions, actions, and accomplishments and recognize appropriate ones to reinforce behaviors consistent with and supportive of this change.

- Determine how, within our organization's culture, to encourage and reward adoption of best practices.

- Identify and target opportunities for our leaders to communicate more broadly.

- Identify major supporters within AOR 5 and 7 and use them to communicate to other AORs (in general) and AOR 3 (in particular).

- Broadly share the readiness assessment conclusions and recommendations with all members of the organization, accompanied (or shortly thereafter supplemented) by a plan for implementing the recommendations.

---

minutes or less. This figure also provides a sample of the types of conclusions and recommendations your strategic team might generate after analyzing the results of an organizational readiness assessment.

CONDUCTING SPOT SURVEYS

Whereas the readiness assessment provides useful information prior to strategy execution, spot surveys provide useful information during and throughout your strategy execution. My experience and observations lead me to believe that conducting and acting on a series of spot surveys will increase the likelihood of your achieving optimal short- and long-term success by providing needed feedback on the extent to which:

- The members of your organization have—
  - Changed the way they think, behave, and perform to match newly prescribed expectations and requirements.
  - Recalibrated their attention and focus and reemphasized or redirected their effort and resources to generate newly prescribed results and outcomes.
- Methodologies, tools, and techniques are helping employees (at all levels) achieve short- and long-term success.
- Organizational technology, systems, and processes are helping employees (at all levels) achieve short- and long-term success.
- The members of your organization—
  - Possess needed capabilities, self-confidence, and self-motivation to achieve short- and long-term success.
  - Consistently apply the effort and produce the results and outcomes required to achieve short- and long-term success.

Actions resulting from spot surveys will help your organization set the stage for your short- and long-term success in several important ways. The individuals responsible for leading and managing your strategy execution will have the information they need to make sound decisions and take responsible action—within the context of constantly changing conditions and circumstances—and thus maintain their credibility. Your executive sponsor will have the information he or she needs to help address the competing priorities and conflicting initiatives inherent in complex organizations responding to a slate of constantly changing needs, expectations, and requirements. The leaders of your organization will have the information they need to shift resource allocations and emphasize priorities or responsibilities to address emerging obstacles, barriers, and impediments; and to strengthen systems and processes to encourage, recognize, and reinforce efforts and actions required to address acute weaknesses and threats. All members of your organization will have the information they need to capitalize on short-lived opportunities and reduce or mitigate those factors that will eventually impede your organization's success if left unnoticed or unattended.

REMAINING "SPOT-ON"

For your organization to effectively and efficiently translate its strategic goals into concrete actions, a multitude of organizational environmental factors must—regardless of changing conditions and circumstances—remain in place to induce and support:

- Employees (at all levels) throughout your organization—
  - To direct their time, attention, and resources to those decisions and actions that contribute to your organization's short- and long-term success.
  - To continuously improve systems, processes, the nature and scope of their personal contribution, and their team's ability to deliver on its value proposition within the context of competing and constantly changing needs, expectations, and requirements.
- Divisions, departments, and units working—
  - In a coordinated and integrated manner to meet competing and constantly changing needs, expectations, and requirements.
  - Together to produce results and outcomes likely to be valued by your customers, clients, and surrounding community.

YOUR ORGANIZATION'S SPOT SURVEY

Your organization's spot survey provides a "snapshot" of your employees' (at all levels) views, perceptions, and attitudes while strategy execution is actually under way. The spot survey supplements your organization's readiness survey in that it evaluates the extent to which employees (at all levels) are adopting and adhering to changes associated with your organization's newly developed or modified strategic plan; exposes changing needs, expectations, and requirements; reveals lessons learned and best practices; and helps uncover pockets of resistance (to address) and commitment (to leverage).

Your planning team will use spot survey results when identifying emergent issues to be considered; impediments, obstacles, or barriers to be addressed; and strengths to be leveraged. Your organization's spot survey will focus on emerging, developing, or rapidly materializing (1) factors likely to contribute to or impede effective and efficient execution of your organization's strategic plan and (2) variables likely to impact (in a positive or negative way) your organization's short- and long-term success. Experience and observations suggest that your spot survey may focus on variables similar or identical to the ones evaluated in your readiness survey:

- Attitudes relating to changes occurring during strategy execution, such as—
  - Changes impacting the employee in a positive, neutral, or negative way.
  - Employees thinking, behaving, and performing in the newly expected way.
  - Progress associated with the strategic plan–related changes taking place.
- Views pertaining to whether employees (at all levels) have accurate information about the strategic plan and how strategy execution has impacted—
  - How they contribute to the organization's short- and long-term success.
  - What they are being asked to do on a daily basis.
  - The emphasis they now place on quality, customer service, product innovation, and process efficiency.
- Views pertaining to whether employees (at all levels) and their colleagues support the changes occurring during strategy execution and the extent to which they are supporting strategy execution, implementation, or deployment.
- Perceptions about the extent to which organizational components (divisions, departments, and units) are working together to produce strategic plan–related change.
- Views about the extent to which division, department, and unit executives and managers are working together to produce strategic plan–related change.
- Attitudes about the extent to which the organizational elements (technology, systems, and processes) necessary to drive and support strategic plan–related change are in place.
- Views about the extent to which the organization's leaders have invested the needed time, resources, and money to support strategic plan–related change.
- Perceptions about the extent to which the organization's executives, managers, and supervisors are managing and supervising in a manner that drives and supports strategic plan–related change.

- Views about the extent to which information about progress, lessons learned, and best practices is being consistently and accurately communicated.
- Perceptions about the extent to which the organization as a whole is achieving its mission.
- Views about the extent to which the organization is identifying and acting on opportunities for continuous improvement.

CONDUCTING YOUR ORGANIZATON'S SPOT SURVEY

A branch of the military, while executing changes associated with its strategic plan, recognized the importance of (1) remaining in close contact with employees (at all levels) and (2) obtaining their views, attitudes, and perceptions on the extent to which they adopt and adhere to changes associated with the organization's strategic plan; prevailing and emerging issues to consider, challenges to address, and strengths and opportunities to leverage or take advantage of during and throughout strategy execution; unexpected or unanticipated factors contributing to or impeding effective and efficient execution of the organization's strategic plan; and variables likely to eventually adversely impact the organization's success if left unnoticed or unattended.

The military conducted a series of spot surveys to:

- Solicit views on the importance of the change taking place and its impact on employees (at all levels) and their colleagues.
- Obtain feedback on the extent to which organizational elements and components impact strategy execution and the organization's ability to achieve its mission and attain its vision.
- Gather information on the effectiveness of communiqués and identify opportunities to strengthen communication throughout the entire organization and within select divisions, departments, and units.
- Ask questions about the current level of buy-in, ownership, and commitment for changes occurring within the organization.
- Obtain feedback on the effectiveness and efficiency of the technology, systems, and processes that are key to the organization's short- and long-term success.
- Gather information on the strengths that need to be leveraged and the weaknesses that need to be addressed.
- Identify silos of leadership, executive, management, and supervisor—
  - Excellence to leverage during strategy execution.
  - Weakness or resistance to reduce during strategy execution.
- Solicit suggestions and recommendations to apply toward the organization's continuous improvement efforts.

- Obtain information—
  - To compare against baseline information obtained in the organization's readiness assessment.
  - Against which future spot survey results will be assessed.

All uniformed and civilian members of the military involved in the strategy execution were asked to complete the spot survey. Respondents were asked to provide information on these demographic variables:

- Position (uniformed or civilian) held within the organization.
- Level (executive, manager, supervisor, or individual contributor) within the organization.
- Length of service with the organization.
- Division, department, or unit to which the respondent is assigned.

The team administering the spot survey analyzed and summarized the results and shared participant statistics and survey results with the strategic planning team. The data across the demographic categories revealed that employees (at all positions, levels, divisions, departments, or units) in general shared consistent views but that there were some differences in opinions across certain divisions. The planning team felt that this information reflected positively on the organization's general management practices but identified opportunities to strengthen communication within various divisions.

Given the complexity of military organizations and the multitude of factors impacting their employees' ability to succeed, it was essential that the strategic planning team take spot survey information into consideration. Figure 11.2 presents the actions the planning team decided to take to further support strategy execution. Please note that some information was omitted from Figure 11.2 and that some of the information was modified to protect sensitive and/or confidential material.

Figure 11.2 presents the kind of information that is typically obtained in a spot survey, although this briefing was designed to be delivered in three minutes or less. This figure also illustrates the types of conclusions and recommendations your strategic team might generate after analyzing the results of a spot survey.

Your strategic planning team's effort to monitor progress and changing conditions and circumstances does not end with the initial spot survey. The timing of subsequent spot surveys will depend largely on the nature and magnitude of the change associated with your strategic plan; the prevailing and emerging challenges and opportunities impacting the organization's ability to achieve short- and long-term success; and the extent to which employees (at all levels) consistently apply optimal effort, exhibit appropriate behavior, and perform in a way (and at a level) that generates needed results and outcomes.

Figure 11.2   Results of Organization Spot Survey

Spot Survey Findings, Conclusions, and Recommendations

We are undergoing wide-scale strategic plan–related change. Such wide-scale change requires us to recognize and respond to changing positions, needs, and expectations. Such understanding will enable us to:

- Identify new and emerging enablers and impediments to change.
- Capitalize on the new and emerging enablers of change.
- Counter new and emerging impediments to change.
- Take steps to—
  - Recognize, reward, and otherwise reinforce positive changes in attitude, effort, behavior, and performance.
  - Correct inappropriate behavior and otherwise improve inadequate or suboptimal effort and performance.

This briefing provides an analysis of the results of the spot survey completed by 5,275 members (about 91 percent) of our organization. Select members of the planning team reviewed the survey results and respectfully provide draft conclusions and recommendations for your review and consideration. NOTE: Spot survey results are detailed in the accompanying document; this briefing only summarizes the conclusions and recommendations.

Conclusions, based on the analysis of the findings and the comparison of spot survey results and readiness assessment results:

- Communication is having a positive effect but needs to be enhanced in several AOR regions.
- Support for strategic plan–related change is fairly strong and is increasing.
- A relatively low level of buy-in and commitment exists in AOR 3.
- Overall confidence in the change remains fairly constant in most AOR regions and continues to climb in AOR 5 and 7.
- A majority of respondents feel that change-related impact has thus far been neutral or somewhat positive.
- There is some optimism—
  - About how people are beginning to work differently.
  - That changing the way our employees work will have a positive impact on their military career.
  - That changing the way our employees work will have a positive impact on their careers once they retire or transition from our military organization.
- Only a few remain unclear about what they should do to support this change.

(Continued)

Figure 11.2   (Continued)

- The buy-in and commitment of—
  - Executives and managers are now stable.
  - Supervisors and sole contributors are now increasing.
- Support is much more widespread than it was expected to be (as was reported in the readiness assessment).
- Attitudes about change in AOR 3 remain largely unfavorable, with the more favorable attitudes occurring in the higher (leader, executive, and manager) levels of the organization.

Recommendations, based on the analysis of the conclusions:

- Show the benefit of strategic plan–related change, and manufacture quick wins by parts and levels of the organization in which support is strong.
- Take concrete steps to understand and address the concerns of those groups in which—
  - Support for this change is currently low and stable.
  - Confidence in this change appears to be stable or sliding.
- Develop a comprehensive communication strategy and execute it throughout the entire organization.
- Direct targeted messages and information to AOR 3—
  - What people throughout the organization are doing to support and facilitate strategic plan–related change.
  - Current levels of support for strategic plan–related change reported in this survey.
  - Increasing pockets of support and growing confidence for strategic plan–related change reported in this survey.
- Address concerns associated with strategic plan-related change in a straightforward manner.
- Have conversations with senior-level uniformed and civilian executives and managers to determine why their buy-in and commitment have remained static while the buy-in and commitment of supervisors have significantly increased.
- Take advantage of the positive perceptions, attitudes, and views of AOR 5 and 7—
  - Capture lessons learned to share and best practices to replicate throughout the organization.
  - Solicit personal testimonials to incorporate into future organization-wide and division, department, and unit-specific communiqués.
  - Arrange for AOR 5 and 7 representatives to coach supervisors, colleagues, and associates working in other AOR regions (in general) and AOR 3 (in particular).
- Broadly share the spot survey conclusions and recommendations with all members of the organization, accompanied (or shortly thereafter supplemented) by a plan for implementing the recommendations.

CONDUCTING PERIODIC STRATEGY REVIEW SESSIONS

Your strategic planning team takes steps—both during and after the strategic planning session—to ensure your organization's short- and long-term success. While these actions will likely yield positive results and outcomes, it is important that your strategic planning team, working closely with your senior leaders, periodically evaluate your organization's performance, results, and outcomes to identify ways to enhance and further improve:

• Its next strategic planning endeavor to help ensure increasingly more effective and efficient strategy formulation.
• The way it deploys and implements its strategies to help ensure increasingly more effective and efficient execution.

It is important that your planning team periodically review the framework, model, or process followed and the deliverables generated throughout the strategic planning effort to identify opportunities for enhancement and improvement and when possible take full advantage of those opportunities (e.g., "course correct") while this planning cycle is still under way. Otherwise, opportunities for enhancement and improvement, along with their associated solutions, should be noted so that they can be applied during your organization's next planning cycle.

It is also important for your planning team to periodically review progress, achievement, and accomplishment to identify ways to:

1. Raise understanding, buy-in, commitment, and advocacy.
2. Enhance the knowledge, skills, and abilities that are key to the organization's short- and long-term success.
3. Strengthen the technology, systems, processes, methodologies, tools, and techniques that assist, support, and otherwise contribute to the organization achieving its mission and attaining its vision.
4. Identify lessons learned to share and best practices to replicate throughout the organization.

I therefore encourage your strategic planning team, working closely with your organization's leaders, to conduct periodic strategy review sessions to:

• Determine how your organization is doing—
   o Review the goals, actions, timeframes and critical dates, and metrics stipulated in the action plan.
   o Review progress to date to determine the extent to which (1) general progress has been made and/or (2) the strategic goals and associated tactics, major tasks, and minor tasks have been accomplished.

- o Review specific actions and activities stemming from previous strategy review sessions to determine the extent to which (1) progress has been made and/or (2) the strategic goals and associated tactics, major tasks, and minor tasks have been accomplished.
- Determine if your organization should—
  - o For tactics, major tasks, and minor tasks that are experiencing optimal execution, identify and note potential lessons learned and best practices.
  - o For each marginal or suboptimal gain or achievement, analyze its impact on the metrics outlined in the action plan and the organization's short- and long-term success to determine whether to invest resources, time, and energy to improve performance.
- Determine how your organization should improve—
  - o As appropriate, further—
    - Analyze the gap between the actual progress or accomplishment and the desired or required performance.
    - Explore underlying factors or factors contributing to the performance gap.
  - o Solicit ideas from other employees (at all levels) on how to effectively and efficiently close the performance gap.
  - o Identify and select the solution(s) most likely to lead to optimal execution.
  - o Incorporate solution(s) into the organization's action and/or contingency plan, assigning a responsible party, a critical date or timeframe, and metrics.
- Determine how your organization should continuously improve—
  - o Review previously enacted remedial actions; determine how to consolidate gains and replicate positive results and outcomes.
  - o Explore actions, situations, and circumstances contributing to optimal results and outcomes; identify lessons learned to share and best practices to replicate throughout the organization.
  - o Determine how to incorporate exemplary methodologies, processes, tools, and techniques into the organization's ongoing continuous improvement effort.
  - o Assign select marginal and suboptimal performance issues to one or more response teams; each response team applies the organization's continuous improvement framework, model, or process to those issues.

The topics and issues your strategic planning team explores during its strategy review sessions will depend largely on how long it's been since you conducted your last strategy review session; the nature and scope of change associated with your strategic plan; prevailing and emerging challenges and opportunities impacting the organization's ability to achieve short- and long-term success; and the extent to which optimal effort is being applied, appropriate behavior is occurring, and performance is generating needed results and outcomes.

One organization in the business-to-business commodities industry recently solicited input from its leaders, executives, and strategic planning team members while preparing for its first monthly strategy review session. Your strategic planning team members might consider the following perspectives and views useful and beneficial as they prepare to conduct your first strategy review session:

- Key expectations regarding the strategy review session—
  - Help further align leaders and executives to the organization's direction, priorities, and accountabilities.
  - Reinforce and add clarity to action items, timelines, and success measures.
  - Reach agreement on challenges we face that are most likely to impede our ability to execute our strategic plan.
  - Given time pressures, prioritize the most realistic things we can do to address the challenges we now face.
  - Provide an opportunity for leaders and executives to hear what other people have to say (and an opportunity for various key stakeholders to be heard).
  - Serve as a check point for ensuring that everyone is on the same page.
  - Garner additional buy-in and commitment to support what we agreed upon during the strategic planning session.
- Critical success factors needed to meet or exceed the above expectations—
  - Involving those responsible for implementing the tactics, major tasks, and minor tasks.
  - Honestly and candidly discussing issues without assigning blame.
  - Reviewing data rather than basing conclusions and decisions on isolated incidents or anecdotal information.
  - Not allowing anyone to monopolize the conversation or overly influence our discussion, conclusions, or decisions.
  - Given the length of the strategy review session, following the agenda and adhering to the pre-established ground rules.
- How people feel about the strategy review session—
  - A clear majority look forward to reviewing the organization's progress and accomplishments.
  - Many feel a bit overwhelmed due to competing priorities and concerns.
  - Many are really excited, realizing that the organization's strategic plan lacks value unless it is successfully acted upon.
  - A few are somewhat concerned, because they know progress is slow and they face a multitude of barriers, obstacles, and impediments.
  - Several are looking forward to the strategy review session because they know it will contribute directly to the organization's short- and long-term success.

- The most important elements, components, or aspects of the strategy review session—
  - Using planning tools and techniques to analyze and solve challenges.
  - Following a process likely to enhance buy-in, ownership, and commitment during the session.
  - Everyone agreeing to the conclusions drawn and decisions made during the review session.
  - All leaders and executives committing to or being able to live with the decisions made during the session.
  - Following a structured process to review actions being taken, determine progress, and assess overall accomplishment.

Figure 11.3 presents topics and issues typically addressed during a monthly strategy review session, with this particular session lasting four hours. This figure also illustrates the types of conclusions your strategic team might draw and recommendations it might generate while conducting a monthly strategy review session.

Strategy review does not end after your organization conducts its first strategy review session. The timing of subsequent strategy review sessions will depend largely on the nature and scope of change associated with your strategic plan; progress being made toward the organization accomplishing its mission and attaining its vision; prevailing and emerging challenges and opportunities impacting the organization's ability to achieve short- and long-term success; and the extent to which employees (at all levels) consistently apply optimal effort, exhibit appropriate behavior, and perform in a way (and at a level) that generates needed results and outcomes.

MOVING FORWARD WITH STRATEGY EXECUTION

The members of your strategic planning team have carefully analyzed volumes of data and information; considered a variety of factors, topics, and issues; reflected on your organization's purpose and reason for existence; factored conclusions drawn on all of the above into the development, refinement, or verification of your organization's mission, vision, sweet spot, and values; and identified the means by which your organization will accomplish its mission and attain its vision. Your strategic planning team has:

- Developed a strategic plan to help your organization accomplish its mission and attain its vision.
- Created a contingency plan to help your organization address unexpected and unanticipated challenges.
- Explored and decided on what your organization will do to ensure constant and consistent execution throughout the entire organization.

Figure 11.3 Strategy Review Session Topics and Issues

Topic: Update on Key Strategies (60 minutes)

- Based upon preparation completed prior to the session, responsible parties report on each of the organization's key strategies, answering the following questions:
  - Using a stoplight assessment (i.e., green, yellow, or red)—
    - How do you feel about the progress you have been making with your key strategy?
    - If your assessment is anything other than "green," why?
  - Having had an opportunity to think more about your key strategy—
    - Do you feel its level of criticality matches the amount of time, effort, and resources it is requiring?
    - If not, what is the mismatch, and what do you think should occur now?
  - Considering that strategic management requires the involvement, contribution, support, and advocacy of the entire leadership team—
    - Have you received the level of involvement, contribution, support, and advocacy your key strategy requires?
    - If not, what additional involvement, contribution, support, and advocacy are needed?
- The goal is for each responsible party to take no more than 15 minutes to report on his or her key strategy.

Issues: Challenges and Countermeasures (120 minutes)

- Participants explore prevailing challenges to the implementation of the key strategies and identify:
  - Root causes.
  - Contributing factors.
  - Potential countermeasures to address the challenges.
- In completing the above analysis, participants revisit and utilize the set of criteria developed during the corporate planning session to evaluate and prioritize strategies. They also refer to and use the tools and techniques introduced and applied during the corporate planning session.

Topic: Resources (30–45 minutes)

- The group discusses the implications of the previous identification of challenges and countermeasures, focusing on how to incorporate the countermeasures into the day-to-day running of the business, in terms of:
  - Time.
  - Financial resources.
  - People.

(Continued)

Figure 11.3   (Continued)

Topic: Debriefing and Next Steps (15 minutes)

- Debrief the above discussions; identify strengths and opportunities for improvement.
- Identify other items, issues, and challenges that need to be addressed (e.g., metrics, tracking systems, ongoing situational tracking capability, etc.).
- Discuss immediate next steps and designate responsible parties, critical dates, and success measures.

- Investigated and decided how your organization will help ensure that everyone has the needed levels of awareness, understanding, buy-in, commitment, and advocacy.
- Laid the groundwork for continuously improving its next strategic planning session to help ensure increasingly more effective and efficient strategy formulation.
- Identified ways to strengthen the way your organization implements its strategies to help ensure increasingly more effective and efficient execution.
- Put tactics in place to help—
  - Strengthen its overall strategic planning, strategy formulation, and strategy execution capabilities.
  - Create a cadre of employees capable of—
    - Planning, preparing for, leading, supporting, participating in, and following up on strategy formulation and execution.
    - Effectively functioning as strategic leader, manager, facilitator, coach, and/ or participant.
- Laid the groundwork for ensuring (1) optimal strategy execution and short- and long-term success and (2) effective and efficient strategy formulation and execution by—
  - Identifying and utilizing an executive sponsor.
  - Developing and utilizing a balanced scorecard.
  - Properly managing its various key stakeholders.
  - Conducting a readiness assessment prior to initiating strategy execution to determine whether success is likely and, if not, what additional actions must occur to properly set the stage for success.
  - Performing a series of spot surveys during strategy execution to identify changing needs, expectations, and requirements, lessons learned and best practices, and pockets of resistance (to address) and commitment (to leverage).
  - Conducting periodic strategy review sessions to—
    - Identify changing external opportunities and threats and internal strengths and weaknesses.

- Explore ways to take advantage of factors impacting the organization in a positive way and address factors impacting it in a negative way.
- Determine progress being made on all fronts and identify ways to leverage the achievement and reduce, avoid, or mitigate barriers, obstacles, and impediments.
- Identify lessons learned to share and best practices to replicate throughout the organization.
- Explore opportunities for enhancement and improvement and when feasible take advantage of those opportunities (e.g., "course correct") while execution is under way.
- As appropriate, note opportunities and their associated solutions to apply to your organization's next planning session or during its next planning cycle.

Chapter 10 presented methodologies, tools, and techniques your organization and planning team can use throughout the strategic planning process to support information and data analysis, interaction, and decision making and to facilitate communication with the broader organization. The Appendix presents resources that readers can use to further explore strategic planning and strategy formulation and execution.

Appendix

Strategic Planning Resources

BOOKS

10 Steps to Successful Strategic Planning. Susan Barksdale and Teri Lund. Alexandria, VA: American Society for Training and Development, 2006.

60 Minute Strategic Plan. John E. Johnson and Anne Marie Smith. Gold River, CA: 60 Minute Strategic Plan, Inc., 2006.

Advanced Strategic Planning: A New Model for Church and Ministry Leaders. Aubrey Malphurs. Grand Rapids, MI: Baker Books, 2005.

Ahead of the Curve: A Guide to Applied Strategic Thinking. Steven Stowell and Stephanie Mead. Sandy, UT: CMOE, Inc., 2005.

Applied Strategic Planning: An Introduction. Timothy N. Nolan, Leonard D. Goodstein, and Jeanette Goodstein. San Francisco, CA: John Wiley & Sons, 2008.

The Competitive Advantage of Nations. Michael E. Porter. New York: The Free Press, 1990.

Contemporary Issues in Leadership, 5th ed. William E. Rosbenbach and Robert L. Taylor. Boulder, CO: Westview Press, 2001.

Enterprise Resource Planning, 3rd ed. Bret Wagner and Ellen Monk. Florence, KY: Course Technology, 2008.

Essential Managers: Strategic Thinking. Andy Bruce and Ken Langdon. New York: Dorling Kindersley Publishing, 2000.

Executing Your Strategy: How to Break It Down and Get It Done. Mark Morgan, Raymond E. Levitt, and William Malek. Boston: Harvard Business School Press, 2007.

The First 90 Days: Critical Success Strategies for New Leaders at All Levels. Michael Watkins. Boston: Harvard Business School Press, 2003.

Formulation, Implementation, and Control of Competitive Strategy, 11th ed. John A. Pearce II and Richard B. Robinson Jr. New York: McGraw-Hill/Irwin, 2008.

Human Resource Strategy: Formulation, Implementation, and Impact. Dr. Peter Alan Bamberger and Professor Ilan Meshoulam. Thousand Oaks, CA: Sage Publications, 2000.

Leadership in Organizations. Gary A. Yukl. Englewood Cliffs, NJ: Prentice Hall, 1981.

Leadership: Enhancing the Lessons of Experience. Richard L. Hughes, Robert C. Ginnett, and Gordon J. Curphy. New York: McGraw-Hill/Irwin, 1999.

Leadership: Managing in Real Organizations, 2nd ed. Leonard R. Sayles. New York: McGraw-Hill, 1989.

Learning to Think Strategically. Julia Sloan. Burlington, MA: Butterworth-Heinemann, 2006.

A Manager's Guide to Globalization: Six Skills for Success in a Changing World, 2nd ed. Stephen H. Rhinesmith. New York: McGraw-Hill, 1996.

Maximum Leadership: The World's Leading CEOs Share Their Five Strategies for Success. Charles M. Farkas and Philippe De Backer. New York: Henry Holt & Company, 1996.

The New Strategic Thinking: Pure and Simple. Michel Robert. New York: McGraw-Hill, 2006.

Project Management: A Systems Approach to Planning, Scheduling, and Controlling. Harold Kerzner. Hoboken, NJ: John Wiley & Sons, 2009.

Simplified Strategic Planning. Robert W. Bradford and J. Peter Duncan with Brian Tarcy. Worcester, MA: Chandler House Press, 2000.

Strategic Management, 11th ed. John Pearce and Richard Robinson. Columbus, OH: McGraw-Hill, 2008.

Strategic Management: An Integrated Approach, 8th ed. Charles Hill and Gareth Jones. Boston: South-Western College Publishing, 2007.

Strategic Management: Process, Content, and Implementation. Hugh Macmillan and Mahen Tampoe. New York: Oxford University Press Inc., 2000.

Strategic Planning for Dummies. Erica Olsen. Hoboken, NJ: Wiley Publishing, 2007.

Strategic Planning for Nonprofit Organizations, 2nd ed. Michael Allison and Jude Kaye. Hoboken, NJ: Wiley Publishing, 2005.

Strategic Planning for Public and Nonprofit Organizations: A Guide to Strengthening and Sustaining Organizational Achievement, 3rd ed. John M. Bryson. San Francisco, CA: John Wiley & Sons, 2004.

Strategic Planning for Public Relations. Ronald D. Smith. New York: Routledge, 2009.

Strategic Thinking: A Step-by-Step Approach to Strategy, 2nd ed. Simon Wootton and Terry Horne. Sterling, VA: Kogan Page US, 2001.

The Strategy-Focused Organization: How Balanced Scorecard Companies Thrive in the New Business Environment. Robert S. Kaplan and David P. Norton. Boston: Harvard Business School Press, 2000.

Strategy Formulation and Implementation: Tasks of the General Manager. Bryant Thompson. New York: McGraw-Hill/Irwin, 1992.

Success Planning: A "How To" Guide for Strategic Planning. Rebecca Staton-Renstein. North Miami Beach, FL: TOBSUS Press, 2003.

Thinking Strategically: The Competitive Edge in Business, Politics, and Everyday Life. Avinash K. Dixit and Barry J. Nalebuff. New York: W.W. Norton & Company, 1991.

Vision: How Leaders Develop It, Share It, and Sustain It. Joseph V. Quigley. New York: McGraw-Hill, 1993.

JOURNALS

The Academy of Management Perspectives
Organization: The Academy of Management
Frequency: Published quarterly
ISSN: 1558-9080
Subscribe: Telephone (800) 633-4931 or e-mail aom@exchange.ebsco.com

The Academy of Management Journal
Organization: The Academy of Management
Frequency: Published six times a year
ISSN: 0001-4273
Subscribe: Telephone (800) 633-4931 or e-mail aom@exchange.ebsco.com

The Academy of Management Review
Organization: The Academy of Management
Frequency: Published quarterly
ISSN: 0363-7425
Subscribe: Telephone (800) 633-4931 or e-mail aom@exchange.ebsco.com

The Academy of Strategic Management Journal
Organization: Academy of Strategic Management
ISSN: 1939-6104
Subscribe: E-mail support@alliedacademies.org

Harvard Business Review
Organization: Harvard Business School
Frequency: Published 12 times per year; includes double issues in January/February and July/August that count as two issues each
ISSN: 0017-8012
Subscribe: Telephone (800) 274-3214 or e-mail hbursubs@neodata.com

International Journal of Business Strategy
Organization: International Academy of Business and Economics
ISSN: 1553-9563
Subscribe: Telephone (702) 560-0653 or e-mail Admin@iabe.org

Journal of Business Strategy
Organization: Emerald Insight
Frequency: Published bimonthly
ISSN: 0275-6668
Subscribe: E-mail Collections@emeraldinsight.com

Long Range Planning
Organization: Strategic Planning Society
Frequency: Published six times a year
ISSN: 0024-6301
Subscribe: Telephone +44 (0) 845 056–3663

Management Science
Organization: Institute for Operations Research and the Management Sciences
Frequency: Published monthly
ISSN: 0025-1909
Subscribe: E-mail informs@informs.org

Sloan Management Review
Organization: MIT Sloan School of Management
Frequency: Published quarterly
ISSN: 1532-9194
Subscribe: Telephone (800) 875-5764 or e-mail SLON@neodata.com

Strategy + Business
Organization: Booz, Allen, & Hamilton, Inc.
Frequency: Published quarterly
ISSN: 1083-706X
Subscribe: Telephone (877) 829-9108 or e-mail strategy_business@neodata
.com

Strategy and Leadership
Organization: Emerald Insight
Frequency: Published bimonthly
ISSN: 1087-8572
Subscribe: E-mail Collections@emeraldinsight.com

ORGANIZATIONS

Academy of Management
P.O. Box 3020
Briarcliff Manor, NY 10510-8020
Phone: (914) 923-2607
Fax: (914) 923-2615
E-mail: aom@pace.edu
Web site: http://www.aomonline.org

Association for Strategic Planning
12021 Wilshire Blvd., Suite 286
Los Angeles, CA 90025-1200
Phone: (877) 816-2607
Fax: (323) 954-0507
Web site: http://www.strategyplus.org/index.shtml

Center for Creative Leadership
One Leadership Place
P.O. Box 26300
Greensboro, NC 27438-6300
Phone: (336) 545-2810
Fax: (336) 282-3284
E-mail: info@leaders.ccl.org
Web site: http://www.ccl.org

Institute for Operations Research and the Management Sciences (INFORMS)
7240 Parkway Drive, Suite 300
Hanover, MD 21076
Phone: (443) 757-3500
Fax: (443) 757-3515
E-mail: informs@informs.org
Web site: http://www.informs.org/

Strategic Management Society
Rice Building, Suite 215
815 W. Van Buren Street
Chicago IL 60607
Phone: (312) 492-6224
Fax: (312) 492-6223
E-mail: sms@strategicmanagement.net
Web site: http://strategicmanagement.net

Young Presidents' Organization
Global Services Center
Hickok Center
451 S. Decker Drive
Irving, TX 75062
Phone: (800) 773-7976
E-mail: askypo@ypo.org
Web site: http://www.ypo.org

ARTICLES

N. Boyd, "Implementing Large-Scale Organization Development and Change in the
    States," *Public Administration Quarterly*, Vol. 33, No. 2 (2009), pp. 233–269.

Paul B. Carroll and Chunka Mui, "7 Ways to Fail Big," *Harvard Business Review*, Vol. 86, No. 9 (2008), pp. 82–91.

T. Crook, D. Ketchen, J. Combs, and S. Todd, "Strategic Resources and Performance: A Meta-analysis," *Strategic Management Journal*, Vol. 29, No. 11 (2008), p. 1141.

F. Duserick, W. Huang, and Z. Dai, "The Impact of Effective Strategic Planning and Leadership on Employee Satisfaction," *Competition Forum*, Vol. 5, No. 1 (2007), pp. 243–252.

Robert Evans, "The Case against Strategic Planning," *Independent School*, Vol. 67, No. 1 (2007), pp. 92–104.

John Hagel III, John S. Brown, and Lang Davison, "Shaping Strategy in a World of Constant Disruption," *Harvard Business Review*, Vol. 86, No. 10 (2008), pp. 80–89.

Lloyd C. Harris and Emmanuel Ogbonna, "Initiating Strategic Planning," *Journal of Business Research*, Vol. 59, No. 1 (2006), pp. 100–111.

G. Hodgkinson, E. Sadler-Smith, L. Burke, G. Claxton, and P. R. Sparrow, "Intuition in Organisations: Implications for Strategic Management," *Long Range Planning*, Vol. 42, No. 3 (2009), pp. 277–297.

H. Donald Hopkins and Tim Swift, "Business Leaders Speak Out: Their Real Strategic Problems," *Journal of Business Strategy*, Vol. 29, No. 5 (2008), pp. 32–37.

Nicolas Kachaner and Michael S. Deimler, "How Leading Companies Are Stretching Their Strategy," *Strategy & Leadership*, Vol. 36, No. 4 (2008), pp. 40–43.

B. Massury, "Helping Leaders Achieve Strategic Alignment," *Strategic Communication Management*, Vol. 13, No. 3 (2009), p. 12.

T. Plant, "Holistic Strategic Planning in the Public Sector," *Performance Improvement*, Vol. 48, No. 2 (2009), pp. 38–43.

Mike Schraeder, "A Simplified Approach to Strategic Planning," *Business Process Management Journal*, Vol. 8, No. 1 (2002), pp. 8–18.

Kim Hua Tan and Ken Platts, "Effective Strategic Action Planning: A Process and Tool," *Business Process Management Journal*, Vol. 11, No. 2 (2005), pp. 137–157.

N. Wasilewski and K. Motamedi, "Insights for Effective Strategic Planning," *Competition Forum*, Vol. 5, No. 1 (2007), pp. 229–235.

ARTICLES AVAILABLE ONLINE

Pankaj Ghemawat, "Managing Differences: The Central Challenge of Global Strategy," *Harvard Business Review*. Published March 1, 2007. Product number R0703C can be downloaded from Harvard Business Review (http://hbr.org).

Daniel H. Gray, "Uses and Misuses of Strategic Planning," *Harvard Business Review*. Published January 1, 1986. Product number 86105 can be downloaded from Harvard Business Review (http://hbr.org).

Robert S. Kaplan and David P. Norton, "Using the Balanced Scorecard as a Strategic Management System," *Harvard Business Review*. Published July/August 2007. Product number R0707M can be downloaded from Harvard Business Review (http://hbr.org).

Peter Lorange and Richard F. Vancil, "How to Design a Strategic Planning System," *Harvard Business Review*. Published September 1, 1976. Product number 76507 can be downloaded from Harvard Business Review (http://hbr.org).

Henry Mintzberg, "Fall and Rise of Strategic Planning," *Harvard Business Review*. Published January 1, 1994. Product number 94107 can be downloaded from Harvard Business Review (http://hbr.org).

Gary L. Neilson, Karla L. Martin, and Elizabeth Powers, "The Secrets to Successful Strategy Execution," *Harvard Business Review*. Published June 1, 2008. Product number R0806C can be downloaded from Harvard Business Review (http://hbr.org).

Michael E. Porter, "The Five Competitive Forces That Shape Strategy," *Harvard Business Review*. Published January 1, 2008. Product number R0801E can be downloaded from Harvard Business Review (http://hbr.org).

John K. Shank, Edward G. Niblock, and William T. Sandalls Jr., "Balance 'Creativity' and 'Practicality' in Formal Planning," *Harvard Business Review*. Published January 1, 1973. Product number 73108 can be downloaded from Harvard Business Review (http://hbr.org).

Notes

CHAPTER 2

1. Hrebiniak, Lawrence G. 2005. *Making Strategy Work*. Upper Saddle River, NJ: Wharton School Publishing.

2. Mintzberg, Henry, Joseph Lampel, and Bruce Ahlstrand. 2008. *Strategy Safari: A Guided Tour through the Wilds of Strategic Management*. New York: The Free Press.

3. Kim, W. Chan, and Renee Mauborgne. 2005. *Blue Ocean Strategy*. Boston: Harvard Business School Press.

CHAPTER 5

1. Porter, Michael E. 1980. *Competitive Strategy: Techniques for Analyzing Industries and Competitors*. New York: The Free Press.

2. David, Fred R. 1997. *Strategic Management,* 6th ed. Upper Saddle River, NJ: Prentice-Hall.

3. *Bloomberg Market Data.* [Online]. (2010). Wilmington, Delaware: Bloomberg. Available: http://www.bloomberg.com/

4. *ORBIS.* [Online]. (2010). Brussels: Bureau Van Dijk. Available: http://www.bvdinfo.com/Products/Company-Information/International/Orbis.aspx

5. *Gartner Research.* [Online]. (2010). Stamford, CT: Gartner, Inc. Available: http://www.gartner.com/technology/home.jsp

6. *Hoover's Business Information.* [Online]. (2010). Austin, TX: Hoover's. Available: http://www.hoovers.com/

7. Nadhani, Sanket. *Selecting the Right Chart for Your Data.* [Online]. (2010). Kolkata, India: FusionCharts. Available: http://www.tutorial9.net/web-tutorials/selecting-the-right-chart-type-for-your-data/

8. Treacy, Michael, and Fred Wiersema. 1997. *The Discipline of Market Leaders: Choose Your Customers, Narrow Your Focus, Dominate Your Market*. New York: Basic Books.

CHAPTER 6

1. *Brainstorming*. [Online]. (2010). London, England: European Union. Available: http://www.usabilitynet.org/tools/brainstorming.htm
2. *Affinity Diagramming*. [Online]. (2010). London, England: European Union. Available: http://www.usabilitynet.org/tools/affinity.htm
3. *Prioritization Matrix: Practical Variations*. [Online]. (2010). London, England: Syque. Available: http://syque.com/quality_tools/toolbook/Priority/vary.htm

CHAPTER 7

1. *Contingency Planning Guide for Federal Information Systems*. [Online]. (2010). Gaithersburg, MD: National Institute of Standards and Technology. Available: http://csrc .nist.gov/publications/nistpubs/800-34-rev1/sp800-34-rev1.pdf
2. Continuous Improvement Framework, personal notes, 2008.

CHAPTER 8

1. Simerson, B. Keith, and Michael L. Venn. 2006. *The Manager as Leader*. Westport, CT: Praeger.
2. Gulick, Luther, and L. Urwick. 1937. *Papers on the Science of Administration*. New York: Institute of Public Administration.

CHAPTER 9

1. Kaplan, Robert S., and David P. Norton. 1996. *The Balanced Scorecard: Translating Strategy into Action*. Boston: Harvard Business Press.

Bibliography

Advance Publications. *Bizjournals*. http://www.bizjournals.com/.

Alcoa, Inc. *Vision and Values*. http://www.alcoa.com/global/en/about_alcoa/vision_and_values.asp

Avon Products, Inc. *Our Vision and Mission*. http://responsibility.avoncompany.com/page-13-our-vision-and-mission

BASF Corporation. *Values*. http://www.basf.com/group/corporate/en/about-basf/vision-values-principles/vision.

BASF Corporation. *Vision*. http://www.basf.com/group/corporate/en/about-basf/vision-values-principles/vision

Ben and Jerry's Homemade, Inc. *Mission*. http://www.benjerry.com/activism/mission-statement/?ref=promo

Bloomberg. *Market Data*. http://www.bloomberg.com/

Bureau Van Dijk. *Mint Global*. http://www.bvdinfo.com/Products/Company-Information/International/Mint-Global.aspx

Bureau Van Dijk. *ORBIS*. http://www.bvdinfo.com/Products/Company-Information/International/Orbis.aspx

The Corporate Executive Board. *Our Corporate Mission*. http://www.executiveboard.com/about_mission.html

Cranes, W. T. *Effective Meetings for Busy People: Let's Decide It and Go Home*. New York: McGraw-Hill, 1980.

Cummins Inc. *Values*. http://www.cummins.com/cmi/content.jsp?menuIndex=1&siteId=1&overviewId=2&menuId=1&langId=1033&

Cummins Inc. *Vision*. http://www.cummins.com/cmi/content.jsp?menuIndex=1&siteId=1&overviewId=2&menuId=1&langId=1033&

David, Fred R. *Strategic Management*, 6th ed. Upper Saddle River, NJ: Prentice-Hall, 1997.

Dell Inc. *Soul of Dell*. http://www.dell.com/content/topics/global.aspx/corp/soulofdell/en/index?c=us&l=en&s=corp&~ck=mn

European Union. *Affinity Diagramming*. http://www.usabilitynet.org/tools/affinity.htm

European Union. *Brainstorming*. http://www.usabilitynet.org/tools/brainstorming.htm

Gartner, Inc. *Gartner Research*. http://www.gartner.com/technology/home.jsp

General Electric Company. *Imagination at Work*. http://www.ge.com/innovation/archive.html

General Electric Company. *Our Company*. http://www.ge.com/company/index.html

General Electric Company. *Why GE*. http://www.ge.com/careers/why_ge.html

Gulick, Luther, and L. Urwick. *Papers on the Science of Administration*. New York: Institute of Public Administration, 1937.

H&R Block. *Values*. http://www.hrblock.com/presscenter/about/mv.jsp

The Hershey Company. *Mission Statement*. http://www.thehersheycompany.com/about/

Hoover's. *Business Information*. http://www.hoovers.com/

Hrebiniak, Lawrence G. *Making Strategy Work*. Upper Saddle River, NJ: Wharton School Publishing, 2005.

Johnson & Johnson. *Our Credo*. http://www.jnj.com/connect/about-jnj/jnj-credo/

Junior Achievement Worldwide. *Who We Are*. http://www.ja.org/about/about_who_vision.shtml

Kaplan, Robert S., and David P. Norton. *The Balanced Scorecard: Translating Strategy into Action*. Boston: Harvard Business Press, 1996.

Kellogg Company. *Our Values*. http://www.kelloggcompany.com/company.aspx?id=35

Kim, W. Chan, and Renee Mauborgne. *Blue Ocean Strategy*. Boston: Harvard Business School Press, 2005.

Land O'Lakes, Inc. *Mission*. http://www.landolakesinc.com/company/philosophy/default.aspx

Land O'Lakes, Inc. *Values*. http://www.landolakesinc.com/company/philosophy/default.aspx

Land O'Lakes, Inc. *Vision*. http://www.landolakesinc.com/company/philosophy/default.aspx

McGraw-Hill. *Capital IQ*. http://www.compustat.com/default.aspx

Mintzberg, Henry, Joseph Lampel, and Bruce Ahlstrand. *Strategy Safari: A Guided Tour through the Wilds of Strategic Management*. New York: The Free Press, 2008.

National Institute of Standards and Technology. *Contingency Planning Guide for Federal Information Systems*. http://csrc.nist.gov/publications/nistpubs/800-34-rev1/sp800-34-rev1.pdf

Porter, Michael E. *Competitive Strategy: Techniques for Analyzing Industries and Competitors*. New York: The Free Press, 1980.

The Ritz-Carlton Hotel Company, L.L.C. *Gold Standards*. http://corporate.ritzcarlton.com/en/About/GoldStandards.htm

Simerson, B. Keith, and Michael L. Venn. *The Manager as Leader*. Westport, CT: Praeger, 2006.

Syque. *Prioritization Matrix: Practical Variations*. http://syque.com/quality_tools/toolbook/Priority/vary.htm

Treacy, Michael, and Fred Wiersema. *The Discipline of Market Leaders: Choose Your Customers, Narrow Your Focus, Dominate Your Market*. New York: Basic Books, 1997.

University of Minnesota. *Body of Knowledge*. http://www.csom.umn.edu/cms/page5508.aspx

U.S. Census Bureau. *American FactFinder*. http://factfinder.census.gov/home/saff/main.html?_lang=en

YMCA of the U.S.A. *About Us*. http://www.ymca.net/about-us/

Index

About the Author

B. KEITH SIMERSON has provided consultation and executive coaching to professional services firms; to clients in the health care, architecture, and engineering professions; to automotive, industrial supplies, paper, rubber, heavy machinery, petrochemical, hospitality, business-to-business merchandising, food processing, and electronics industries; and to branches of the U.S. military and foreign governments. He has consulted throughout the United States and in Iraq, Canada, Argentina, Mexico, Germany, Italy, Bermuda, France, and the Netherlands.

Dr. Simerson helped develop and implement a five-year strategic plan for a $6 billion professional services firm; led integration teams for the merger of two petrochemical industry giants; helped develop the consulting framework and an electronic consulting "toolkit" for a leading professional services firm; established consulting organizations in two leading health care systems; helped lead an internal-consulting organization within a $40 billion oil and gas company; served as a global human resources leader in a top-tier professional services firm; and has helped branches of the military transition through wide-scale ("flag-to-flag") change.

Dr. Simerson is on the faculty of Northwestern University's Master of Science in Learning and Organizational Change (MSLOC) Program, where he instructs courses and conducts research in the areas of strategic planning, strategy formulation, and strategy execution. He earned his EdD with emphasis in management and organization development from the University of North Carolina at Greensboro and an MA with emphasis in administration, supervision, and higher education from Appalachian State University.

Dr. Simerson is the coauthor of *The Manager as Leader* (Praeger Publishers, 2006), *Fired, Laid Off, Out of a Job: A Manual for Understanding, Coping, Surviving* (Praeger Publishing, 2003), and *Evaluating Police Management Development Programs* (Praeger Publishing, 1990). He has also authored and coauthored book chapters and journal articles; been featured in regional newspaper articles and syndicated newspaper columns; and been cited in international magazine publications.